ALSO BY MARK JACOBSON

American Gangster
Teenage Hipster in the Modern World
12,000 Miles in the Nick of Time
Everyone and No One
Gojiro

THE
LAMPSHADE

A Holocaust Detective Story
from Buchenwald to New Orleans

MARK JACOBSON

Simon & Schuster
New York   London   Toronto   Sydney

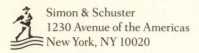 Simon & Schuster
1230 Avenue of the Americas
New York, NY 10020

First Simon & Schuster hardcover edition September 2010

SIMON & SCHUSTER and colophon are registered trademarks
of Simon & Schuster, Inc.

For information about special discounts for bulk purchases,
please contact Simon & Schuster Special Sales at
1-866-506-1949 or business@simonandschuster.com.

The Simon & Schuster Speakers Bureau can bring authors
to your live event. For more information or to book an event,
contact the Simon & Schuster Speakers Bureau at
1-866-248-3049 or visit our website at www.simonspeakers.com.

Designed by Akasha Archer

Manufactured in the United States of America

10   9   8   7   6   5   4   3   2   1

Library of Congress Cataloging-in-Publication Data is available.

ISBN 978-1-4165-6627-4
ISBN 978-1-4165-6630-4 (ebook)

PHOTO CREDITS (by page number):
Courtesy of Mark Jacobson: 12, 63, 82, 95, 212, 287, 299, 313, 327
Courtesy of Skip Henderson: 33, 192, 310
Courtesy of Ken Kipperman: 136
Photograph used with permission of the Musée de la
     Résistance et de la Déportation: 10
Photograph by Ruben R. Ramirez, used with the permission of the *El Paso Times*: 162, 165
Courtesy of Sovfoto: 106

And after my skin has been destroyed, yet in my flesh I will see God.

Job 19:26

THE
LAMPSHADE

PROLOGUE

I must say I didn't put much stock in the possibility that a Dominican spiritualist working out of a basement in Union City, New Jersey, would have much to say about a human skin lampshade reputedly made in a Nazi concentration camp. But there I was sitting across from Doña Argentina, a large woman wearing a ceremonial headdress and smoking a pair of cigars, one on either side of her mouth. A friend of mine, a devotee, had recommended the medium, saying that if the lampshade had truly once been part of a person, "the spirit" would still be present. If so, then Doña Argentina would make contact with it, bring its secrets to light.

There was a bit of desperation in my visit, an anxiety that had been mounting since I had first come into possession of the lampshade, which a friend had purchased at a rummage sale in New Orleans, Louisiana, in the aftermath of Hurricane Katrina. Later, after DNA testing proved that the lampshade had been fashioned from the skin of a human being, I'd spent many, many months attempting to track down its true nature, its origin and meaning, a search that had taken me halfway around the world. So I was willing, if not too excited, to drive the ten miles from my Brooklyn home, through the Lincoln

Tunnel, to Union City, where everyone speaks Spanish, to hear what the mystic had to say.

Doña Argentina, who said she had learned the ways of contacting the dead from her mother, whose portrait could be seen on the wall behind a six-foot-tall plaster of Paris likeness of the Virgin, began the session auspiciously. Taking the lampshade from its box, she took one look and said, "Oh, they kill him." This was quite possibly accurate, considering there was every chance the shade had been constructed from the skin of one of the eleven million people, six million Jews among them, who had been killed by the Nazis during their twelve-year reign of terror. On the other hand, spiritualists had their tricks. They like to impress their needy supplicants. I did not know what my friend had told Doña Argentina about the lampshade before I'd arrived.

A few moments later, Doña Argentina placed a candle beside the lampshade, which was alarming. After making a number of trips to Buchenwald, the Nazi camp most associated with the lampshade story, and spending much time in New Orleans, where the object had been scavenged from an abandoned building wrecked in the catastrophic hurricane, I had no desire to see it incinerated in the basement of a Jersey spiritualist's parlor. This seemed a real possibility as the candle flame grew higher.

"*Mira!* The spirit is strong," Doña Argentina said, taking a chug of rum. "It is speaking . . ." There was a pause now, as she stiffened in her velveteen chair. Her eyelids were fluttering. "He says . . . he says . . ."

I'd always assumed the skin of the lampshade came from a male, but this was the first time I'd heard it identified by the pronoun. Until this moment it had always been an *it,* a frightening, intentionally depersonalized *it.*

"He says . . . they are all bad to him. They hurt him. They cut him. Stab him with knives. They throw him in the closet. Lock him away. But you . . . you are different. You are kind to him. You give him attention."

"Yes." I was paying attention to the lampshade. For months I'd thought of little else.

The candle flame shot higher. Doña Argentina swigged more rum. The picture of her mother loomed above. "He says he feels safe with you. He wants to stay with you."

"Stay with me?"

"He says he wants to stay with you always. He never wants to leave you."

"You're kidding." Ever since the lampshade had arrived at my door as an unsolicited parcel of terror, I'd been trying to get rid of it. It was, I thought, like the black spot in Robert Louis Stevenson's *Treasure Island,* a dark circle inscribed on a page ripped from a purloined Bible, a floating accusation of ultimate guilt a pirate might find shoved in his breeches some bad night. The idea was to divest yourself of the spot before its curse took hold, to pass it to the next unsuspecting fool, if need be.

"He can't stay with me. That's crazy."

Doña Argentina leveled her gaze at me. For the moment it seemed as if she'd separated herself from her trance and had returned to the temporal world. She lowered her voice, as if to keep her thoughts from the spirit.

"*Por qué?*" she asked. "*Por qué* he can't stay with you?"

"Because . . . because it is a Nazi lampshade. It doesn't belong to me. I can't keep a Nazi lampshade."

"You don't want him? He is not a Nazi."

"I know he's not a Nazi. I know that." Doña Argentina was recommending I keep the lampshade near me as much as possible, to keep it at my bedside. "I can't have a Nazi lampshade in my house."

"But this is what he wants. You cannot do it? You want me to tell him that he cannot stay with you. That you don't want him."

"It isn't that I don't *want* him. I just can't . . . keep him."

Suddenly this trip to Union City had become very complicated. I couldn't become the permanent guardian of a human skin lampshade. It—or should I now be referring to the shade as he?—was a dead person. A murder victim, a former human being, not a curio, a grim collector's item. I'd spoken to rabbis, to museum officials, professors, geneticists, policemen, politicians. Dozens of serious people had weighed in with opinions concerning the lampshade and what should be done with it. Now this spiritualist, this lottery number picker, was advocating this radical course of action.

"I will tell him," Doña Argentina said, in the manner of a neutral messenger. The candle flame shot higher again. Doña Argentina stared into the fire. She let out a barking sound. If it was a performance, it was a good one. It was a while before she spoke again.

"He says there is nothing he can do. It is your choice. He says he leaves his fate to you . . . but it is good."

"Good?" I replied meekly.

"It is good because he trusts you. You're the only one he has now."

PART 1

ONE

In the fall of 1827, as he was completing his masterwork *Faust,* Johann Wolfgang Goethe, greatest of all German writers, took a walk through the Ettersberg forest near his home in Weimar. "This is a good place to be," the seventy-eight-year-old Goethe told his secretary and biographer, Johann Peter Eckermann, as the two men paused to admire the view. "Of late I have thought it would be the last time I should look down from here on the kingdoms of the world, and their splendor. We tend to shrink in domestic confinement. Yet, here we feel great and free . . . as we always ought to be."

One hundred and ten years later, in the spring of 1937, Theodor Eicke, the *Obergruppenführer* of the Waffen-SS Totenkopf Death's Head division, and Fritz Sauckel, soon to be in charge of the largest contingent of forced workers since the African slave trade, sought to pay tribute to Goethe. As they cleared the Ettersberg forest for the construction of the Buchenwald camp, where fifty-six thousand people would die before April 1945, they ordered that one large oak be left standing. This was said to be Goethe's *Eiche,* or Goethe's Oak, the very tree under which the great poet had written his great work. The camp, at the time the largest in the Reich, was built around the tree. It was an arbitrary decision on Eicke's part. After all, there was no way of knowing which oak Goethe had actually sat under; the Ettersberg is full of the trees. Indeed, in *Conversations of Goethe,* Eckermann recounts how *Faust's* author carved his initials into not an oak but a beech tree, the dominant species in the forest (the name Buchenwald, chosen by SS leader Heinrich Himmler, means beech forest). But a beech is a spindly thing compared to an oak. Its roots do not plumb as deeply into the earth, its wood is not as hard, its fruit is not so plentiful.

For the Nazis, it was important to lay claim to the poet's legacy. Hitler himself had sat beside these same trees. The Führer loved—and was loved in—Weimar and the Thuringia state that surrounds it. A grand hub of Western culture for three centuries, onetime home to Martin Luther, Friedrich von Schiller, Franz Liszt, Johann Sebastian Bach, Friedrich Nietzsche, Richard Strauss, Paul Klee, Wassily Kandinsky, Hector Berlioz, Arthur Schopenhauer, Walter Gropius, Rudolf Steiner, Marlene Dietrich, and Richard Wagner, Weimar was an early center of Nazi popularity. In 1926, following Hitler's release from prison after the Munich Beer Hall Putsch, when he was prohibited from speaking in much of the country, Weimar welcomed him. Before becoming chancellor, he often addressed crowds in front of his beloved Hotel Elephant. In 1933 the Nazis won a majority of the votes in the area. It was here that the Hitlerjugend, the Hitler Youth, was organized. To the Führer, the Thuringian hills, and the great works produced there, were "the embodiment of the German spirit."

A truly new society, especially one as revolutionary as that envisioned by the Nazis, could not spring from nowhere, based on abstract ideas alone. Goethe's Oak provided a powerful foundation for a perfect ancestral line, unsullied by the "bacillus" the concentration camp was designed to weed out. Here was Nature's own living icon, connecting the glorious German past to the magnificent thousand-year future to come.

But iconography, fudged or not, can be difficult to control, even for Nazis. If Goethe's Oak represented for the SS a connection to a more perfect blood and soil, it also held special significance for the Buchenwald prisoners.

This owed to the singularity of the Buchenwald camp. Central hub to dozens of smaller, satellite prisons in the immediate area, Buchenwald was considered a "mild" camp in comparison to the death factories to the north and east. Buchenwald inmates might expire in the quarry, be starved to death, or perish from rampant disease, but straightforward murder, the shot to the back of the head, was never the intended purpose of the place. The population was diverse, including a high proportion of educated, often well-known inmates. Over the course of its eight-year existence, the once and future French prime minister Léon Blum, child psychologist Bruno Bettelheim, Jakob Rosenfeld, who would become Mao Zedong's personal physician and health minister, historian Christopher Burney, Albin Grau, producer of F. W. Murnau's film *Nosferatu,* French sociologist Maurice Halbwachs, aviation pioneer Marcel Dassault, future Nobel laureates Léon Jouhaux and Imre Kertész, Netherlands prime minister Willem Drees, Elie Wiesel, and Princess Mafalda, daughter of King Victor Emmanuel III of Italy, were imprisoned at Buchenwald.

These people knew who Goethe was. They'd read *Faust.* They had their own interpretations of how and why humanity makes its deals with supernatural evil. Goethe's story was so big that everyone in the camp could envision its author on their side. So when the anointed oak burst into a pillar of fire during the Allied bombing of the camp in July 1944, inmates and SS guards alike rushed to hoard flaming chips of pith and bark, collaborating for a moment, in hopes of salvaging pieces of the once-mighty tree.

The stump remains at Buchenwald today, to be seen by those who visit this forlorn place.

•　•　•

Buchenwald, Goethe's Oak, 1943

The journey to wartime Buchenwald has been described as an interminable winter train trip, prisoners shoved so tightly into a wooden cattle car that their skin froze to the person next to them, turning the unfortunate passengers into one giant, barely squirming block of ice. This living death was interrupted by arrival at the camp, the sudden iris shock of the car doors flung open in a vicious chaos of SS men screaming, cudgels flying, guard dogs baring teeth.

More than six decades later, the trip is appalling mostly in its ease. The two-hour jaunt on the lickety-split Deutsche Bahn from Berlin to the Weimar train station, cheery for the Christmas season, where smiling, rosy-cheeked ladies in white puffy hats sell tasty bratwursts and warming *Glühwein* in paper cups, is followed by a fifteen-minute ride on the number 6 bus. Like clockwork the bus arrives, bright red and shiny, the destination spelled out in yellow blinking electronic letters: *Buchenwald, Buchenwald*—as if it were going anyplace, anyplace at all.

Halfway up the hill the bus makes a left turn onto the so-called Blutstrasse, or "Blood Road," which was built by the prisoners in 1939, eventually stopping in a parking lot in front of the old SS barracks, now the museum's administrative offices. From there the visitor walks down the Carachoweg (*caracho* is Spanish slang for "double time"), where arriving prisoners, half dead from their journey, were made to run as fast as they could by SS men with clubs. Ahead, its outline barely visible in the enveloping fog, the squat chimney of the crematorium lurches into the sky.

Just outside the electrified barbed wire fence, into which desperate inmates would sometimes hurl themselves in vain attempts at suicide, is a zoo, where on Sunday afternoons, in full view of the starving prisoners, SS men often came with their wives and young children to feed the bears and monkeys. Unique to Buchenwald, the zoo was created, according to an order issued by Camp Kommandant Karl Koch, to provide camp officers with "diversion and entertainment . . . viewing the beauty and peculiarities of various animals which they will hardly be able to meet and observe in the wild." SS men were expected to "refrain from anything that might not be good for animals," as the camp commander had "again received reports saying that SS men have tied the deer's horns to the fence, where the animals were found to have had tinfoil shoved in their mouths. Perpetrators of such loutish acts will be reported to the SS chief to be punished for cruelty to animals."

Passing the empty zoo, the visitor arrives at Buchenwald's main entrance. At the Auschwitz death camp the sign said *Arbeit Macht Frei,* or "Work Will Set You Free," the sickest of all Nazi jokes. At Buchenwald the message is more subtle, the cast-iron letters on the iron gate reading *Jedem Das Seine,* or "To Each His Own."

Again, *Kultur,* the very mention of which was said to make Reichsmarschall Hermann Goering remove the safety on his Browning pistol, appears to have been at work in the Thuringian hills. Bach, a former Weimar chamber musician, called his 163rd cantata *"Nur jedem das Seine!".* But the phrase dates back to Plato and Cicero, who wrote, *"Justitia suum cuique distribuit":* "Justice renders to everyone his due."

This was the big Nazi laugh at Buchenwald, since the letters of the sign, designed by Franz Ehrlich, an inmate and former Bauhaus student, face inward. You might delude yourself, as so many Jews and others did before the war, that you were as German as anyone else. You might hold on to the fantasy of belonging even as they marched you off to the camp. It was only when the camp gates slammed behind the prisoner that the phrase *Jedem das Seine* became clear. *To each his own.* You could harbor whatever illusions you wished about yourself, but it was the Nazis, the Supermen, who decided who you really were.

I was at Buchenwald to see about the lampshade. If you are interested in lampshades allegedly made out of human skin, Buchenwald is the place.

Facts pertaining to the so-called Nazi human skin atrocities remain a topic of debate, yet there is testimony indicating that the practice was widespread. During the Nuremberg war crimes trials, Dr. Franz Blaha, a Czech Communist surgeon arrested by the Gestapo, spoke of his forced participation in various Nazi experiments at Dachau. This included, Blaha said, being made to perform over twelve thousand autopsies.

"It was common practice to remove the skin from dead prisoners," Blaha testified with clinical precision, saying Nazi doctors like Sigmund Rascher and Klaus Schilling were particularly interested in "human skin from human backs and chests. It was chemically treated and placed in the sun to dry. After that it was cut into various sizes for use as saddles, riding breeches, gloves, house slippers, and ladies' handbags. Tattooed skin was especially valued by SS men. Russians, Poles, and other inmates were used in this way, but it was forbidden to cut out the skin of a German. This skin had to be from healthy prisoners and free from defects.

"Sometimes we did not have enough bodies with good skin and Rascher would say, 'All right, you will get the bodies.' The next day we would receive twenty or thirty bodies of young people. They would have been shot in the neck or struck on the head so that the skin would be uninjured. Also, we frequently got requests for the skulls or skeletons of prisoners. In those cases we boiled the skull or the body. Then the soft parts were removed and the bones were bleached and dried and reassembled. In the case of skulls it was important to have a good set of teeth. When we ordered the skulls, the SS men would say, 'We will try to get you some with good teeth.' So it was dangerous to have good skin or good teeth."

Similar details turn up in the often disputed deathbed "confession" of Franz Ziereis, commandant of the Mauthausen camp, who was shot by American troops in May 1945 while trying to escape dressed in civilian clothes. "I have personally killed about four thousand prisoners," the suddenly remorseful Ziereis was reported to have said before dying from his wounds. In the realm of "the use of bodies," however, Ziereis passed the blame to other, otherwise anonymous individuals like "Chemielskwy and Seidler in Gusen," who, he claimed, "had human skin specially tanned on which there were tattoos. From this leather they had books bound, and they had lampshades and leather cases made."

Nonetheless, when it comes to Nazi use of human body parts, particularly the flaying, stretching, and tanning of tattooed skin to make lampshades, one name stands out among all others. That is Ilse Koch, aka "the Bitch of Buchenwald," the red-haired, legendarily hot-blooded wife of the aforementioned Kommandant Karl Koch.

The former Ilse Köhler was born in 1906, daughter of a lower-middle-class factory worker in Dresden, then, as now, a stronghold of rabidly right-wing politics. After studying to be a librarian and working as a secretary, Köhler joined the National Socialist Party in 1932, when women made up only 7 percent of the membership. A picture of the young Ilse taken around this time shows a somewhat zaftig young woman sitting on what appears to be a table in the corner of a wallpapered room. Her wavy, shoulder-length red hair is parted with obvious care on the right side of her roundish face. She wears a billowy white blouse with a ruffled plaid bow, a skirt that falls slightly below her knees, and black pumps. There is little to suggest that this is the woman who would soon be reviled the world over as an evil succubus. On the contrary, the way she leans forward, lipstick on the slightly pursed lips of her smallish mouth, a faint sense of dare in her canny eyes, she appears a slightly naughty 4-H girl, up for coy fun but nothing more.

With Hitler's rise to the German chancellorship the following year, Köhler took a job as a guard at the Sachsenhausen concentration camp outside Berlin. It was there she met the camp chief, Karl Koch, a former bank clerk and World War I vet with a reputation as a harsh administrator. A Nazi Party member since 1924 and favorite of SS leader Heinrich Himmler, Koch was soon transferred to the Gestapo's notorious Columbia House prison in Berlin, where he reputedly ordered prisoners to be shackled by the neck and fed from bowls on the stone floor. When Koch entered the room, inmates had to bark and howl like dogs.

Perhaps Koch's zeal was a compensation for his somewhat deficient pedigree. Considered a vanguard force of the coming racial state, SS men were supposed to be paragons of German masculinity, the cream of the genetic crop. In the early days, no man standing less than six feet tall need apply. Koch was not quite all that. A barrel-chested man with a pronounced, pointed chin who often wore dark glasses over his deep-set eyes, there was a gnomishness about him. Not that this mattered to Ilse Köhler, who, according to her biographer Arthur L. Smith, had a distinct weakness for men in uniform, especially those with the Death's Head insignia on their cap and collar. Ilse became Karl Koch's personal secretary, and in May 1936 they married.

Ilse and Karl Koch were wed in a verdant grove outside the Sachsenhausen walls at midnight. Everything was done according to protocols set forth by the 1931 Engagement and Marriage Order aimed at ensuring that the SS would remain "a hereditarily healthy clan of a strictly Nordic German sort" and sanctioned by the Main Office of Race and Settlement. Karl Koch wore his uniform and a steel helmet. Ilse Koch, in a long white dress, was anointed as a "custodian of the race," from whose womb would come forth genetically pure representatives of the glorious evolutionary future. An eternal flame burned in an urn as the betrothed exchanged rings decorated with runic signs. The newlyweds were given gifts of bread and salt, emblematic of fruitfulness and purity. A copy of *Mein Kampf* was taken from a wooden box and presented to the groom, after which the couple walked hand in hand past an array of saluting white-gloved SS men.

Koch's appointment as Kommandant at Buchenwald, the largest and most elaborate of the camps at the time, was a plum. An ugly, vicious man with a beautiful wife, he may not have been popular with his fellow officers, but he was under Himmler's wing and that was enough. Upon arriving at the new facility, one of Koch's first orders of business was to confer upon Ilse the title of *Oberaufseherin*, or "senior overseer," a rank accorded no other SS frau.

From the start, Koch imposed a reign of relentless cruelty at the camp, marked by innovative tortures, including the infamous "tree hanging," in which prisoners were strapped to a ten-foot-tall pole with their hands tied behind their necks, sometimes for days. Another practice was a particularly noxious form of waterboarding in which victims were pushed facedown into the vile open latrines. The Koches' domestic extravagance was an obscene counterpoint to these horrors. At the grand Villa Koch, where dozens of prisoners were employed as plantation-style domestics, dinner was served on the best china and eaten with the finest silver. It would later be proved that the ex-banker Koch and his cronies financed much of this opulence by embezzling camp money and stealing from terrorized inmates.

No small amount of this loot went toward keeping up with Ilse Koch's ever expanding needs and desires. The former Dresden working-class girl took to the highlife of a concentration camp overseer. Anxious to keep his wife happy, Koch showered her with gifts—from fine clothes to inlaid wood furniture to diamond rings—mostly made by or stolen from prisoners. If Frau Koch desired to take a bath in Madeira, as she reportedly did, the wine was provided. In 1939, thinking his wife might like to learn to ride a horse, Koch commissioned the construction of a thirty-thousand-square-foot private riding hall with mirrored walls and a sixty-foot vaulted ceiling outfitted with dramatic skylights. According to the *Buchenwald Report,* compiled shortly after the war by the U.S. Army and former prisoners, as many as thirty prisoners died in the rush to finish the hall, which cost in excess of 250,000 marks. When the Kommandeuse, as Ilse Koch was called, took morning canters around the ring, the Buchenwald prisoners' band provided musical accompaniment.

For many, this would be the enduring image of Ilse Koch: provocatively seated atop her favorite steed (usually remembered as milky white), riding crop at the ready, black leather boots to her knee, and all that red hair. Later, after the war, there would be much talk of the scantily dressed Kommandeuse, riding through the camp, stopping only to accuse men of lasciviously staring at her breasts and her bottom, a crime for which the punishment was a beating or death.

It must have seemed an incredible dream to the Kommandant's wife, a prize not unlike that granted by the forces of darkness in a dozen retellings of the Faust myth. Saved from drudgery by becoming a Nazi, she was soon accompanying her frog prince husband to Himmler's Wewelsburg castle with its eighteen soaring towers. Declared by the Reichsführer as *"das Zentrum der neuen Welt,"* or "the center of the new world," Wewelsburg was a place where Ilse, as a member of this all-powerful new Chosen People, would always be welcome.

It was sometime in the summer of 1938, according to Harry Stein, the chief historian at the present-day memorial at Buchenwald, that Ilse Koch gave her husband a special gift. Many of the SS wives had become fascinated with the work of the SS camp doctor, Erich Wagner, a former student of "race science" at the then Nazi-run Friedrich Schiller University in nearby Jena. Wagner, apparently a dashing sort, was in the middle of compiling his Ph.D. thesis, *"Ein Beitrag zur Tätowierungsfrage,"* or "A Contribution on the Tattooing Question," a report on the relationship between tattooing and criminal behavior. In the process of his research, Wagner and other doctors in the camp pathology block reportedly began to remove the skin of prisoners with particularly colorful and/or lewd tattoos. Inmates would later say that many of these dried and tanned tattooed skins were stitched together into gloves, bookcovers, and lampshades. It was one of these lampshades, Harry Stein said, that was given by Ilse Koch to Karl Koch as a present for his birthday.

"It was considered the most favorite of all the presents given to Karl Koch," Harry Stein said. "All the guests applauded." It seemed, at the time, a token of love between husband and wife.

The first published account of the Ilse Koch "Lady of the Lampshades" story appeared in the U.S. Army publication *Stars and Stripes* on April 20, 1945, Adolf Hitler's fifty-sixth birthday, nine days after the liberation of Buchenwald. Ann Stringer, a UPI correspondent, filed a story from the camp saying she had seen a lampshade, "two feet in diameter, about eighteen inches high and made of five panels . . . made from the skin from a man's chest. Along side were book bindings, bookmarkers, and other ornamental pieces—all made from human skin, too. I saw them today. I could see the pores and the tiny unquestionably human skin lines."

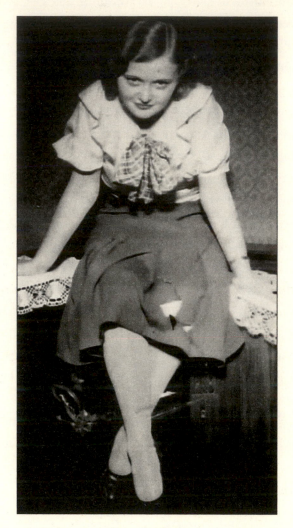

Young Ilse Koch

This was the first time people outside the Buchenwald camp had heard of Ilse Koch and her alleged passion for objects made from human skin. One prisoner, identified in Stringer's story as "a Dutch engineer," described how the former Kommandeuse "would have prisoners with tattoos on them line up shirtless. Then she would pick a pretty design or mark she particularly liked. That prisoner would be executed and his skin made into an ornament."

By the end of 1941, the Nazi dream-life of the former Ilse Köhler began to collapse around her. Karl Koch was transferred from Buchenwald to Lublin, Poland, to oversee the construction of Majdanek camp, where eighty thousand people would die, most of them Jews and Soviet prisoners of war. In 1943, Koch, his largesse with Himmler used up, was convicted by an SS court of corruption and murder charges. He was returned to Buchenwald in chains and executed by a firing squad on April 5, 1945, only a week before the American troops arrived at the camp. By then, Ilse, her fabulous riding hall now a shabby warehouse, had fled to the small town of Ludwigsburg, where she was recognized by a former Buchenwald prisoner and turned over to the Allied authorities.

By 1947, at her trial before the war crimes tribunal at the former Dachau camp, Ilse Koch no longer resembled the ingénue who married Karl Koch just a decade before. She looked haggard and worn, in part due to the fact that despite being incarcerated for months, Koch was, shockingly, pregnant, father unknown. Some months later, when she gave birth to a son, the child was not greeted into the SS clan as one more potential Norse god on earth. Listing the event in its Milestones section, *Time* magazine noted, "Born, to Ilse Koch . . . a male bastard."

The trial of Ilse Koch was a worldwide sensation. She was, after all, the perfect defendant, perfectly pregnant, perfectly sourpussed, bearing the perfect nickname, "the Bitch of Buchenwald," a cannily alliterative mistranslation of her prison epithet, *die Hexe*—"Witch"— *von Buchenwald*. She was the "Lady of the Lampshades," whose crimes—the blithe defilement of the human body—struck many as even more indicative of Nazi evil than the killing of millions. The fact that she was a woman, a red-haired black widow, made it all the more shocking.

The testimony was properly lurid. "I had several occasions to see Ilse Koch and also to have personal business with her," testified Kurt Froboess, a prisoner at Buchenwald from its opening in 1937 until liberation, describing an incident in which he and a Czech chaplain were digging a ditch to lay cables. The chaplain tossed some dirt out of the hole, Froboess said. "Suddenly someone was standing on top of the ditch and was yelling, 'Prisoner, what are you doing down there?' Someone was standing with her legs straddling the ditch. We looked up to see who it was and recognized Mrs. Koch. She was standing on top of the ditch without any underwear and a short skirt. As we did this, she said, 'What are you doing looking up here?' and with her riding crop she beat us, particularly my comrade."

Describing another encounter, Froboess testified, "It was a hot day. Some of them [the prisoners] were working without a shirt. Mrs. Koch arrived on a horse. There was a comrade there—his first name was Jean, he was either French or Belgian—and he was known throughout camp for his excellent tattoos from head to toe. I particularly recall a colored cobra on his left arm, winding all the way up to the top. On his chest he had an exceptionally well-tattooed sailboat with four masts. Even today I can see it before my eyes very clearly. Mrs. Koch rode over until she came pretty close and had a look at him. And she told him, 'Let's work faster, faster.' She took his number down. Jean was called to the gate at evening formation. We didn't see him anymore."

About a half year later, Froboess continued, he had occasion to visit a friend of his who was working at the Buchenwald pathology department, and there he saw "the skin and to my horror I noticed the same sailboat that I had seen on Jean."

On August 14, 1947, Ilse Koch, guilty of participating in a "common plan" to violate "the Laws and Usages of War" during her tenure as Kommandeuse of the Buchenwald Concentration Camp, stood before the court in a frumpy checkered dress and was sentenced to life in prison. Despite all the testimony about human skin lampshades and bookbindings, no such object was introduced in evidence. For her part, Ilse Koch steadfastly denied ever owning a human skin lamp-shade or ordering one made. She claimed the first time she ever heard of any lampshades was when "I read about it in *Life* magazine."

TWO

But we are getting ahead of ourselves, if not in time, in terms of telling this story. To get to the beginning we have to back up some seventeen years from today, to a beastly hot summer day in Clarksdale, Mississippi, a ramshackle town of about twenty thousand in the heart of the Mississippi Delta, which isn't a river delta at all but rather a diamond-shaped expanse of topsoil-rich land once home to the American South's largest cotton plantations. It might not look it at first glance—the landscape flat as a board, and the magnolia trees growing wild in unkempt backyards—but Clarksdale has a lot in common with the Thuringian hills of Weimar, home to both the most brilliant flowering of German humanism and abject Nazi barbarism.

This assertion stems, in part, from Clarksdale's indisputable position as the epicenter of early African-American blues music, a shriek of syncretic pain born during the dislocation of slavery that eventually morphed into rock and roll, which along with Hollywood came to dominate the cultural life of the twentieth century much as Weimar held sway over the eighteenth and nineteenth. Charley Patton, John Lee Hooker, Muddy Waters, Son House, Howlin' Wolf, and many other artists spent large parts of their lives in Clarksdale. Sam

Cooke was born here. After a car crash one night on a lonely stretch of blacktop, Bessie Smith died in the makeshift emergency room of the Clarksdale colored people's hospital, which later became the Riverside Hotel, where Ike Turner lived as a boy.

More specific to this story, however, is Clarksdale's close proximity to the intersection of U.S. highways 49 and 61. This is the famous "crossroads" where, legend has it, bluesmen came to sell their soul to the devil in exchange for becoming the best guitar player and singer anyone had ever heard.

This is the often-quoted testimony of Tommy Johnson, who, like Robert Johnson, author of the iconic song "Cross Road Blues," claimed to have undergone the process. "If you want to learn how to make songs yourself," Johnson said, "you take your guitar and you go to where the road crosses that way, where a crossroads is. Be sure to get there just a little before twelve that night so you know you'll be there. You have your guitar and be playing a piece there by yourself . . . Then a big black man will walk up there and take your guitar and he'll tune it. And then he'll play a piece and hand it back to you. That's the way I learned to play anything I want."

Tommy Johnson, Delta bluesman

It is a narrative that Goethe would have recognized, sitting under his oak tree, the poet's bemused Mephistopheles being archetypical kin not only to Tommy Johnson's "big black man" but also the Celtic Puck, the Norse Loki, the Hopi Kokopelli, and a dozen more supernatural trickster/soul barterers. For the Clarksdale bluesmen, the story almost certainly accompanied their forebearers on the slave ships. Called Eshu by the Yorubans, Anansi among the Ashantis, Legba throughout the Caribbean, the god of the crossroads appears in many African mythologies. He waits at the spot where pathways come together, that existential point where options become palpable. Often depicted leaning against a rock, sometimes chewing on a long reed, the crossroads god asks the arriving traveler what direction he's going, if perhaps he needs a little help finding his way. Not that his advice can be trusted: the riches he claims are down the road come with an even greater toll. But the human sojourner—be he Faust or Peetie Wheatstraw, another bluesman who supposedly went to the intersection of highways 61 and 49 at midnight—is no fool; he knows who he's up against. That's the trick of it, an inbred human trait, a cocky hubris of sorts, trying to beat the devil at his own game, if you can.

My voyage to Buchenwald began at the Crossroads. The Crossroads Bar, that is, then located at 224 Sunflower Street in what passes for downtown Clarksdale, where, on the aforementioned breathlessly hot July afternoon in 1995, I first encountered Raymond Henderson, who, along with everyone else, calls himself Skip.

Thinner then, raw-boned almost, his long, straight brown hair flung about with each herky-jerk gesture, Skip was standing behind the rutted wooden bar, talking six times faster than anyone else in the entire state. Hearing his jackhammer diction, so discordant compared to the slurred molasses patter of the locals, I asked, "Hey, you're not from here, are you?"

"Fuck no," Skip replied, his Sicilian–Scotch-Irish roots unconcealed. "I'm from New Brunswick, New Jersey."

Sliding forth a bottle of Blackened Voodoo, the preferred dark brew of the Crossroads, Skip, who started the bar in an old warehouse with the dementedly romantic notion that he'd give the few remaining Clarksdale musicians a place to play, continued his harangue to the two or three assembled drunks. As usual, Skip was exasperated by the shortcomings of his fellow human beings. This particular rant involved the long-abandoned Clarksdale railway station that he wanted to turn into a blues museum. It was at Clarksdale Station that Muddy Waters, who'd grown up picking cotton on Stovall's plantation, laid his money down at the colored people's ticket window (located in the baggage department just so no one forgot his place) to ride the Illinois Central Railroad to Chicago, where he and other Southland bluesmen would plug their instruments into the electric socket and shake the world. This made Clarksdale Station an important place not only in the annals of the blues but also in the overall account of African-American migration northward following the demise of the sharecropping system, Skip explained loudly and not for the first time.

The train station project grew out of Skip's larger mission in and around the Mississippi Delta. Back in Jersey, before the breakup of his first marriage, he split his time between his social work day job and his equally time-consuming passion for the collection and preservation of classic, often neglected, elements of pop culture. In the 1970s and '80s his social work function took the less-than-ideal form of high school counselor/truant officer ("a school pig," in the vernacular), a hectic position for which the state of New Jersey felt the need to issue Skip a badge and a .38 revolver. It was not a job guaranteed to ensure popularity, and one time Skip pulled in to the school parking lot to see eight-foot-high letters on the building wall spelling out "Mr. Henderson Is A Big Prick." As Skip walked by, the Polish janitor who was scrubbing off the graffiti seethed, "You—you make them do this."

Skip took refuge in his guitar business, restoring and selling vintage instruments, usually his beloved Fender Telecasters and Stellas. In this capacity he learned that many of the greatest blues artists, like Charley Patton, Sonny Boy Williamson, Mississippi Fred McDowell, and Memphis Minnie, geniuses all, were buried in unmarked graves.

To Skip, this was an outrage. A national shame. It could not stand. Establishing the Mount Zion Memorial Fund, he started calling successful white singers like John Fogerty and Bonnie Raitt to remind them that they could relieve part of their acknowledged debt to these bluesmen and -women by paying for their tombstones. R. Crumb, known to Skip through the obsessive record-collecting world, contributed a drawing to crown the obelisk dedicated to Robert Johnson at Morgan City, Mississippi. Skip had the Crumb drawing printed on a piece of porcelain, which he affixed to the monument. When the medallion was stolen, Skip made another one. When that one was taken, he had the picture engraved in the stone. This was a lot of work, especially in light of the fact that every blues fan knows Johnson's body is not to be found at Morgan City. Neither are the singer's remains buried at the two other Mississippi locations that purport to be his gravesite. In fact, despite leaving behind some of the most evocative American music ever recorded, no one has ever ascertained what happened to Robert Johnson or his mythically sold soul.

The success of the gravestone project was followed by the difficulties with the train station. The day I met him, Skip was railing that this was sheer Neanderthal prejudice. Only the week before he'd presented his proposal to the Coahoma County supervisors, detailing how the train station would not only memorialize the area's invaluable cultural legacy but also bring considerable tourist dollars to the chronically depressed local economy. Clarksdale, in case anyone on the board had failed to notice, was a mess. Over on Issaquena Avenue, the black neighborhood's main drag, the roof of the movie theater had blown off. A giant ailanthus tree, at least fifty feet tall, was growing up right between the derelict seats. Many lived without indoor plumbing. Couldn't an influx of blues-loving Yankee greenbacks help that? The board, all white, was not impressed.

"Let me tell you something, son," said one member. "There ain't nobody we know who is gonna drive all the way over heah to hear about some Negro man playing a ghee-tar. Your project is just for the blacks. I can't support it."

It was insane, this tyranny of the skin, Skip declaimed that hot day in Clarksdale, the way the outermost layer of a man was all that could be seen and judged by other men. When would the decent and reasonable impulses of the species, the beating heart of brotherhood, finally break through the surface that kept us apart? It was an admirable but futile screed, as Skip and everyone in the bar that day, a motley assemblage that included a drunken blues singer who called himself Rocking Daddy Juking on the Corner, or "R.D.J.C. for short," readily agreed. You could scream all you want about the way skin—what could be seen from the outside—had caused so much misery in this world. But it was a hard thing to get around. It was something you were born with, as dictated by God, or some trickster devil juking at the Crossroads who just liked to stir things up.

One thing that could be done, however, was to mess with it. To paint upon it. Make yourself a canvas. To declare that no matter what anyone else thought, the bigots and those who might think you old and ugly, this skin, this personal parcel of living real estate, belonged to you, no one else. This brought up Skip's tattoo, the most remarkable one I'd ever seen, a bit of ink that would almost have certainly attracted the attention of Dr. Erich Wagner and Ilse Koch.

"Weird tattoo you got there," I mentioned to Skip, referencing the image on his right bicep depicting an astronaut, wearing a NASA suit, floating free beside a Gemini space capsule. "Who's that?"

"Who?" Skip replied, ever peeved at the ignorant, poking an index finger at his upper arm. "That's Ed White, my *hero*."

"Ed White, the astronaut, is your hero?"

"First American to ever walk in space. Ed fucking White."

It was at this point that Skip's version of the Ed White spacewalk diverged from the official NASA account. As per many published stories at the time, Skip believed that when White made his historic jaunt on June 3, 1965, the astronaut was subject to a condition known to scuba divers as being "narked," or so one theory goes. This occurs when the change in external pressure makes nitrogen more soluble in the body tissues, causing the diver, or in this case the spacewalker, to experience sensations not unlike ingesting several drinks or breathing nitrous oxide. In other words, while floating amid the boundless expanse of the universe, Ed White was stoned out of his mind.

He was enjoying himself so much that he refused to return to the space capsule. When fellow astronaut James McDivitt signaled that the walk should conclude, White replied, "No way." "McDivitt had to drag White back in," Skip recounted. When White was finally pulled back into the ship, he said, "This is the saddest moment of my life, coming back in here."

"You think you're sad now, wait until we get down to earth," McDivitt supposedly replied.

After White was killed in a training accident, Skip memorialized him on his arm. It was a tribute, Skip said, "to the man who would not come back in." Who cared what sort of ass-covering story NASA put out about the incident. When it came to tattoos, it was the metaphor that mattered. Times had moved from when all you saw were Popeye's anchors and a sallow "Mom" on the saggy arms of afternoon drinkers. All over, nineteen-year-old suburbanites were walking around looking like yakuza who had fallen asleep in the inkman's chair. Everyone had a tattoo now, some of them really stupid, picked out of a catalog like a paint chip. This was wrong, Skip thought. A true tattoo was a statement of faith. If you were going to mark yourself, commit it to your permanent record, you had to make it count.

Over the following decade, I saw Skip on and off. He remarried, had three more children to go with his four grown boys—the grandiloquently monikered Michelangelo, Dominic, Alessandro, and Antonio—left Clarksdale, and moved four hundred miles down Highway 61, to New Orleans.

It seemed a crackpot notion to put down roots in a place where the water table makes it impossible to bury a body below the ground, but to Skip it made sense. For a former altar boy equally lapsed and devout, New Orleans was much like the Church, or what the brothers of the Sacred Heart taught him was "the one true faith." Intellectually you knew it was all lies—the Anne Rice bedsheet-waving crapola and the storied decay—but once you walked into St. Louis Cathedral in the Quarter and smelled the incense, or heard the second-line band going down Rampart Street, Lord have mercy! The place wasn't what it once had been—even Fats Domino, who preferred sitting on the porch of his Ninth Ward yellow and brown house with the letters *FD* embossed on the front, had to play the Vegas lounges to make a living—but still the city offered shabby, irresistibly noncorporate redemption, a chance to be part of something, however hokey, bigger than yourself.

Morons call New Orleans the Big Easy, but this is one more carny ruse to keep those out-of-town suckers drinking. The Big Anxiety is more like it. Once the second-largest city in the United States, for years the biggest in the South, the place has always been hanging by a thread. Founded in 1718, the fledgling settlement was completely wiped out by a storm in 1722. In 1788, 856 of the town's 1,100 structures were destroyed by fire. Yellow fever epidemics were rife throughout the nineteenth century. In 1853, more than 12,000 people succumbed in a matter of months. The only noteworthy outbreak of bubonic plague, the apocalyptic medieval "black death," in the United States, hit the city in 1914, causing widespread terror.

The willful illogic of building a city largely below sea level, on swamplands sandwiched between the Mississippi River and Lake Pontchartrain, the second-largest saltwater lake in North America, has long flummoxed sober-minded urban planners. According to *National Geographic,* the city has been subject to major floods twenty-seven times since its founding, which breaks down to nearly once every ten years. The Great Flood of 1927 displaced 700,000 people along the Mississippi, including more than 300,000 African Americans, who were duly rounded up and herded into refugee camps. In response to the deluge, the City of New Orleans, employing a time-honored race/class-based theory of emergency management, notoriously dynamited its overburdened levee system, diverting the high waters from the rich, "uptown" areas to the poorer downriver precincts.

In his resonant tune "Louisiana 1927," Randy Newman sings, "President Coolidge come down in a railroad train," but that never happened. In a precursor of more recent history, Coolidge, who refused to extend federal funds to deal with the calamity, remained in Washington. In his stead, he sent Commerce Secretary Herbert Hoover (whom Newman refers to as "a little fat man with a notepad in his hand"), who vowed to resettle the refugees. Later, as president, Hoover reneged on this promise. In a move that would become the template for such disasters, authorities spent federal money to increase the size of the levees, a hit-and-miss approach that failed most notably in September 1965, when the storm surge from Hurricane Betsy breeched the walls, inundating the town for two weeks.

This was what you bought into by moving to the Crescent City, Skip Henderson knew well, the deal you made for getting to eat real good oyster po' boys and smell the night-blooming jasmine in your backyard. There was a point where simple tolerance for impermanence crossed over into fetishization, but that's what attracted people like Skip Henderson to New Orleans. They hazarded a glance at the sky, waiting for the other shoe to drop yet again. Between 1999 and 2004, with globally warmed Gulf waters churning at an unprecedented rate, Skip and his family evacuated their home four times.

New Orleans evacuations have a rhythm, a routine. A hurricane is not like an earthquake, a sudden heart attack from out of nowhere and then you're dead. Tracked by long-range meteorological projection, the hurricane approaches as a dread-drenched creep. From the moment the storm is identified, usually as an anonymous "tropical depression" somewhere off West Africa, and begins moving west, through the Sargasso Sea, onward toward the de rigueur destruction of Haitian shantytowns, now with a name just to make it personal, the tension builds. When it gets into the Gulf, that's showtime. The doomsday weathermen are waving their laser pointers and here it comes, that buzzsaw Rorschach blot, like a teratoma blanched blue and green by the radar scans, a telegraphed haymaker you can't quite duck. And there, in the middle, at the center of the swirl, is the eye. The unblinking, Old Testament eye in the sky, *malocchio* in the Italian, *kin-a-hora,* as my Yiddish mother used to say: the evil, evil eye.

Of course, this being New Orleans, there are always those who simply will not go. The phlegm coughers, the black tooth types, blustering how they rode it out then and they were going to ride it out now, and the only way they are leaving is when some cop pries their stone-cold ass cheeks from the bar stool. It is a rap so stupid, so indolently hell-bent, you could almost envy it, Skip Henderson often thought. But what was a family man to do? Three little kids and a wife. Who wanted to be that one last fool who, upon seeing the birds flying inland, or hearing the crash of a brownshirt's brick through the shopkeeper's window, didn't get while the getting was good?

For Skip, the last few moments before the evacuation, with the boxes packed and kids safe in their car seats, were painful triage. In the collector's life, what could be left behind? Which Fender? How many of the wristwatches bought from unaware or desperate second-hand dealers? A framed ticket stub from the sixth game of the 1986 World Series? Collecting was a life-defining joy, but hoarding was a sin. It was against what Luke said in his Gospel, 12:15, an admonishment about "covetousness." There was virtue in traveling light, but it didn't take away the heartbreak of leaving things behind.

The worst of all the evacuations was Ivan, the category 3 storm in 2004. Skip and his family were on the Crescent City Connection, the double-span bridge over the river, when one of his wrinkle-faced English bulldogs, Ike, brother to Tina, began wheezing and then dropped dead in the front seat. Stuck in panicked, unmoving traffic, hours passed before Skip could get off the bridge and pull the animal's body out of the car. It was awful, but in the end Ivan veered off, to Alabama or some other redneck wherever. The bullet had been dodged. New Orleans was saved, yet again spared by the grace of God to continue its cheesy cycle of decay.

Skip Henderson

Still, who could have foreseen Katrina? Certainly the storm was big, hundreds of miles across; on the radar it pulsed like a medicine ball of pain, its outer bands extending from Pensacola all the way to the Yucatán. On the TV screen it seemed to cover the entire Gulf, and the Gulf was a thousand miles wide! The National Weather Service had released that mind-boggling warning that should the hurricane maintain its strength, most of New Orleans would be "uninhabitable for weeks, perhaps longer," that "all gabled roofs will fail," that "water shortages will make human suffering incredible by modern standards."

But that had been said before, Skip thought, packing the car one more time. Why should this time be any different?

For Skip Henderson, as for so many others, what had happened in New Orleans during Katrina didn't fully sink in until he returned to the city nearly two months after the storm. It was one thing to sit numb in front of the TV at his in-laws' house in Alabama, watching the merciless timeline unspool: the bungling, frightened response by the city government, the breaching of the levees, the failure of the pumps, the horrors of the Superdome and the Convention Center, the people on the roofs, the bodies in the water, the looting and the shooting, Bush in his plane, Brownie doing "a heck of a job." Sixteen hundred people dead, the beloved city shattered, its population dispersed, often at gunpoint, throughout the country; the news was too horrible to take in all at once.

To be back, however, in the first wave of those to return: that was the real shock.

After eight weeks without power, his refrigerator was so foul that Skip hauled the box out onto the sidewalk and blasted it full of holes with his pistol grip shotgun. This was pretty much his only damage, besides some downed trees. Along with the French Quarter, Marigny, and parts of the Garden District, the Bywater, where Skip had bought his place because the area reminded him of a sketchier circa 1981 East Village in New York, is part of the "sliver by the river"—higher ground, if only by a foot or so. That made Skip a survivor, at least real estate–wise, whatever that was worth in the decimated town. In those early days, with his family still in Alabama and the town so closed up you had to go to the Quarter just to drink a beer, Skip started driving around. He drove around every day for weeks, from morning until the nighttime curfew, when he locked himself inside his house and sweated.

He called it the Magical Misery Tour, not that there was any set itinerary. Nothing was where it should be. Houses were in the water and boats were on dry land, sometimes on top of houses. On Napoleon

Avenue, an ultrasound machine sat in the middle of the street for weeks. Over on Martin Luther King Jr. it was a dentist's chair, the spit bowl still attached. With the streetlights out and the stop signs blown away, these objects created a new traffic pattern. Life, as it had been lived, was gone. Skip drove past Robert's Supermarket, where he had shopped twice a week, and Charity Hospital, where half the city's babies had been born, and one look told him: they'll never be back.

You never knew what might turn up. One day Skip passed a burning house in the Central City section and was amazed when a fire truck tore around the corner, sirens blaring. After the storm, many fires went untended. But there they were, the NOFD, hatchets in hand, pulling hose, just like the firemen kids dream of growing up to be, in real cities. The problem was there was no water pressure in the hydrant. The firefighters stood there looking at the dribbling nozzle as if it were the end of a kinked garden hose. Then, seemingly from nowhere, a helicopter appeared overhead. Dangling from the chopper's bottom was a giant canvas scoop, which opened, dropping thousands of gallons of water on the blaze. With the house transformed into a steaming hulk, the firemen and helicopter departed. Why this particular house, modest at best before the storm, had been chosen to receive special treatment from the local authorities and then was left to rot away along with the rest of the neighborhood was hard to figure, but Katrina was full of mysteries.

One day in early 2006 the only thing Skip Henderson planned to do was go over to Mickey Markey Park at Royal and Piety streets in the Bywater to see if he could stand to vote for Ron Forman in the upcoming mayoral election. Forman was shaking hands and giving out balloons to the kids at the park. Ordinarily, Skip would never consider supporting a moneyed candidate like Forman, head of the decidedly uptown, if relatively liberal-minded, Audubon Nature Institute, which watched over the zoo and aquarium. But only months after Katrina, with the National Guard driving around the neighborhood in Hummers, this was a different sort of election.

For a hundred years people have said if you want to know what's up in New Orleans politics, see who parades with whom on Mardi Gras. The fact that everyone wears a mask didn't really hamper identification. You knew who they were. Of all American cities, there's no place where the circumstances of one's birth count so much as in New Orleans. The rich St. Charles Avenue white people are most often found marching with the elaborate old-line krewes, Proteus and Rex. In earlier times some of these celebrants might have paraded, as a good number of their grandparents no doubt did, with the Mystick Krewe of Comus. Named for the Greek god of revelry and nocturnal dalliance, Comus was the first of the Mardi Gras parading societies. Founded in 1856 and long the voice of upperclass racialism—in 1877 the theme of the parade was a celebration of "the Aryan Race"—Comus always held the biggest balls and rolled the grandest floats. One of the last openly segregated organizations in New Orleans, Comus refused to allow blacks in their processions. In 1991, served with a court order restraining them from parading unless they disclosed their membership—seen as a de facto order to integrate—Comus's response was simply to stop parading.

If New Orleans politics are pretty much race politics, the opposite number to the uptown white parades has long been the Zulu Social Aid and Pleasure Club, since 1909 the primary African-American Mardi Gras krewe. Zulu, as everyone calls it, presents itself as an all-inclusive, solidarity-based event, but this is misleading, given the complex history of race mixing in New Orleans, where light-skinned "Creoles" have long enjoyed social and financial benefits not readily available to their darker-hued brethren. In political terms, this caste system is expressed in "the paper bag test": the large majority of the town's African-American leading businessmen and politicians tend to be lighter in color than a UP #3 paper bag. From this circle came people like Dutch Morial, who was elected the city's first black mayor in 1978, his son Marc, who served from 1994 to 2002, and the holder of the office during Katrina, C. Ray Nagin.

Skip had to admit that, all things being equal, he retained a reflex to vote for black candidates on the off chance they might turn out to be another Martin Luther King, Jr. However, Ray Nagin, a cable TV executive who promised to run New Orleans like "a buisness" was another matter. Skip didn't trust him. Elected by a thin margin, Nagin would prove a bitter disappointment, most disastrously during Katrina. A memorable image from historian Douglas Brinkley's book *The Great Deluge* describes the mayor cowering in a twenty-seventh-floor bathroom at the Hyatt, "rearranging knickknacks and toiletries" while the storm raged outside. Skip now regarded Nagin as a clueless buffoon at best. When the mayor expressed the opinion that "hope" might just be the city's best chance for salvation after the storm, Skip spray-painted "Hope Is Not a Plan" on the wall of an abandoned building in the Bywater. Later, when Bush came to town and greeted the mayor by rubbing his gleaming, shaved head, prompting colleagues at the State Employment Office to exclaim, "You see what Ray let that fool do?" Skip reproduced the front-page picture of the head rubbing from the *Times-Picayune* with the caption "That's My Good Boy" and stuck it up on telephone poles around town.

This was where Ron Forman came in. Forman occupied a unique position in the Venn diagram of New Orleans power. He was Jewish. The NOLA Jewish community has rarely exceeded ten thousand, but it has played a significant role going back to the town's patron pirate saint, Jean Lafitte, the supposedly half-Sephardic rogue hero of the Battle of New Orleans. Judah Touro, another Sephardim who fought in the Battle of New Orleans, built a small dry goods store into a fortune and became one of the city's most generous philanthrophists, with streets, hospitals, and synagogues named after him.

On the other hand there was Judah Benjamin, a slave owner and Jefferson Davis's secretary of state, whose picture was printed on the Confederate two-dollar bill. Benjamin gets a mention in Stephen Vincent Benét's epic poem "John Brown's Body." "Seal-sleek, black-eyed, lawyer and epicure," Benét writes of Benjamin, picturing the politician questioning himself: "The eyes stared, searching. 'I am a Jew. What am I doing here?' "

For Skip Henderson, though, one name stood out from the rest—Morris Karnofsky, a Russian Jew whose family owned a dry goods store on South Rampart Street. In what stands as one of the truly great culturally enabling moments in American history, Karnofsky advanced his young employee, Louis Armstrong, the money to buy his first cornet. Armstrong writes about the incident in his essay, "Louis Armstrong + the Jewish Family in New Orleans, La. . . . A Real life story and experiences at the age of seven years old with the Karnofsky (Jewish) Family, the year of 1907."

Employing his own offbeat syntax, Armstrong wrote: "The Karnofsky Family kept reminding me that I had Talent—perfect Tonation when I would Sing. One day when I was in the wagon with Morris Karnofsky—we were on Rampart and Perdido Streets and we passed a Pawn Shop which had in its Window—an old tarnished beat up B Flat Cornet. It only cost *Five* Dollars. Morris advanced me Two Dollars on my Salary.

"I had a long admiration for the Jewish People. Especially with long time courage, taking So Much Abuse for so long. Seven years old but I could easily see the *ungodly treatment* that White Folks were handing the poor *Jewish* family I worked for . . . Of course we are all well aware of the *Congo* Square—*Slavery*—*Lynchings* and *all* that *stuff.* Maybe the Jewish people did not go through *All* of those *things* but they went through *just* as *much. Still they stuck together . . .*"

Mindful that one of Armstrong's sacred cornets was among the items damaged when the roof blew off the old U.S. Mint museum on Esplanade Avenue, Skip went to Mickey Markey Park in hopes that Ron Forman might be a Jew in the mode of Morris Karnofsky. It was not to be. Forman mentioned that afternoon that in the storm's aftermath he'd gone the extra yard to save the Audubon Aquarium's penguin colony. Nothing against polar avians, Skip thought, but how out of it could one guy be?

Half the parish was sleeping in FEMA trailers full of formaldehyde. In St. Roch people were shooting each other in turf wars over roofless squatter shacks. Just mailing a damn letter was a major project. Things were nasty and getting nastier. In the wake of incidents like Jefferson Parish deputies firing over heads of New Orleans residents to keep them from crossing the Gretna Bridge during the height of the poststorm flooding, race talk was taking on a cosmic tone. There were stories of how Blackwater mercenaries, seizing control of the streets in the absence of the NOPD, had killed dozens of alleged looters and dumped their bodies in the river. No less ominous was the fact, as pointed out by the classically inclined, that the name Katrina had its roots in the Greek *katheros,* or "cleansing." The *ethnic* prefix didn't even have to be mentioned, not with much of the black community banished to the decommissioned Houston Astrodome, where George Bush's mother would cluck how much they'd moved up in the world. This attitude dovetailed with commentary from mean-minded idiots like John Hagee, then John McCain's religious-right point man, who, calling attention to the annual "Southern Decadence" gay parade scheduled for a few days after the storm hit, said, "I believe that New Orleans had a level of sin that was offensive to God, and they were recipients of the judgment of God for that." Dennis Hastert, then Speaker of the House, said that for the life of him, he couldn't see why anyone would want to waste a nickel of taxpayers' money rebuilding a sewer like New Orleans.

The world wasn't coming to an end—it *had* ended, Skip thought, and here was Forman, this hapless guy in a Brooks Brothers shirt and tan chinos standing in the middle of Mickey Markey Park, surrounded by piles of garbage that used to be people's furniture, talking about penguins, not one of which had ever been seen in a bayou.

The handshake closed the deal. With Forman's hand lying in his own like a limp mackerel, Skip's attention was diverted to the rummage sale on the other side of Piety Street.

• • •

The drum. That's all Skip wanted. A drum to beat on for Mardi Gras.

Skip had been looking for a drum, but it wasn't until he left Ron Forman's rally to cross the street that he realized he'd been searching for *a particular drum*—this one. It was a fairly new-looking Yamaha model, with a three-inch-wide horizontal smudge bisecting the drumhead. Skip recognized the brown-green stain immediately: he'd been looking at variations of it for months while driving around the ruined city. It was the waterline, the gauge by which the height of the toxic flood could be measured, a malevolent, citywide bathtub ring. Streaked across building walls, visible on the doors of the thousands of cars stockpiled underneath the elevated I-10, in some places the ring was as much as ten feet off the ground, way over your head. The line was Katrina's mark, like the familiar Xs spray-painted on the walls of almost every building in town by the National Guard. A code like the voodoo *veves* they resembled, the Xs, called "Katrina crosses," told what day the house was inspected, which Guard unit had entered the building ("TX 1" for Texas number 1), and how many dead bodies had been found inside.

The skin of the Yamaha drumhead bore the storm's watermark. That, and the fact that it didn't seem too warped, made it a perfect noisemaker for the Bywater Bone Boys, Skip thought. Founded by Skip and a few Bywater locals during the Mardi Gras before Katrina, the Bones, whose charter said only "No dues, no officers, no meetings, not bound by circumstance," claimed none of the lineage of the white uptown krewes or the black second-liners from Treme. Composed primarily of recent arrivals, the Bones nonetheless had their place in the shattered New Orleans power structure. These were the fresh recruits, the wide-eyed Americorps do-gooder types, the drifting, crusty post-hippies, the Williamsburg artist transplants, the real estate speculators. They arrived along with the hundreds of Mexican day laborers who waited in the parking lot of the Lowe's out on Elysian Fields Avenue hoping for a construction job—all of them ready to buy into the tattered romance of the city even as the absent masses of homegrown refugees considered new lives in Atlanta or Houston. It wasn't ideal, this post-apocalypse party scene, but it beat the wretched petro-Vegas plans the Republicans had for the next incarnation of the former French river fort founded by Jean-Baptiste Le Moyne de Bienville in 1718.

Besides, the Bones were not without roots. "Boneman" groups had been rising at dawn to wake up the town on Mardi Gras morning for more than a century. For neotraditionalists like Skip and his Bywater buddies, this was the attraction—the connection to the mystical New Orleans gone by, a place where the seamless merge of life and death was celebrated with happy funeral music. This was the essence of the carnival, Skip always said, dredging up his altar boy Latin. *Carne* means "meat," *vale* means "good-bye." Lent was coming, things would be given up. Carnival was the festival of the flesh and you might as well drink up because after Fat Tuesday came Ash Wednesday with its cold reminder of the dust to which you will return. It was like the refrain in the song the brass bands sang at the traditional second-line funerals—life was merely a ramble, an ephemeral ramble around the town, until the butcher cut you down.

So why not be a Bone Boy, paint a skeleton on a black hoodie and run into the street at the crack of dawn banging drums and screaming things like "Wake up, future dead!" and "Who next? *You next!*"

After the storm, some said Mardi Gras should be suspended, even if that had never happened except for world wars and when the NOPD went on strike. The Bone Boys did not agree with this sentiment. On the contrary, Skip thought, the storm had done much to repurpose their mission, to purge it of unfortunate hipster irony. Instead of proclaiming the old-news inevitability of death, it was important to wake up the town so everyone knew they were still alive. That was why Skip had to have that water-stained drum. Spiritualized by the Flood, it was the perfect post-Katrina thing to bang on.

The drum was part of a rummage sale, mostly a pile of storm-ravaged junk haphazardly displayed along the paint-peeling walls of the house at the corner of Piety and Royal. It was a motley, obviously scavenged array of mismatched things: a couple of waterlogged Allen Iverson jerseys, a pair of andirons, a Weber grill, some flowerpots, a bed frame, an adding machine covered with dried mud. Nothing anyone would want.

"How much for the drum?" Skip asked the man standing there with his back turned.

At the sound of Skip's voice the guy turned around. He was tallish but bent over, probably in his forties, but that was hard to gauge with dark bubble shades covering his eyes. Over a greasy New Orleans Saints T-shirt, he wore a thin black leather jacket with the sleeves rolled up to reveal arms covered with what Skip immediately recognized as prison tattoos, blue, black, and blotty. Those must have hurt, Skip thought, picturing a commingled stream of blood and ink dripping onto the cement jailhouse floor. On his right arm the man bore the likeness of a hundred-dollar bill complete with a blurred head shot of Benjamin Franklin. Beside the bill was the inscription "BY ANY MEANS NECESSARY." Tattooed onto the guy's stomach, visible between the hem of his too-small T-shirt and his beltless jeans, was simply "NOLA."

To Skip, this second tattoo seemed redundant. Where else could this individual be from? The way he looked, like some unhinged brigand, his haircut a whacked-off Mohawk in the front and long and stringy in the back, his river rat amalgam of off-angled Brooklynese with the occasional flowery Southernism thrown in, the guy was a *yat*—the tag stemming from the universal greeting "Where y'at?"— a species of Orleanian more indigenous than that army of termites munching away at the foundation of your house.

"How much for the drum?" Skip repeated.

"Can't you read?" the man replied, pointing to a nearly illegible handwritten sign reading, "$100—take it all away."

Skip had no need for any of the trash splayed across the sidewalk. "I'll give you a hundred for the drum alone," he bargained. "Keep the rest of the stuff and sell that for a hundred."

The man just kind of hung in space the way becalmed video game characters do, awaiting instructions from a joystick. On the small nearby stoop was a gaunt, almost concave woman, with henna red hair and chalk-colored skin. The girlfriend, Skip surmised. Beside her, sitting on folding chairs, were two men, one white, one black, both in what looked to be their late sixties, wearing those plastic-brimmed nautical caps aging jazzmen favor. They were drinking Pabst Blue Ribbon out of coffee mugs, or so it seemed from the number of empty beer cans at their feet.

"Take it or leave it," the man finally said, pointing at his sign.

That about tore it from Skip's perspective. He'd already made his best offer. Walking away, he heard the man's voice behind him. "Wait a minute," the man said. "I've seen you around here. You're a *neighbor*. That's a whole different story. I got a lot of things. Interesting pieces."

It was then, Skip remembers, that the man, who had now introduced himself as Dave, Dave Dominici, reached under a mottled table and pulled out a small lamp. "Check it out, *neighbor*. This isn't part of the other deal. It's separate," Dominici said, flashing a gap-toothed, leering jack-o'-lantern carny smile. "This is going to be right up your alley. There's a man for every product, and this is the thing for you. I *know* it."

The lamp in his hand, Skip felt his collector's impulse, his reverence for a particular object seen within the proper context, a talent cultivated in backdate magazine stalls, guitar salesrooms, and a thousand hours on eBay, click in. A quick scan revealed what appeared to be a beaux arts–style lampshade (the plastic fixture, from China, was of no interest) likely made in the mid-twentieth century. Ten inches across the top, a foot at the base, composed of panels, eight around, the shade's condition far from perfect but not too bad. Skip's first thought was he might be able to use it in his guest room.

Then something caught his eye about the lampshade frame, how the thin metal latticework was held together. When he was running his guitar shop back in Jersey, Skip often handled vintage German instruments, Höfners and Framuses for the most part. Both brands made a high-quality product (Höfner's jazz models and the hollow-body violin bass Paul McCartney played were especially good), but many players complained about the so-called popsicle stick structure of the guitar neck. Rather than a single piece, the German necks were composed of thin layers of wood sandwiched together with glue. The necks never warped, but to some ears they didn't resonate like the single-piece models. This made the German guitars sound, Skip thought, a little dead.

One other thing Skip noted about the German guitars whenever he obsessively dismantled and reassembled his stock was the solder. Funny how little details stick in your mind. The solder on American-made Fenders and Gibsons looked silvery and a little blobby. German solder had a darker, bluish appearance, with a liquid, almost oily sheen. The lampshade solder looked like that.

Now he began to grok it, the material of the lampshade itself. The warmth of it. The greasy, silky, dusty feel of it. The veined, translucent look of it.

"What's this thing made out of, anyhow?" Skip asked.

"That's made from the skin of Jews," Dominici replied.

"What?"

"Hitler made skin from the Jews!" Dominici returned, louder now, with a kind of goony certainty.

With that, the two old Pabst drinkers suddenly came to life. "Nazis! Adolf Hitler!" said the white guy.

"That's right. World War Two! Motherfucking Nazis!" said the black guy.

"Believe me, *neighbor*," said Dominici, a half smile on his bumpy face. "Hitler made skin from the Jews. It's a *historical fact!*" He pointed at the lampshade Skip now held in his hand. "You want it? Thirty-five dollars. That's a heck of a good deal."

A human skin lampshade for thirty-five dollars. That was a deal, all right.

• • •

Dave Dominici's claim about the provenance of the lampshade was unsettling, not that Skip believed it. New Orleans was full of wacky people with scary, implausible stories, more every day since the hurricane. But just because your worst nightmares were coming true on a regular basis was no reason to believe everything you heard. Was there any reason to believe *anything* Dave Dominici said? The man was seemingly not stable, a potential substance abuser of the first order. That very day, Dominici revealed that, along with his girlfriend, the thin and pale Gaynielle—*Gaynielle Dupree, was that New Orleans enough for you?*—he had slept right through Katrina.

"Out like a light. Dead to the world," he said, matter-of-factly. They didn't even wake up when the storm winds tipped his house on its foundation, leaving spidery cracks in the plaster walls. The next morning Dominici was puzzled to find himself walking uphill to get to the bathroom, as if he'd been transported to an antigravity room in a funhouse. It was only when he looked out the shattered window to see the uprooted trees and overturned cars that it occurred to him to inquire, "What the hell happened here?"

Dave Dominici was a character, all right, a true New Orleanian gone cat. As Skip was walking away with the lampshade, Dominici called after him. Did Skip want to buy some "house columns"? Two eight-foot wooden faux-Doric columns had held up the roof of the small porch in front of Dominici's house. One had been knocked down during the storm and lay in the yard. The other was in place. "*Neighbor!* Fifty for the pair," Dominici shouted, tugging at the still-standing column as Skip walked away.

Skip didn't believe it. Not at first. Still, even if he once had sold the skeleton of a human hand to one of his guitar shop clients, rock and roller Willy DeVille, Skip wasn't about to argue when his wife, the lovely Fontaine, told him there was "absolutely no way that thing" was going on any lamp in her house. Not with that story attached to it.

Skip could have thrown the lampshade out at that point, as much as it was preying on his mind, sending out those bad vibrations, real or imagined. He meant to throw it out. But he didn't. He let it sit there, in his closet, festering.

Once, during his "school pig" days in northern New Jersey, Skip was handed the case of a nine-year-old girl named Jessica. She hadn't shown up at school for a week and there was no answer at her home. Skip went out to the house to find out why. When he got there he found the house had been burned down ten days before. It was a crime scene. Someone had torched the place. Jessica and her grandfather were dead, burned alive. As it turned out, the whole thing was a big mistake. A female drug dealer in the area had been ripped off by another dealer, so she gave her crackhead boyfriend a can of gasoline and told him to burn down the rival's home. He got the wrong house. Jessica's body was nearly unrecognizable by the time it was recovered. The cops had Skip look through pictures of dozens of burned children, trying to get some kind of identification.

What made people do things like that, Skip often wondered, kill other people out of sheer stupidity and greed? On another truant case he showed up at the kid's address to find her three-year-old sister lying in a snowbank in her underwear. The mother had thrown her out of the house because she wouldn't stop crying. Skip wrapped her up in his trench coat and took her to the emergency room. When the doctors finally came to attend the child, Skip just stood there in the hospital hallway screaming.

These things stayed with you. They scarred you. Twenty-five years after the incidents, Skip could remember the names of all the victims, the colors of the rooms they lived in, the way the rugs in their houses seemed to be alive beneath your feet until you realized it was roaches, the bugs in shag carpeting that made it look like it was moving. What made seven-year-olds shoot other seven-year-olds in the face at the Iberville projects? Sociology was one thing, evil another. Evil was a magnetic force, Skip thought. It was as ubiquitous as the broken glass beneath your feet, the stale air you breathed. This was what priests had taught him, and Skip saw no reason to stop believing it now.

One morning, after a restless sleep, Skip packed up the lampshade and sent it to a drum maker he knew, a person with a taste for the macabre. A few days later the lampshade came back. "I've been beating on skins my whole life," the drum maker told Skip, "and I never saw anything like this. The animal that came from never had any fur on it."

A few days later Skip packed the lampshade up again and sent it to a pathologist he'd known for years. Once more the lampshade came back. "Don't send me shit like that," the pathologist said.

It was around then that I happened to call Skip. We'd gotten closer over the years, especially since I'd joined the Bywater Bone Boys and spent Mardi Gras morning making as much noise as possible, waking the "predeceased." Skip told me about the lampshade, the whole saga more or less.

"That's a weird story, Skip," I said.

"Well," Skip replied, "it isn't my problem anymore."

"How's that?"

"Because I just sent it to *you*. You're the journalist, you figure out what it is."

A few days later a box arrived at my door in Brooklyn. It came U.S. mail, covered with forty or so first-class stamps bearing the likeness of the great boxer Sugar Ray Robinson. Sugar Ray was Skip's way of saying he was sorry for sending the thing. He knew Ray was my all-time favorite, the way he moved. Like that was supposed to soften the blow. I opened the box and looked inside.

"Gevalt," I said.

THREE

Half a century before Skip Henderson's package arrived at my door, before the word *holocaust* was spelled with a capital *H,* my subteen friends and I, growing up in the "fresh air zone" of Flushing, Queens, knew the lampshade was a bad thing, not that any of us thought about it very much. Beloved child actors in the then fully functioning American Dream theater, we rode our bikes and bounced our Spaldeens in our own personal Utopia. If anyone said it wasn't so, we had Utopia Parkway, a nice six-lane road with its own exit off Robert Moses's (our Albert Speer) newly constructed Long Island Expressway to prove it. Just about everyone's dad worked for what civil servants always called "the City of New York," got his house on the GI Bill, and made the same amount of money. It was probably as close to socialism as there ever was in the United States, not that we Cold War kids, who one day gathered by the expressway to boo as Khrushchev's car drove by, were supposed to know anything about that.

The Italians were the tough guys, of course. Mostly they were okay, but there were those times when you'd hear that ominous chorus of fake sneezing. "Ah-ah-ah . . . *Jew!*" And there'd they be—Vito,

Joey, and Willie, the Romanos, the Littelis—bouncy in their continental pants, hairless chests thrust out, waiting to see what you'd do.

There were two choices. You could ignore them, hope they found someone else to hassle. Or you could reply, as I sometimes did, "*Guinea*-sundheit." Screaming and yelling followed, maybe some pushing. Sometimes the conflict would escalate. Then it would come out: "Shut your fucking mouth or I'll turn you into a lampshade. You heard me, *Jewboy. A lampshade.*"

This could not be ignored. "Take that back!" was the only acceptable response, and when it was not, there'd be no choice but to start swinging. It was crazy, because back then, at age ten, none of us knew exactly what we were fighting about, except that the lampshade had something to do with what the Nazis had done to the Jews—or more important in the universe of training-wheel machismo, something the pussy Jews *had let* the Nazis do to them, a really terrible, unspeakable thing.

In America, the story of the Nazi lampshade peaked following the 1948 commutation of Ilse Koch's sentence by General Lucius Clay, then military governor of the U.S. Occupation Zone in Germany. Stating "the evidence just wasn't there," Clay, accepting the recommendation of his staff, reduced the life sentence Frau Koch had been given at the Dachau trials to a mere four years, with credit for time served.

Stateside, reaction to the prospect of the skin-flaying, lampshade-making Bitch of Buchenwald walking free was instant and loud. New York congressman Emanuel Celler attacked Clay's decision as "an outrage . . . This woman has been responsible for the making of hundreds of innocent people into lampshades." The sentiment was echoed in the press and the fledgling television industry. Ed Sullivan, still on the Broadway beat for the New York *Daily News* in the early days of his Sunday-night variety show, wrote, "Maybe our Army has revised the conviction so that Ilse Koch can get back into the lampshade business again." Dorothy Fuldheim, a popular news figure of the time and the first anchorwoman to appear on television, expressed a common opinion, saying, "If Ilse Koch is not guilty, then Himmler and Hitler are also not guilty!"

The protest crossed political lines. Woody Guthrie, whose guitar bore the legend "This machine kills fascists," wrote a song called "Lucius Clay and Ilsa [*sic*] Koch." The lyrics were sung from the point of view of a camp prisoner. "I'm here in Buchenwald, my number's on my skin," Guthrie sings, describing the horror of the bodies being dumped in piles, the SS officers cracking their skulls and stealing the gold teeth from their mouths. Telling of "lampshades made from skins," Guthrie goes on, ending by saying the "stink is killing me" because "old Ilsy Koch was jailed/Old Ilsy Koch went free."

With Walter Winchell, then the most powerful newsman in the country (and a strange bedfellow for Woody Guthrie), attacking Clay's decision and demanding to know "What kind of friend does Frau Koch have in the Berlin High Command?" the U.S. Congress convened highly publicized hearings chaired by Michigan Senator Homer Ferguson to investigate the matter. Much of the damning testimony from the Dachau trial was read into the record, further cementing the image of Koch as a horseback-riding, lampshade-making Nazi monster. The hearings were front-page news for days. Treading a tenuous path between further embarrassment of the Army, which had just won the war after all, and troublesome possibility of double jeopardy, the Ferguson committee recommended that the fledgling West German government try Frau Koch for "crimes against German nationals," a category of offense that had not been covered by the Dachau proceedings. Eager to please the Americans at little expense to itself (who was going to come to the aid of someone like Ilse Koch?), the West German government quickly reconvicted the Kommandeuse, who was again given a life sentence.

What he called "that Ilse Koch business" would hound Lucius Clay for years. In 1950, he delivered a speech at New York's Town Hall and was interrupted by shouts of, "Let's ask General Clay about Ilse Koch and the human skin." Clay, who still has a street named for

him in Berlin, claimed never to have regretted his decision to com-
mute Ilse Koch's sentence, saying, "My judgment might be wrong but
it fits my conscience." His comment that the famous Buchenwald
lampshades were "absolutely proven" to be made of "goat-skin"—even
though there is no record of any proof of this claim—would later become a staple of Holocaust-denier rhetoric.

How much of this history filtered down to our preadolescent
brains is difficult to recall, except that I remember one evening
sneaking my parents' copy of Leon Uris's *Exodus,* a book found in
every Jewish household at the time, in hopes of reading some of the
dirty parts my friends had told me about. I never got past the sentence where Uris writes about how "Ilse Koch used the skin of Jews to
make lampshades." That sent me to bed with the covers over my head.

Then again, the 1950s were an odd time to be Jewish in the United
States, at least in my family. Culturally we were Jewish, willing to
assimilate as long as the seltzer man still brought the Dr. Brown's
Cel-Ray soda to the door. The religious aspect, outside of no Christmas tree, however, remained only a hollow but ensnaring echo of the
past. My parents never went to temple, even on the High Holy Days
(not riding in a car on Yom Kippur was their single act of atonement);
nonetheless I was made to attend Hebrew school three days a week
until my bar mitzvah in 1961. Our temple was of the Conservative persuasion, a sensible middle-class path between Unitarian-style Upper
West Side Reformists and the long-black-coated ultra-Orthodox. Still,
as the temple was relatively new (how we resented their building the
rabbi's house on our best baseball field!) and not well established,
many of the instructors were bussed in from more observant Brooklyn
neighborhoods.

Rabbi Adler was one of my teachers. Older than the others, with
hooded eyes, unkempt beard, and shabby coat, he was a scholar. He'd
grown up studying in unheated European yeshivas and did not keep
secret his humiliation at being so needy in this foreign land that he
was forced to make a living teaching a classroom of faux-*goyishe pish-
ers* like us. One time my friend Stewie forgot his yarmulke and was

wearing a Yankee cap instead. Adler snatched it from Stewie's head and threw it out the window.

"You!" Rabbi Adler yelled in his nearly impenetrable inflection. "You are not a Jew! *None of you are.*"

I was afraid of Rabbi Adler, his fright-wig hair and mottled skin no doubt fulfilling many of the anti-Semitic touchstones that had been drilled into my young, unknowing Yid head. Consequently, I wasn't thrilled one afternoon to find him standing beside me at the next bathroom urinal, specks of food in his scraggly beard, smelling like an old kitchen. Things had not been going well in class. Well aware that I, like most of my doo-wop-regarding, baseball average– memorizing classmates, could not read a word of Hebrew, Adler had been calling me to read from the prayer book. "Ha-ga-la . . . na . . ." was all I usually could muster, to his mounting rage.

Rabbi Adler stood there a moment, staring at me. "Mordecai," he finally said, using my Hebrew name. "Do you have any idea?"

"Excuse me, Rabbi, idea of what?"

Adler did not answer but instead pulled up the sleeve of his black coat to reveal a series of tattooed numbers on his forearm. He stuck the numbers in front of my face and held them there. "Idea of this," Adler spat before zipping himself up and leaving the bathroom.

That night I mentioned this incident to my father, who to my surprise seemed really angry about it. "He had no business doing that," my father said, agitated. Previously Dad's attitude toward my "Jewish education" was that I was to shut up and simply do it, get bar mitzvahed so everyone in the family could come to the party, and that would be that. This was the old man's basic approach to most parenting issues, in keeping with the standard operating mode of the stoic World War II vet. Arriving in Europe a few days after the Normandy landing, he'd fought with Patton's Third Army, in the Battle of the Bulge, up and down the Rhine Valley.

These were the facts, not that I heard them from my father. I read about them in old issues of *Yank* magazine and other Army publications that kept track of his unit, the 133rd Engineers Division.

I always asked him if he'd killed the soldier whose German helmet, complete with swastika decal above the rain curl, he'd brought back from the war. His standard answer was "He saw me, I saw him, we both fainted, but I woke up first." My mother, though, said Dad had killed the guy. "Shot him. Dead. The Nazi," she said, which definitely provided me with bragging rights down at the park.

What was true I never knew, but my father didn't care if we used the helmet for our war games. One day Dad saw me carrying my air rifle with the helmet on my head. "Oh, so today you're the Nazi," he said with a shrug, and went back to pruning his rosebushes.

Rabbi Adler's act, however, got under my father's skin. Later that night I heard him and my mother arguing about it. "He did that *on purpose*," my father said to my mother, who told him to keep his voice down. The incident was not mentioned again. It was near the end of the school year and Rabbi Adler did not return, replaced by other scary bearded men from nightmare worlds across the sea. But still, I think about why my seeing Adler's number tattoo upset my parents so. What was he showing me, after all, but history, what had happened to people for no other reason than that they were Jewish—Jewish like me, regardless of what the rabbi thought?

I didn't quite get it until many years later, after both my parents were dead. I went to a funeral for a great-aunt of mine, the sister of my father's father, Harry. There were twelve of them to begin with, eight boys and four girls. Some I knew, some I had never met, like the celebrated Uncle Larry, the family gangster who once, as the story went, won a Mott Street Chinese restaurant playing craps in a downtown opium den. The fact that he lost the restaurant to another gambler a couple of weeks later mattered little. For decades after, when anyone in the family craved a bowl of yat gaw mein, we always went to "Uncle Larry's," out of loyalty.

My great-aunt was the last of them, well into her nineties when she died. I drove out to the cemetery for the funeral and there they were: all the headstones, one for each brother and sister, none on this earth for less than sixty years. Their parents had bought that one-way ticket to Ellis Island in the nick of time; they'd all gotten out, not one of them had ever been sent to a death camp or had their skin turned into a lampshade by Ilse Koch. It was something to feel good about: their bones planted in the dispassionate earth of Nassau County.

This, I decided, was the key to my father's long-ago rage. It wasn't as if our family was so smart. There were plenty of others way smarter than us and they had been caught and killed. You couldn't just call us lucky, either. Dad would spend long afternoons playing blackjack in Atlantic City casinos when he was dying of kidney failure and wound up having a heart attack instead. He knew the limits of luck. The reason we had survived to thrive in this, our wondrous Queens Utopia, transcended luck or brains. You couldn't call it a smattering of benevolence on harsh Yahweh's part, either, because my father never believed in any of that. The way things worked out was beyond any accounting, not to be taken for granted but simply accepted. What had happened to Rabbi Adler and his people was their problem. We were Americans, citizens of the true promised land. Adler had "no business" trying to infect me, the blessed son, with their misfortune.

I appreciate my father for this sentiment, if indeed that was what he was thinking. No doubt he felt he was looking out for me. But as the sign on the Buchenwald gate says, *Jedem Das Seine*, you are who you are. And now that this stupid lampshade had arrived in my life, certain existential details could no longer be overlooked.

New York has gone through many changes since I ran free with my friends in as yet unsubdivided Queens. One thing remains the same, however. Even since Rudolph Giuliani supposedly cleaned up the town, there are still a lot of ways to wind up dead in the big city. Anyone who spends any time working at the Office of the Medical Examiner—what most people call "the morgue"—gets used to seeing all kinds of bodies. Shot bodies, stabbed bodies, poisoned bodies, strangled baby bodies, beaten-to-death bodies, to say nothing of so-called naturally diseased bodies and bodies whose vital parts are simply too far out of warranty to keep on ticking.

No morgue worker, however, had ever seen anything like September 11, 2001. From the first moments after the planes smashed into the Trade Center towers, the medical examiner's office was on full alert, ready for the unprecedented carnage certain to follow. Early estimates said as many as ten thousand people could be dead.

"That was the eeriest thing," says Shiya Ribowsky, who was Director of Special Projects at the ME's office on 9/11, "standing around on Thirtieth Street at the office waiting for the bodies. Bodies that never came. That's when we began to realize the scope of what had happened. We weren't going to get any bodies. Not intact, anyhow. What was coming would be pieces of bodies, if that." Over the next several months Shiya Ribowsky and his coworkers at the examiner's office spent as many as sixteen hours a day attempting to sort the remains of the people killed at the World Trade Center, some of whom would take years to identify.

I got Shiya Ribowsky's name from a former NYPD homicide detective who spent a long time working on missing persons cases. "Try this guy. I met him at the ME's office," the cop said, in his cop way, offering the name, the phone number, and nothing else.

Truth be told, I'd been dragging my feet on the lampshade. In fact, I'd done almost nothing about it in the four months since it had arrived from New Orleans other than to stick it in a closet. When Skip Henderson called, as he often did, to find out "What's up with the lampshade?" I told him I was working my way up to it. After all, I was busy, a working man with things on my mind. Even if what Dave Dominici had said was true, a long shot at best, the thing had been lying around for more than sixty years. Another couple of months wouldn't hurt. No need to rush into things.

Every so often, however, I'd take it out of the box, give it a once-over. On the surface, the thing didn't look all that creepy. If you didn't *know*—if the idea hadn't been planted in your head—it would have been very easy to walk past the shade in some dusty secondhand store. Even if you did stop to pick it up and inspect the oxidized metal frame and the parchment panels, what would you see? Just a vaguely antiqueish table lampshade with some cheesy boudoir tassels in the shape of little bells hanging off the bottom.

Not knowing the story, a person might easily enough confront the lampshade armored with the rational. After all, if there was one thing everyone had heard about human skin lampshades, especially the human skin lampshades associated with the so-called Bitch of Buchenwald, it was that they were made of tattooed skin. That was the whole decorative scheme, so to speak. The lampshade that the heavily tattooed Skip Henderson bought from the equally heavily tattooed Dave Dominici had no such markings. It was tattoo free. Beyond that, the standard opinion among scholars (it is now possible to get a Ph.D. in "Holocaust studies") had long been that Ilse Koch did not make "hundreds" of human skin lampshades as Emanuel Celler had contended. In fact, as with the equally celebrated case of the soap the Nazis supposedly made from "Jewish fat," many historians now believed the lampshades, if they existed at all, were quite peripheral to the vast story of the Holocaust, that they were possibly even illusionary tchotchkes of terror, the product of Allied propaganda and the brutalized imagination of prisoners.

This was how the rational person would regard the lampshade. But knowing the story, just having the suggestion inside my head, changed everything. It preyed on your mind, as Skip Henderson said. Knowing the story made it almost impossible not to feel what Skip felt when he picked up the shade: the warmth of its touch, the strange, greasy smoothness, how diaphanous it looked when placed near the light, the way the stretched panels looked to be marked with striations similar to the ones I saw on my own skin. Knowing the story brought up unsettling questions beyond even the obvious ones of who made the shade and how it had come to be in New Orleans. For instance, what about those tassels, which at least to the untrained eye appeared to have been affixed to the bottom of the frame at a later, perhaps even significantly later date? Why would someone go to the trouble of adding them onto an old lampshade? And what did that person know?

About five minutes of that was enough to make me stick the lampshade back into its Sugar Ray Robinson–plastered box and lock it in the closet for another few weeks. Still, what was I to do? I could have sent the box back to Skip Henderson when it arrived, as the drum maker and the pathologist had. But I hadn't. I had kept it. I had put it inside my home, where my wife and I raised our three children. Skip was desperate to get rid of the thing and he had. He'd passed it on to me, and the fact that it was inside my closet, and inside my head, was proof enough that I'd accepted the assignment.

My first idea was to send it to a friend of a friend who worked at the American Museum of Natural History. My friend said this guy was a genius with taxidermy. Certainly he would be able to tell human skin from that of other animals. A few days later the man called me and said he couldn't help me.

"Look," he said. "A lot of my relatives were killed in the camps. This isn't something I need in my life. You understand, right?"

"Yeah, sure. I understand." It wasn't something I was about to insist on. I asked him if there was someone else there who might help me.

"No," he said, and hung up.

Shiya Ribowsky, despite his seriously Jewish name, had no such compunctions on this account. I called him and told him the story about Skip and Dave Dominici and how the thing had come to me. "I'd be *very* interested to see that," he said with a friendly eagerness. He lived on Long Island, but today being Friday, he was in New York. He had a free hour late this afternoon. Could I bring the thing over right now? Did I know that synagogue in Gramercy Park?

"Yeah," I said. My dentist happens to be on that block. I passed the synagogue, located in a former Quaker meeting hall, all too often. Why did he want to meet at a shul?

"I'm the *chazzan* there."

"You're the *cantor*? I thought you worked at the ME."

"I *did* work there. But I've always been a cantor. I do both."

"A forensic cantor—that's a trip."

"Tell me about it."

Now forty-three but still sporting the boychik good looks to make the Hadassah ladies swoon, Shiya Ribowsky has been saying the kaddish, the Jewish prayer for the dead, for more than thirty years now, ever since his debut as a boy cantor in the Flatbush synagogue his father had helped found back in the early 1970s. Put this history alongside his fifteen years in the medical examiner's office, where twelve thousand dead bodies arrive every year, eight thousand of which are autopsied, and you could say that Shiya's relationship with death is more nuanced than most, on both the spiritual and the physical plane.

In Shiya's view, his twin professions coincide paradoxically. When he sings in his exquisite, neo-operatic tenor and recites the Kaddish, it is for the benefit of the living. Inside the tiled walls of the medical examiner's office, there's only the dead.

"It is job one of every religion ever invented," the cantor said with his characteristic matter-of-fact, somehow uplifting manner, "to make us feel better about what we will inevitably become, which is for most people, let's face it, a mass of rotting flesh under the ground. You could say I work both sides of that street."

In the months and years following 9/11, more than twenty-two thousand separate fragments of what had once been human beings arrived at the medical examiner's office. In the beginning the parts were large—sections of legs, whole hands—but gradually the pieces were smaller, sometimes so tiny as to be seen only under a microscope. To be working at the ME's office then, Shiya says, "was about as close to Auschwitz as I'll ever get, a total onslaught of death."

Even for the forensic cantor, someone who for years often spent all day Friday walking up housing project staircases to see the aftermath of domestic violence, blood and entrails splattered against the apartment wall, and then, mere hours later, found himself singing to his well-heeled congregation of the immortality of the soul, the unprecedented interface between the living and the dead on 9/11 was traumatic.

"In this world we will do anything to isolate ourselves from the dead, to pretend that these are two completely disconnected states," Shiya said. "Nine-eleven removed that barrier. So many of the people killed that day were simply pulverized, turned to dust. They were there, in that cloud that hung over Ground Zero. *They became the very air we breathe.* Chances are if you were in downtown Manhattan back then, every time you inhaled you were taking in the dead. If you were a jogger, you were lining your lungs with them."

Then, in his impish way, Shiya smiled. "You could say I have a special insight into death, being dead myself."

Shiya was talking about a wholly other kind of death, one that spoke of his existence as a New York Jew, an experience very different from my own. Born into a Brooklyn family that was "as *frum* as they come" (*frum* being the name the ultra-Orthodox Jews give to themselves), Shiya is descended from a long line of clerics. "When my family got together, you couldn't throw a prayer book without it hitting half a dozen cantors or rabbis." There was no doubt that Shiya, despite his father's demeaning contention that he had "a small voice" that "couldn't reach the back row of the shul," would follow in these hallowed footsteps.

"This was the future, I thought. I had no reason, none at all, to think any differently," remarked Shiya, who lived the life of a young Orthodox boy, wearing only black pants and white shirts, attending yeshiva fourteen hours a day from the age of seven, studying Torah. "That was going to be me," Shiya said, "one of those stooped-over young men with the Coke-bottle glasses, twenty-five going on sixty, cashing a small check—that's what they call them, 'check cashers'— from a rabbinical organization to read Torah and think about Jewish law all day long . . . except my mother made a big mistake, or at least I know she *thinks* it was a mistake, one she regrets to this day.

"You see, my mother was something of an anomaly in the *frum* community, partially because her mother was born in the U.S., in Lowell, Massachusetts, but mostly because she went all the way through secular schooling and got a doctorate. In most *frum* communities that simply never happens. Whatever schooling most women get stops at the point when they're ready to start having children. You won't find very many women in Borough Park with a Ph.D., believe me. But this didn't affect my mother's religious zeal, which has only kept growing to this day. Fundamentalism is an odd thing. It gives you this special sight, the ability to be on the lookout for any and all invading impurities. On the other hand, it makes it so you can't see your nose in front of your face. So I don't think my mother ever considered the risk she was taking, dropping me off at the public library once a week while she did her errands."

It was at the Flatbush library that Shiya first encountered Robert Heinlein, Ray Bradbury, and many other science fiction writers whose ideas often clashed with what he was hearing in the yeshiva. Soon he was reading straight science writers like Stephen Jay Gould and Carl Sagan. "Carl Sagan," Shiya said. "Carl Sagan caused a lot of spiritual warfare inside my head.

"I was in a bind; as my thinking got more liberal and secularized, the community, the Orthodox community, was getting more Orthodox. The first generations of Jews that came to America, like your relatives, wanted to fit in, to assimilate. They succeeded. Jews were more confident, secure that the knock on the door in the middle of the night was really a thing of the past. That was truly wonderful. It also made the Orthodox feel free to become more Orthodox. They became more protective of what they felt were their true roots, although very few Orthodox practices would have been recognizable to Moses, or at least a Moses who had never been to the shtetls of Europe in the eighteenth and nineteenth centuries.

"The past, the life of the shtetl, this whole kind of imagined life with its fundamentalist attitude, took over and gradually I began to realize that religiously I'd become this totally run-of-the-mill, nicely well-adjusted Conservative *American* Jew, living among these aliens. I was reading evolutionary biology and they were telling me the world began fifty-seven hundred years ago and believing otherwise was a *chil' hashem,* or an affront to God."

It all came to a head when Shiya's marriage to his first wife began to break up. "We were married in the Orthodox tradition, but increasingly I felt no longer part of that. My ex and I fought bitterly about it, how I was no longer religious enough. I decided I didn't want to be there anymore. The problem is, the way the community had become, once you leave, the door slams behind you. All of a sudden my ex was making it very difficult for me to see my three children.

"My parents took her side because at a certain point, in the transformation from the rationalist thinker to the fundamentalist, religion and a specific way of practicing is all that matters. That way of thinking is beyond me. I would never presume to know exactly what God wants for humanity and the Jews. The zoom on my Google Earth doesn't pull back that far. The fact that I was a cantor and had been for years, leading services every Friday and Saturday, every High Holy Day, the fact that I *have* to sing, that for me singing is something totally necessary, and that the cantorial liturgy is the music I want to sing—that in many ways I felt *more Jewish in spirit* than ever didn't matter. I might have been singing the same prayers they sung, but I was doing it in a Conservative temple, so that wasn't good enough."

The end, as far as his family was concerned, occurred when Shiya remarried, to his wife, Jen, who was raised Catholic. "Jen converted, she went to the *mikvah,* consulted with many rabbis, but this was never going to cut it for my family. They declared me dead.

"Believe me, you haven't lived until you've had your mother and father sit shiva for you."

This was the man who greeted me at the door of the shul on Gramercy Park South that late winter day in 2007. He was just saying good-bye to some hip-looking Manhattan kids he'd been tutoring for their bar mitzvahs, just like Rabbi Adler and his successors had tutored me. We sat down in the temple banquet hall and talked for a few moments before Shiya said, "So let's see."

The lampshade was still in the box with the Sugar Ray stamps. Shiya lifted it out and held it in his hands, then turned it around. He held it up to the overhead light.

Shiya Ribowsky in shul

"It's parchment, that's for sure." Shiya has handled a lot of parchment in his life, parchment inside tefillin, mezuzahs, and the Torah itself. The lampshade material reminded him of all that. "But it is thinner, much thinner." He held the lampshade closer to his face and turned it around again. Then he took a deep breath and sat heavily into a chair, placing the lampshade on the table in front of him.

"This is the saddest thing I've ever seen in my life," he said.

He looks at twenty thousand pieces of murdered human beings, and this lampshade Skip Henderson bought from Dave Dominici on Piety Street in New Orleans is the saddest thing he's ever seen in his life? "You don't really think this is real, do you?" I asked.

Shiya kept staring at the lampshade on the table in front of him. "There's one way to find out. The DNA."

He went out to his car and came back with a surgical scissors and some small plastic bags. "Mind if I take a couple of samples?" No, I said, I didn't mind.

• • •

With *Shabbos* soon approaching and a few of the congregation members beginning to arrive for services, I left Shiya and headed back to Brooklyn. The F train was packed with the usual multihued crew. The blacks—harried office workers getting looser for the weekend, mixing with slouchy high school hip-hoppers—would mostly get off at Jay Street to change for the A train out to Bed-Stuy and beyond. With them went the various Caribbeans, headed to the far reaches of Crown Heights, to Utica Avenue. The few straggler Hasidic black-hat Jews, cutting it too close for comfort on a Friday afternoon, would stay on until Borough Park and Midwood, along with Bengalis and Pakistanis. Ditto the Dominicans and Puerto Ricans, who lived up on McDonald Avenue. The Russians, more of them every day, it seemed, their outward demeanor stolid and put-upon, would ride to the last stops, where Brighton meets the ocean. There were the "professionals," too, mostly white and mostly young, slogging home from midtown cubicles. Many of them would get off at my stop, which is Seventh Avenue in what used to be called South Brooklyn but now like everything else around, is called Park Slope, a nomenclature dictated by the real estate market.

Sitting among the daily gaggle, the lampshade in its box on my lap, it was no great reach to assume that many of these people, myself included, might never have been born had Hitler's killers succeeded in winning the war. In the brand-new world envisioned by the Reich planners, this trainful of supposed *Lebensunwertes Leben*—"life unworthy of life"—would be replaced by a whole other kind of humanity, riding not in the subway but in the sleek comfort of a Deutsche Liner, a posture-perfect array of second- and third-generation *volk* in their Hugo Boss tailored daywear, medicated for extreme performance by I.G. Farben, checking their holdings in a tightly edited merger of the *Wall Street Journal* and *Der Stürmer*.

This subway cacophony, with its sticky floors and zombie iPod listeners, was so different from the Valhalla the Nazis foresaw for themselves. Down here, nobody needed Plato, or Darwin, to tell them

the world was a finite place, without enough to go around for everyone with the deluded temerity to call themselves human. Democracy, even the illusory sort practiced in America, was a dangerous,
inevitably suicidal thing. Sooner or later these F-train *untermenschen*
would rise up like the nasties in *Metropolis,* demanding their wholly
undeserved share. But in the dream-life of the Reich, with all of Africa and the Russian commies dead or forced into slave labor, some
already working on moon colonies organized by Werner von Braun
and other rocket wizards, there would be no commodities crisis, no
global warming, no economic criminality. It was a fact of natural law
that superior groups would triumph over and subjugate the inferior.
So why not just make it the law of the land, remove the hypocrisy?
And when this happened, the planet would be returned to a primally
clean Eden for the New Chosen People, at least after the perceived
competition, the viral Jews, with their rootless, conspiratorial culture,
had been eliminated.

With the lampshade samples already on their way to the DNA
lab, it was no stretch for me and my fellow riders to count ourselves
lucky that the Nazis had made their grab for racial hegemony when
they did. A mere seven decades after the promulgation of Laws for
the Protection of German Blood and German Honor in 1935, which
among other things forbade "the extramarital sexual intercourse between Jews and subjects of the state of Germany or related blood," it
was sobering to imagine what the Hitlerites might have accomplished
had they cracked the genetic code. With their zealous Teutonic genius for organization, what chance would supposed lesser beings
have had if Mengele's mad alchemist notions of turning brown eyes
blue had been replaced by a technology capable of producing a complete chromosomal profile from a single strand of hair?

Shiya sent the lampshade samples to the Bode Technology Group, a
well-known genetic analysis laboratory in Lorton, Virginia, outside

Washington D.C. In the aftermath of the 9/11 disaster, the New York medical examiner's office had done a lot of business with Bode and Shiya had been impressed by the results.

"Medical knowledge tends to expand during wartime, and nine-eleven was no different. The science of DNA identification grew up on the back of nine-eleven," Shiya explained, adding that despite the lab's distressing address on Furnace Road, Bode had the best chance of making an analysis of the aged and desiccated lampshade cutting. "Nobody can do what they do," he said.

A quick look at the corporate history of the Bode company, however, was a bit unsettling. Founded by Tom Bode in 1995 as a midsized laboratory providing DNA identification primarily to law enforcement agencies in sexual assault and paternity cases, the lab was purchased in May 2001 by ChoicePoint, a leading "data aggregation" company with strong ties to Republican Party heavyweights in both the public and the private sectors. Onetime CIA operative and Bush administration undersecretary of state Richard Armitage was a former CEO; John Ashcroft served as the firm's main Washington lobbyist after his run as U.S. attorney general. Despite involvement in a number of controversial episodes, including the 2000 Florida presidential vote counting, by 2005 ChoicePoint was maintaining seventeen billion separate records dealing with individuals and businesses. In 2007 Bode was sold again, this time to the GlobalOptions Group, another Pynchonesque-named concern whose advisory board included two former FBI directors, William Sessions and William Webster. At this point, Howard Safir, once Rudolph Giuliani's largely ceremonial police commissioner, now head of the GlobalOptions Security Consulting and Investigations division, became Bode's CEO. Although primarily known in law enforcement circles for once busting acid guru Timothy Leary and being related to Louis Weiner, the detective who arrested bank robber Willie Sutton, Safir was a strong advocate of the commercial possibilities of DNA typing in the security industry. Shortly after he took over at Bode, the New York *Daily News* ran a story questioning whether $20 million of NYPD contracts with the lab during Safir's tenure as police commissioner had been "extended without competition from other bidders."

Asked if he worried about the potential exploitation of such a powerful identification tool as DNA sampling for political, commercial, and/or privacy-invading reasons, Dr. Robert Bever, vice president and head research and development officer at Bode Technology, sat in his office on Furnace Road and offered only a small smile. A cautiously friendly man whose wire-rimmed glasses and short-sleeved white shirt give him the aspect of an earnest colonial missionary, Bever is not given to making global comments, especially when they might reflect upon his boss.

Originally trained as a microbiologist, Bever, now in his early fifties, began in the forensic DNA business working on paternity cases in a lab he set up in his garage. "It was all test tubes and used Volvo parts," he said. Author of many peer-reviewed articles with titles like "Utilization of a Robotic Workstation, Fitzco FTA Paper and the Promega Powerplex to Optimize Laboratory Procedures for the Analysis of STR Loci," Bever first came to Bode in the late 1990s and has been head of R & D for the past half dozen years.

"I think about the implications of this work, the way it might possibly be misused," said Bever in between phone calls with technicians. "We're dealing with the structure of life itself. You can't approach that from a totally technical point of view. This is something I think about—the big picture, the context of our world within all of Creation. In the office, however, we must look through a different lens. Here, all that matters is what can be seen at the end of the microscope. The results. As a scientist and a believer, I don't have any problem with this juxtaposition. There's no real contradiction to me."

When it came to the lampshade, however, Bever acknowledged an added complication, offering a personal note about how a number of his family members had just managed to escape the Nazis. "They left only a couple of weeks before Hitler closed the border . . . That disrupted their lives forever. Sometimes I think how my own life would have been different if that hadn't happened," Bever related, in his measured tone. "When you bring in something like this, a lampshade, with all the stories attached to it, you can't call it just another sample. But it is our job to treat it like that." Still, it was something of a coincidence, my bringing the lampshade to Bode, Bever added, since Jared Latiolais, the research scientist who would be doing the actual DNA testing, was from New Orleans and still had many family members there, several of whom had been displaced by Hurricane Katrina.

Bever would not guarantee any success. He agreed with what Shiya Ribowsky had told me: "With a sample from a living being or someone recently deceased, there will always be a lot of genetic information. The human body is like a wet sponge, DNA-wise. You just have to squeeze it. With this lampshade, the age of it and state of degradation, that's very problematic. With these kinds of samples, what we're doing is trying to wring a bit of life out of death. Some things are more dead than others."

From the start, Bob Bever was fairly certain that any meaningful DNA identification of the lampshade would be of the mitochondrial variety. There are two varieties of DNA to be found in every cell. The vast majority of genetic information is in the nucleus. This is the nucleotide DNA, the site of Crick and Watson's double helix, the full ledger of a being's hereditary dossier. However, as Bever made clear, nuclear DNA is relatively fragile, susceptible to degradation in the face of excessive moisture and sunlight, which was a problem since if there was anything New Orleans had in abundance, outside of *bon temps* and drive-by shootings, it was heat and humidity.

This left the mitochondrial, or mtDNA, the feminine ghost in the genetic machine. The DNA in the cell nucleus is the product of equal contributions, twenty-three chromosomes each from the offspring's mother and father. MtDNA, on the other hand, is descended solely from the female, a matrilineal linkage that has given rise to the often debated concept of "the mitochondrial Eve," the idea that all humans can trace their origins to a "most recent common ancestor," conjectured to be a woman who lived 140,000 years ago in East Africa. While that is not an evolutionary scenario to cheer a *blut und boden*

Nazi eugenicist, mtDNA has nonetheless proved a boon to modern-day forensic detectives. It has been especially useful in the search for so-called ancient DNA, since even if the genetic information found in the mitochondria is less varied than the nuclear, it tends to be hardier and more stable.

Certain that the age and condition of the shade precluded much recoverable data, Bever said he hoped to "amplify the mito" in the lampshade sample, thereby enhancing the remaining DNA sequences. One major hurdle would be to eliminate "contaminates." You didn't want to pick up genetic material from the various handlers of the shade. Buchenwald, if that was indeed where the thing had come from, was liberated in 1945. It was now 2007. Who knew how many individuals might have touched the lampshade in its prospective journey from the Ettersberg forest to New Orleans? At the time it was impossible to know even how long the lampshade had resided with Dave Dominici before he sold it to Skip Henderson. By the time I came to see Bever, Dominici had already changed his story three times as to how and where he had come upon the lampshade. To get a verifiable reading on the DNA of the "base material" of the shade itself, the "competing profiles" of its handlers would have to be stripped away. The sample would have to be bleached and bleached again. This was a laborious process, Bob Bever said. It would take some time.

Meanwhile, the lampshade, snug in its box, sat quietly in my closet, biding its time.

Having written that cool five-thousand-dollar check to Bode Technology, a true point of no return, I figured there were only three ways it could go:

A) The lampshade could be "fake," made of Lucius Clay's unverified "goat skin" or perhaps pig bladder—the bladder of a pig being apparently so similar in molecular structure to human tissue that doctors have used it to reattach severed fingers.

B) Very likely the lab would be unable to make a definite identification. Bob Bever had already said that even if DNA could be retrieved from the sample, it would likely be at the "picogram" level. Asked what a picogram was, Shiya Ribowsky said, "Think of it like this: if the universe is so large as to be beyond imagining, then the picogram might be smaller than we can conceive of."

Then, there was C) The tests would come back saying the thing was real: made out of human skin. This would change things quite dramatically.

After all, you could look at paintings like Fritz Hirschberger's pastel nightmare *Arts and Crafts in the Third Reich*, which shows a demure-looking Ilse Koch seated at an ochre-colored table with Karl Koch, a long-stemmed floor lamp with a pinkish shade bearing the image of an innocent girl in a forest green bonnet. You could read "Lady Lazarus" by Sylvia Plath, surround yourself with the poet's wrenching sectioning of her soon-to-die body, her right foot "a paperweight," her face featureless and fine like "Jew linen," her skin "bright as a Nazi lampshade."

However, to possess such a thing, to be able to hold it in your hand—a *real human skin lampshade*—this was an emotional and intellectual bridge not yet crossed. It was news. And, I had to confess, a large part of me wanted it. That was the shock, how much I wanted that object in the closet to have once been part of a walking, talking human being. It wasn't only me. Nearly everyone I spoke to about the lampshade said, given a choice, they would, with grave reservations of course, rather it be real. It was more than the fact that pig bladders aren't what you call a good story. Here, even in the age of 9/11, after a century of genocide from Guatemala to East Timor, was an opportunity to grasp the unthinkable.

The phone call came soon enough. You couldn't say it was a eureka moment because someone as sober as Bob Bever does not have eureka moments, at least none that show. The lab had done the testing several times, all with the same result. It wasn't much, a level barely above what could be measured definitely, but it was there.

"The report says it's human," Bever said evenly.

"You're sure? No mistake?"

Bever exhibited a sense of irritation. Yes, he said, a mistake was possible, but he was not in the business of making mistakes.

Bever said, "Right now, if I had to stand up in a court of law, as I often do, I would testify that we have found evidence of human origin."

"Huh."

The report emailed from Furnace Road arrived in my in-box a few moments later, dated April 20, 2007, which would have been the Führer's 118th birthday, sixty-two years to the day after Ann Stringer's story about the Buchenwald lampshade broke. A number of items jumped out. Comparing the mtDNA haplotypes found in the lampshade samples to "standard Cambridge Mitochondrial sequences," it was ascertained that the "NCBI database . . . came back with a 0.0 e-value signifying a 100% probability that the cyt b sequence is human." Two such human profiles were found, one major and one minor. It was the opinion of the lab that the minor profile might be due to the handling of the lampshade, but "the major profile is most likely from the lampshade material itself."

A few hours later, Bever called again to make sure I had gotten the report. Yeah, I told him. I did.

FOUR

When I called Skip Henderson to tell him about the results of the DNA test, he was driving down North Claiborne Avenue under the I-10 in "the Bus."

The Bus, a $400,000, forty-five-foot-long converted RV with thirteen Internet-ready computer terminals and a $20,000-plus satellite dish on the roof, was a gift to the City of New Orleans, part of the Bush administration's scattershot Hurricane Katrina recovery plan. The original idea was to create a mobile center to help the handicapped and those otherwise unable to travel find employment. However, with the ravaged city short of cash and unsure how to properly deploy the extravagant vehicle, the Bus remained parked out at Louis Armstrong Airport for more than a year. When Goodwill Industries arrived at a public-private arrangement with the city to organize new post-Katrina employment services, the Bus became part of the deal. It was supposed to be a two-person unit, staffed by a computer-savvy employment counselor and a driver. However, there was only enough money for one salary, which is how Skip, ace employee of the Louisiana Department of Labor, wound up doing both jobs.

Planning was somewhat free-form. Basically, Skip was given the key and told to park in various parts of the largely deserted city and teach whoever happened to straggle in how to log on to Craigslist and other employment sites. There were difficulties from the start. When Skip went to pick up the RV for the first time, he found all the tires of the eight-ton vehicle completely flat. There was no spare. Skip warned the Goodwill people the satellite dish was going to get stolen, but no one listened. One day parts of the thing slid off, crashing to the pavement. Apparently some thieves, trying to remove it, had loosened the bolts.

The presence of Mayor C. Ray Nagin's name on the side of the Bus, part of a complicated municipal takeover of the program, didn't help. On one occasion an outraged citizen started banging on the door, demanding to talk to the mayor. His life in shambles since the storm, the man hadn't received any of his promised state or federal relief and wanted to make sure the mayor knew of his frustrations. "I know he's in there. It says so right there," the man screamed, pointing to the mayor's name on the vehicle. "Send that motherfucker out here! *Right now!*" The Craigslist thing was also problematical, with several would-be job seekers saying, "List? You ain't gonna put me on no list."

Still, Skip forged ahead, testing the Bus's loosely strung suspension system in the ruined sections of town, attending to those he called "America's Least Wanted." When I reached him with the news about the lampshade, Skip was returning from Gentilly, where the still-visible Katrina waterline ranged as high as ten feet in some spots. Skip listened to what Bob Bever had told me, then, barely audible, said, "Let me call you back."

I didn't speak to him again until the next evening. After hearing the news, he had immediately driven the Bus to its lot, locked it up, gotten in his car, and driven home, where he drank quite a bit of Jack Daniel's and several beers. Then he went to his computer to retrieve a picture he'd downloaded of Masha Bruskina, a seventeen-year-old Byelorussian Jewish Communist partisan being hanged by a laughing Nazi SS officer, an image that had haunted him for decades. Skip stared at Bruskina's dead face, impassive, unrelenting beneath the hair she'd bleached blond to pass as an Aryan, and began to weep. Then he stumbled into his living room and fell asleep on the couch. When he woke up several hours later, both his young daughters were perched on top of his prone body as if it were a bleacher seat as they watched an episode of *SpongeBob SquarePants*.

Getting up, Skip drove the five blocks to Piety Street, where Dave Dominici lived. Reaching through the padlocked iron gate, Skip knocked on the wood door, which bore a sign saying, "Trespassers will be shot, survivors will be shot again." There was no response, so he knocked again, harder this time. He heard the sound of someone stirring, followed by a shout of *"Identify!"*

Being, as he later described himself, "pretty much out of my mind by this point," Skip screamed, "It's me! Skip. Remember me? I bought the lampshade!"

The door opened a crack. Dave Dominici's face appeared, a New Orleans Saints fleur-de-lis skull wrap askew across his forehead. Dominici opened the door wider. He was wearing boxer shorts. In his hand, underneath a folded newspaper, Skip could see what he imagined to be the barrel of a large pistol.

It was late now, and there was no one around except for a couple of drunks exiting Markey's Bar a block down Royal Street. "You remember me," Skip said again. "The guy who bought the lampshade. You know, your *neighbor.*"

A glimmer of recognition set in. "Oh . . . *Neighbor!*" Reaching through the gate, Dominici opened the padlock. "Come on in, *neighbor,*" he said, suddenly as friendly as can be.

The door opened into the kitchen which was lit by the glare of a single floodlight clipped onto a nail beside the refrigerator. Running around the room barking her head off was Dixie, Dominici's shepherdlike mutt. A beige rug covered most of the kitchen floor. Dominici told Skip not to step on the rug because it was covering a four-foot-square, three-foot-deep hole in the floor.

"Don't want to lose you, *neighbor,*" Dominici said.

"That lampshade you sold me—remember that lampshade? *It's real!*"

Dominici looked out of it. Totally fried. He didn't seem to have any idea what Skip was talking about.

This angered Skip. When he first got the lampshade, he entertained, for a moment, the notion that Dominici might be some kind of neo-Nazi, a rump follower of David Duke, Louisiana's foremost fascist, who'd run for governor and senator a number of times back in the 1990s. Skip had met those freaks in the various jails where he'd worked trying to save the prisoners from themselves. But Dominici didn't fit that bill. He looked like a hophead, not a Nazi, unless it was possible to be both at the same time, which Skip doubted in a place as lethargic as New Orleans. Still, you couldn't just lay a human skin lampshade on a guy, along with all those sleepless nights, and then claim to have forgotten all about it.

"The lampshade—the damn lampshade," Skip screamed, his ire dissolving to pleading incomprehension. "It's made out of *a person*."

Now Dominici was engaged. "A person?"

"A human being. They did DNA testing on it. In a lab. It's human."

"Human," Dominici echoed, and began walking around the kitchen, stopping in front of the stove, where he squatted and placed his hands on his head as if trying to ward off a migraine. He stayed balled up like that for several seconds before catapulting himself forward, barely missing falling into the hole covered by the rug.

"I knew it. I knew it was Jew flesh!" he screamed.

It was not long before more came to light about Dave Dominici. As I would find out when I visited him at his Piety Street home, the hole in his kitchen floor now covered by a pair of nailed-down exterior doors. Dominici was something of a local celebrity. He was, as he said, "The famous cemetery bandit. The most hated man in New Orleans."

Dominici opened a battered leatherette valise and pulled out a handful of creased clippings from the *Times-Picayune*. "These are all about me," he said, with a salesman's pride. There were two dozen or so articles, from 1998 up through 2002, with headlines like "A Grave Injustice," "Stolen Artifacts' Worth Could Run into Millions," and "Cemetery Thief Pleads Guilty."

The story was this: In February 1998, a groundskeeper at the Lake Lawn Metairie Cemetery, one of New Orleans's celebrated "cities of the dead," from which a large number of decorative statues, brass urns, and benches had been disappearing, spotted what he termed "a suspicious-looking Chevy van with white curtains" moving slowly along the narrow roadways between the graveyard's rococo tombs. The groundskeeper noted the van's license plate and called the police. The vehicle was traced to one Carl Campo, the twenty-six-year-old son of a St. Bernard Parish handyman. After some questioning by New Orleans police detectives, Campo confessed his part in a cemetery robbery gang, fingering Dave Dominici as an alleged "ringleader" in what *Times-Picayune* columnist Chris Rose, writing in *People* magazine, called "a gothic netherworld of crime and greed involving people on all levels of Big Easy society, from petty criminals to the *beau monde*."

Local color writers have been milking the spiked treacle of New Orleans's seedy hoodooism for more than 150 years, but this was hard to beat. Dominici, in the role of a forty-year-old subtropical Fagin, had rounded up a dope-fiend krewe of yats and entered into a compact with a number of French Quarter art dealers, notably one Peter Patout, a descendant of a leading antebellum Louisiana sugar plantation family, to steal and sell a large parcel of the city's most treasured commodity: the dead, or at least the accoutrements of the dead. The dealers kept some of the stuff, sold the rest. A six-foot-tall statue of the Virgin Mary taken from Lake Lawn was selling at a French Quarter shop for $5,200. Other items taken from Orleanian cemeteries began turning up in antique stores in Los Angeles and London, some going for as much as $50,000. According to the *Times-Picayune,* cops had recovered artifacts estimated to be worth a million dollars but

believed that there was "still ten times that out there." The thefts pro-
voked public outcry across class and racial lines.

Perhaps it has to do with those bodies entombed above the ground,
never quite consigned to the finality of having stern Protestant dirt
flung across their face, but even a newbie Bywater Bone Boy calling
out to the predeceased on Mardi Gras morning knows that in New
Orleans, you can stomp someone in a bar, spray bullets from a passing car, murder your parents, and that's just a call to the NOPD, who
may or may not get around to it in due time, blue lights flashing. But
you do not mess with the dead. You do not, no matter how desperately
depraved you may be, desecrate those waterlogged, moss-covered
cemeteries, trash those marble-lined pathways that Walker Percy, the
greatest of the New Orleans local color writers, even better than the
obscurantist Faulkner, called, in his best tourist pamphletese, "tiny
lanes as crooked as old Jerusalem, meandering aimlessly between the
cottages of the dead."

These were not just any dead. As the *Times-Picayune* reported,
"The thieves hit the final resting places of some of the best-known
New Orleans families, including the restaurant-owning Brennans;
the Brocatos, known for dispensing Italian ice cream; and the jazz
musician Louis Prima, of Louis Prima and Keely Smith fame."

If the bandits had raided only the graves of Comus, the sarcophagi
of the uptown rulers, expensively capped teeth might be gnashed, but
few hoi polloi tears would have been shed. But this was a violation of
the eternal rest of the immigrants, the Irish and Italians who came to
the city in the late 1800s when New Orleans was the second-largest
port of entry in the country behind Ellis Island, the dead of those
who'd arrived with nothing and made the new money that kept the
place going beyond the stink of the Confederacy when to be called a
dago in the Quarter often meant running for your life right behind
the blacks. No doubt the immigrants who made it big had profited
handsomely from Jim Crow laws, becoming rich during those soul-
deadening times when the only nonwhites seen around the hot spots
of the city's famous heart-attack cuisine were smiling, always smiling

waiters. But at least they redistributed the wealth from the hands of the plantation class, extending democracy by running businesses based on providing pleasure, even if it was often tourist pleasure.

These were the dead plundered by Dave Dominici, whose grandfather, Papa Tony, came to New Orleans from Palermo in 1910 and, in the manner of so many immigrants who made good, sold enough pasta out of his Colonial Macaroni factory to advertise on New Orleanians' favorite horror movie TV show, *The House of Shock,* hosted by Morgus the Magnificent.

Eight years after his cemetery bandit arrest, kicking back in "the sitting room" of his Katrina-ravaged house, Dave Dominici flipped through his cemetery bandit clippings with a mix of regret, nostalgia, and bravado. "Twenty-two times we were mentioned on the front page, twenty-two," he intoned, pausing over a photo of the distraught Brennan family in front of their desecrated Lake Lawn mausoleum.

"I know I shouldn't have done it and I don't blame these people for getting upset. I'd feel the same way if someone stole from my gramps's tomb. But I was broke and I had this habit, so do the math on that." The haphazardly colored images from Dave's malfunctioning big-screen TV flitted across the cracked ceiling. When he was first arrested, they said he was looking at life in prison, on account of his two previous felony convictions, on drug and burglary charges. This prospect was reduced due in part to the contrite Dominici's efforts to help recover the stolen objects. But still, five years is like forever when you're ticketed for Angola.

"Angola Prison," Dominici said, with dread befitting the fearsome 18,000-acre "farm" in West Feliciana Parish, the largest maximum-security prison in the United States, home to as many as 5,000 bad men at a time, many of whom will never again walk free.

Angola was no picnic; you did what you had to to survive. If this included alliance with the Aryan Brotherhood, Angola's leading white-power gang, so be it. "I'm as proud of my race as the next fella, but I wasn't into that stupid Nazi shit," Dominici said. "But if you had two thousand black guys trying to punch a hole in your scrotum with a sharpened Bic pen, you'd be Heil Hitlering all over the place, too. Moses would have done the same."

Dominici had no complaints about his punishment. What bothered him was how the art dealers like Peter Patout "got off light" and left him holding the bag. "It was all their idea," Dominici moaned, his eyes bulging slightly from his head. "All along they're buying this stuff from me for like a hundred dollars apiece, marking it up a hundred times, sending it all over the world. Then I'm in Angola reading a month-old newspaper and I see Patout is out of the joint and he's so fucking repentant he's joining some Save Our Cemeteries bullshit because all that matters to him is preserving New Orleans's heritage. I'm like, '*Nigga, please!*'"

Since getting out of prison in 2004, he said, he'd turned over a totally brand-new leaf. The house on Piety was an integral part of that. "I got it from a little old lady for thirty-nine thousand before the storm, a real steal." Just two blocks from the river, soon enough the place would be worth "five times that," thanks to the coming Mississippi "Riverwalk" park that Mayor Nagin and his fatcat buddies were talking about building along the levee with the federal money supposedly pouring in for storm relief. His house had the value-added aspect of having "a historical location," since the long-defunct streetcar named *Desire* used to pass right by his kitchen window making its run down Royal Street. It all made sense, Dominici said, since way back to Chalmette High School the girls were always saying he reminded them of Marlon Brando before he started playing those fat-guy parts. Who was Stanley Kowalski, anyway, but a yat?

All he ever wanted, Dominici said, with junkie earnestness, was a chance to prove himself. To be "a normal person." The house was the big first step, "the nest egg." Even if the Riverwalk thing got bogged down, he could still rent out the back half of the place to some strippers he knew. Sure, it needed some "cosmetics," but that was no problem since he was a wizard at interior decoration.

"I'm not just another guy with a head on his shoulders. I'm a guy with a *head* on my shoulders.

"Back in school all I cared about were science and history. Logic. Not that faith business, that pie-in-the-sky religious baloney. The rest of the class is reading Dick and Jane and I'm going through Einstein. The theory of relativity. E equals MC square, Jack, that's what I'm talking about! Teachers said, 'David, you're a sleeping giant, so why don't you wake the fuck up?' People are always underestimating me. I got a knack for innovation. I ever tell you how I was the first chicken spicer at the first Popeye's? Ask Al Copeland if you don't believe me. I was the one who mixed up the spicy and the mild, the fucking flour and cayenne powder all stuck up in my eyebrows like Elmer's glue. Who knows, I'm a hell of a cook, I could have put something in there, that one missing ingredient that clinched the whole deal. People might be eating Popeye's all over the world for no other reason than that little dash of paprika I threw in. I should have gotten something for that! I should have gotten a high-volume franchise in a good location. An honorarium. Something! But fuck it, I'm patient. My time will come. Like the cemetery bandit thing. That wasn't nothing. It wouldn't have made the papers so much if it was nothing. You think it's easy running through a pitch-dark cemetery with a hundred-fifty-pound marble angel under your arm?

"If there was one thing I tried to instill in my krewe, it was some appreciation of art history and taste. You just can't walk in there and start loading up, grabbing the first thing you see. You got to know the difference between the Italianate styles, because Sicily ain't Florence, Florence ain't Rome. You got to check the fingers and the toes, the thin parts, see if it's marble all the way through. Because a lot of people are cheap. God bless them, but they're cheap even in death. It could be just cement covered with marble. You don't want to be out there in the middle of the night stealing fakes. But I know . . . I can tell things. When it comes to the value of things, what they *really* are, I got a sixth sense. I'm never wrong."

That was how he knew about the Nazi lampshade. "I got an eye for antiquities, spot them right off. But you got to find the right buyer, you know. The person who is really going to appreciate an object. The proper fit."

This was where Skip Henderson came in, Dominici said. "When I saw him coming across the street from Mickey Markey Park, I thought to myself, Oh, here comes one. A fish. All I got to do is put out the line and it'll be gobble, gobble, gobble. He looked just like the kind of guy who'd buy a Nazi lampshade."

Dave Dominici in front of his home

Over the next few months I spent a fair amount of time with Dave Dominici, trying to get him to tell me where he got the lampshade.

Originally Dominici told Skip Henderson that he got the lampshade from his dead father, Ralph Dominici, who'd fought his way through Europe after the D-Day landing. His father didn't talk about the shade much, Dave recalled, only said that it was a "trophy of war" to be handled with extreme care. The problem with this story was that Ralph Dominici, who died in 1975, fought in a war, but it was the Korean War. Later Dominici told me he'd been given the shade for "safekeeping" by a ninety-year-old "Jewish fellow named Cohen with one of those tattoos on his arm" who'd moved to Terrebonne Parish to be the rabbi of a synagogue and "live out his twilight years with his people." Told there was no synagogue in swampy Terrebonne Parish (Jewish population, circa 2000: 936) with a ninety-year-old rabbi named Cohen, Dominici said, "Okay, I'll tell you the truth."

The truth was, he said, that he had been given the lampshade by a legless, wheelchair-bound World War II vet, Master Sergeant Peter Patrick Francis Walsh III, whom he and Gaynielle Dupree had met while they were living in a trailer park on the other side of Lake Pontchartrain outside of Covington, Louisiana. It was an act of forgiveness, Dominici said, explaining that he, being "dope sick," had robbed Walsh's trailer, stealing his credit cards. "But I felt bad about it," Dominici said. "I gave back the stuff. And apologized." This was why Walsh, then near death, gave him the lampshade, Dominici said. "He wanted to show that he wasn't mad."

The farfetchedness of this story, plus the fact that no local veterans' organization, the VFW, or the American Legion had any record of a Peter Patrick Francis Walsh, did not deter Dominici. Sticking to his story, he wrote out "an affidavit" attesting its truthfulness. Set down in looping cursive on a piece of lined loose-leaf paper, the statement was titled "How I Met Mr. Walsh."

It said: "Sr. Peter Francis Patrick Walsh III (Covington) (War Vet.) . . . Bobby Bartholomew, sometimes boyfriend of Mr. Walsh's drinking buddy, Mrs. Ann Willie Lester. Bobby Bartholomew met his end at the bottom of a railroad track when he decided to end his (considered) worthless life. Committed suicide (alcoholic). This is how I met Mr. Walsh." Signing the document with his middle name, Ralph, "just to make it more legal," Dominici said that Bobby Bartholomew had actually died by putting his head on the tracks and having the train run over it, but he didn't think that was important to

mention in his statement. All the rest, however, was gospel, and he offered to go over to Walgreens to get it notarized. I told him this would
not be necessary.

I'd about given up on getting anything more out of Dominici when
he called me one Sunday morning. Sounding strangely upset, he said
if I wanted to hear "the *real* truth" about how he got the lampshade,
I should come over to his house right away.

Meeting me at the door in his Saints wear, Dominici was a wreck.
He'd lost his sunglasses and looked like he'd been crying. I don't know
what calamity had befallen him, but something had stolen his swag-
ger. He apologized for sending me on "so many wild goose chases"
but said he had no choice after Skip Henderson had come by to tell
him about the DNA test. "He said that and I got so freaked out. Ask
Gaynielle, it was keeping me up. I was sweating, going nuts."

He was already the most hated man in New Orleans on account
of the cemetery caper, a longtime loser. "If it got around that I had a
human skin lampshade, I'll tell you what would happen. The cops
would be over here trying to hang some Hannibal Lecter rap on me.
Like I was some kind of sick maniac, a disemboweler and whatnot.
Believe me, I have fucked up enough in my life. My moms don't need
to be reading that in the *Times-Picayune* with the morning coffee."

The truth was, Dominici said, "It came from the storm. *Katrina*.
That's how I got it. From Katrina."

To hear Dominici tell it, the hurricane had left him in a "state
of shock, a temporary insanity." Yes, he'd slept through the storm,
but that just made it worse, waking up to a ruined world. "We get
up and we're totally out. No dope. No works. Talk about your junkie
nightmare. I come out the door and it's like everything is destroyed.
Trees gone, cars upside down. But when you got to cop, you got to cop.
Down here we weren't flooded. I didn't have much street water. That
kind of fooled me, because the TV is out, so I didn't hear anything
about the levee breaks, I didn't know about the floods. I just know
I got to see Momma Hilda. She was an old black lady with diabetes
who sold syringes for one dollar. To her house is just a straight walk

up Piety; I done it a thousand times. But now, as I go, I'm seeing the water is getting higher. By St. Claude it's all over my feet. By Robertson it's up to my waist. I'm going, what the fuck is this? Because now I'm swimming. I'm swimming through these tree branches, all these articles of clothing. Shoes, eyeglasses, a whole damn shed went by.

"So I finally get up to Momma Hilda's place, where the water is, like, ten feet high, and I see what looks like this gray bush just bobbing in the water between the shotgun houses. Right away I know it's Momma Hilda, 'cause she's got that color hair. She must have fallen off the porch because she couldn't walk too good and drowned. *Poor dear!* I pulled her out of the drink. I'm crazy dope sick, but what can you do? She was such a nice lady. I just stayed there crying because it was really awful what was happening. After that I went around, trying to save people, getting into houses, seeing who was alive. I was obsessed, because when it comes down to it, I hate death."

A couple of days later the National Guard came by Dominici's house and told him he had to get out. "They got ten guys there with M16s telling us to get our toothbrushes and jump in the truck. That's all they said. 'Get in the truck.' They took us to the airport and put us on a plane. Never said where we were going. I'm screaming, 'Ain't this supposed to be America?' Nobody gave two shits about that. They took us to Knoxville, to some fucked-up Beverly Hillbillies housing project. I'm yelling I got to go back to New Orleans, New Orleans, Louisiana, that's my home. They said to shut up, there was no such thing as New Orleans anymore and I should be glad to be in Tennessee."

Soon after, Dominici and Gaynielle were moved up to New York. "They put us in a Ramada Inn near the airport, room 702 in LaGuardia, New York. I could hear the planes flying by, could see Shea Stadium out the window, and I'm screaming, 'Hey, Bobby Bonds, bust one my way.' We got arrested for not paying the subway fare, but they let us go on account of being refugees.

"New York was cool. But I missed New Orleans too much. I bought this fucked-up little Amigo pickup truck with our relief check and drove back down here. Car was a piece of junk. Every hundred miles or so something would fall off it. But we had to get home, you know? It started making really loud noises around Hattiesburg, Mississippi. But I told Gaynielle, we're so close, we can't stop now. The thing finally died, right out here, coming down Piety Street. We just cruised the last two blocks and shut it off right where you see it now. My house was a mess. Some squatter kids had been in there, dog shit all over the floor. I ran them out of there with shotguns. But at least I was back, you know."

That was when he started "finding things," Dominici said. "There were so many abandoned buildings. People just left everything and got out of town. Plenty of it was ruined, but not all of it. It wasn't like stealing. No one was coming back for these things." It was in one of these houses, Dominici said, that he found the lampshade.

"There was this whole pile of stuff piled up in the front room. Everything nobody would ever want. And there it was, right on top of the pile, balanced up there, like a cherry on top of an ice cream sundae. There wasn't any electricity. Not for months. But I had my flashlight. I remember it was raining. Kind of a mist. The rain was coming in because the roof of the house was ripped off. The way it looked in the flashlight, glistening, it caught my eye. Don't ask me where I got the idea of what it was. But I'd been watching some Hitler stuff on the History Channel. I've always been a history buff.

"You have to trust your instincts, know when something's special . . . That's why I say it was from Katrina. If it wasn't for the storm, I never would have found it."

For the life of him, Dominici could not remember in which house he had found the lampshade. It was part of his post-traumatic shock from the storm, he said. There had been so many houses. Nothing, not even a hundred-dollar bill, could jog his memory. It had long been a bad problem with him, remembering things. One time he shot himself in the leg by accident. Sometimes it still hurt, but when he'd roll up his pants to show the scar, half the time he'd have the wrong leg.

He chalked it up to his ADD. All he could recall was that the house where he got the lampshade was in the lower Bywater, past Alvar Street, not across St. Claude.

Dominici was born in the neighborhood, on Mazant Street in the late 1950s, before the whites moved out to St. Bernard and Jefferson parishes when the feds forced the schools to integrate. Katrina's impact on the area had been erratic—not a lot of flooding, but a lot of wind damage. In the middle of 2007 the piles of debris were still in the streets. Maybe half the buildings were inhabited. A knock on about fifty doors followed by a couple of increasingly labored questions as to whether anyone was missing a human skin lampshade produced mostly puzzled looks.

A meeting with Terry Fredericks, a local contractor who'd employed Dave Dominici briefly to gut wrecked houses after the storm, provided a lead. Fredericks said he'd known the Dominicis for a long time and gave Dave a job "only because his mother begged me . . . I had to fire him after my chain saw suddenly disappeared. He said he didn't know anything about. But I knew he stole it."

Hearing the lampshade story, Fredericks said Dominici wasn't the type to have something "creepy" like that. "He's just a thief, if you know what I mean." Fredericks did, however, have a thought. Right on the other side of the Industrial Canal, in the Holy Cross neighborhood, there was a house that Dominici had worked on. "Someone weird must have been living there. We found a crossbow and some knives. I saw David poking around in the debris, like he always does," Frederick said. "I'd check there."

The house was on Lamanche Street, in the Lower Ninth Ward, the neighborhood that bore the brunt of Katrina's worst devastation. St. Claude Avenue on this side of the canal had never exactly been the Miracle Mile, but two years after the storm there wasn't a single store open for business, not even a gas station. Tourists could still see many of Katrina's most photographed sights—the boats in the middle of the street, the broken church cross stuck in the upper branches of a leafless cypress tree, a white limo on top of a Mitsubishi pickup truck. At nightfall, the place became forbidding, what with the squatters and the unreliable electricity. Even in midafternoon the desolation of the place, its near-total abandonment, was appalling.

It took a few passes to find Lamanche, its street sign was nothing but a Magic Marker scrawl on an eight-inch piece of broken picket fence nailed to a post. The flooding had been severe here, and fifty feet down the street, nature was taking back the land. Tall reeds had grown up on either side of the narrow, potholed road and slapped against my rental car as I drove through. Amid the runaway growth it was possible to forget the surrounding destruction, to discount the entire man-made history of Louisiana back to its purchase in 1803, when the territory made up, as most people here are happy to remind you, more than half the United States.

Throughout nearby St. Bernard Parish, where the prestorm population of about seventy thousand now had fallen to less than twenty-five thousand, you could drive along the curving streets of devastated subdivisions and occasionally come upon a ranch home that had been renovated. The house looked like a totally normal American suburban dwelling, with the pickup in the driveway, bicycles on the porch, a happy face sticker on a shiny mailbox announcing the family's name. The homeowner himself might be out front, watering his resodded lawn, seemingly oblivious to the fact that every other dwelling on the block was abandoned, many with fading Do Not Demolish signs in front.

The house on Lamanche where Terry Fredericks suspected Dave Dominici might have found the lampshade was in the middle of a slo-mo fix-up. Work had been done on the roof; the windows were new. Water-damaged Sheetrock leaned against the porch; a tattered plastic sheet covered the side door. Sitting on the porch was a teen-ager, probably fifteen or so, holding a sleeping baby. Light-skinned in the manner of what is called Creole down here, she was talking on a pink cell phone. She was laughing when I pulled up, but my unannounced presence put a stop to that.

"Do something for you?" the girl asked, warily.

I said I was doing some research on the area and did she know anything about the people who might have lived in the house before the storm.

"Before the storm? Don't know nothing about before the storm." Her aunt, whose house in New Orleans East was wrecked in the flood, had just moved in a couple of weeks before. Their stuff, what they had, was still packed in boxes. Asked if she had found anything "strange," like some old military stuff, or anything foreign, the girl's mood brightened. Yes, she said. Her aunt had found "this weird money" behind the house. "It's foreign. I don't even know where from."

She got up, taking the baby with her, and returned a few moments later with a canvas bag containing maybe twenty coins. "They might be from anywhere."

I dumped a couple into the palm of my hand. "They're Canadian."

"You mean, like, from Canada?"

"Says it right on there."

The girl looked at the coin. "Guess I didn't see that. Shit. Canada's next door. I thought it was far," she said, deflated. Sullen once more, she said she couldn't give me her aunt's number, but I could leave mine. "What am I supposed to say you want?" Seeing no downside, I explained a bit about the lampshade.

The girl looked horrified. "You think it was in this house? They found it here? That's terrible!"

"I didn't say it was from here," I said, attempting to backtrack. "I'm trying to find out about a story I heard."

The baby started to fuss as the girl gave me that look, like if she lived to be a thousand, she'd never understand why white people say and do the things they do. "You looking for something that used to be a person," she said. "People I know—they're looking for people that are still people."

• • •

In his book *The Theory and Practice of Hell,* the first comprehensive account of life in a Nazi concentration camp and in many ways still one of the most informative, Eugen Kogon, a conservative Austrian Catholic who was a political prisoner at Buchenwald from 1939 to 1945, describes the daily routine of the place. Awoken as early as four in the morning by whistles, prisoners were given a meager breakfast of weak coffee and a piece of bread and then made to assemble in the *Appellplatz,* the wide-open field between the inmate barracks and the entrance gate, for roll call.

Prisoners at Buchenwald roll call

"Thousands of zebra-striped figures of misery, marching under the glare of the floodlights in the haze of dawn, column after column— no one who has ever witnessed it is likely to forget the sight," writes Kogon, describing how the various categories of prisoners were de- noted by color-coded SS-issued triangular patches sewn onto their clothing. The "politicals" bore a red triangle, "criminals" green, black was for the "work shy" and the "asocial," purple for Jehovah's Witnesses (described in camp parlance as "Bible researchers"), and pink for homosexuals. Jews wore the infamous yellow triangle. If a Jew was deemed to also fall into any of the other groups, the appropriate colored triangle would be sewn over the yellow one to make a Jewish star. At the morning roll call, the prisoners would line up—as many as twenty-five thousand forced laborers, slaves, really—to be sent out to their various work details in the quarries, machine shops, and pigsties, and in the evening were reassembled in the same spot.

The evening roll call included the dreaded head count, which often took hours, since if anyone was missing, the entire camp was made to stand at attention until the absent prisoner was found. Kogon recounts one such occasion. In December 1938, the prisoners were assembled on the *Appellplatz* for nineteen hours in subzero temperatures, motionless except for incessant commands to remove their caps from their shaven heads and put them back on again.

"Twenty-five had frozen to death by morning; by noon the number had risen to more than seventy," he writes. Kogon describes a similar situation the preceding winter when prisoners were forced to strip naked for a number of hours, a sight which attracted "the wife of Kommandant Koch, in company with the wives of four other SS officers," who came "to the wire fence to gloat at the sight of the naked figures."

One recurring feature at roll call was the singing of "The Buchenwald Song," always accompanied by the camp band. The song was commissioned by SS Major and Deputy Camp Kommandant Arthur Rödl, an alcoholic Karl Koch crony and member of the Nazi "Blood Order," indicating party membership dating back to the days of the Munich Beer Hall Putsch. Other camps had songs, so Buchenwald should have one as well, Rödl declared, offering ten marks to any prisoner writing an acceptable tune. Many proposals were turned down before an entry submitted by a "green" criminal but actually written by a pair of Austrian Jews was accepted. Apparently either unaware of or unconcerned with the underlying subversiveness of lyrics like "O Buchenwald, I cannot forget you/For you are my Fate . . . We will say yes to life/For the day will come when we are free!" Rödl ordered each prisoner to learn the song. Appearing at roll call "stinking drunk," he would snap, "Sing 'The Buchenwald Song'!" He'd require the inmates to stand for hours in driving rainstorms until the piece was rendered to his satisfaction.

The Jews had their own song, which they were forced to sing repeatedly, often at the command of the SS officer Hermann Florstedt, who, after the transfer of Karl Koch to Lublin, was widely reported to have been Ilse Koch's lover. Entitled "The Jew Song," it went, "For years we wreaked deceit upon the nation/No fraud too great for us, no scheme too dark/All that we did was cheat and swindle/Whether with dollar, pound, or mark/But now, at last the Germans know our nature/And barbed wire hides us safely out of sight . . . And now, with mournful crooked Jewish noses/We find that hate and discord were in vain/An end to thievery, to food aplenty/Too late, we say, again and yet again."

At one time, anyone standing on the *Appellplatz* could have seen most of the camp. It would have been possible to scan the array of prisoner barracks, small wooden shacks called "blocks," fanned out in lines of eight and ten, the "children's blocks" set behind them. To the side would have been the medical experiment blocks, with their tile-topped tables on which Nazi doctors went about their harsh rounds of yanking gold teeth and stripping skin from the dead. Also visible, of course, would be the crematorium and its squat smokestack, where, prisoners grimly joked, the exhaust of their existence would soon be rising.

I thought that seeing these things would provide context, a way to collate the experience of standing in the cold wind with what can be read in books and seen in movies. It was in and around those doom-laded bunkhouses that Margaret Bourke-White, traveling with Patton's army, took her famous photos of the bodies that Edward R. Murrow, in an anguished on-site radio broadcast, said were "stacked like cordwood." But most of the camp structures were torn down by the Soviets in the early 1950s before they turned the place over to their East German clients, who, in the interests of their "antifascist" cause, memorialized the vanished buildings by filling their footprints with piles of stones.

On the day I arrived, I saw nothing from the *Appellplatz*. The winter Ettersberg fog had descended and was so thick I could barely make out my feet. The last, sparse tourist group had long since filed onto their bus and gone down the Blood Road, and I was alone, marooned on the *Appellplatz*, enveloped in the fog like a gauze-wrapped mummy.

Years before, in Phnom Penh, I'd visited Tuol Sleng, a former high school that became the notorious S-21 prison, where the Khmer Rouge tortured and murdered more than fourteen thousand people between 1975 and 1979. What happened at Tuol Sleng ("Hill of the Poisonous Trees" in Khmer) was as hideous as anything ever attempted by the Nazis. The chilling photo gallery of the victims and the list of "security regulations" still hang on the wall: "4: You must answer my questions without wasting time to reflect." "6: When getting lashes or electrification you must not cry out at all." Still, when the harrowed visitor leaves Tuol Sleng, he steps back into the world. On the other side of the fence, outside the prison entrance, people bustle by, deliverymen go about their business, motorcycle taxi–men hang out beside their scooters smoking cigarettes, the bougainvillea blooms. The Buchenwald *Appellplatz* was not like that. Socked in by the fog, it was as if the end of the line had been reached, with nothing but abyss ahead.

Who knew what manner of ghosts lurked out there in the gray swirl? So many had died here. At any moment I expected them to assemble in their striped pajamas for yet another roll call. I could join right in, singing "The Jew Song."

I'd lived a charmed life, I knew, growing up in America, removed from the terror of my roots. In Romania, where half my family comes from, they didn't even need Nazis. The Romanian army competed with the *Einsatzgruppen*, SS "mobile killing teams," to see how many

Jews they could murder. It was in the blood there, too. But I'd been spared, much as I'd gotten out of so much other misery, the Vietnam War included. Past sixty now, and they hadn't laid a glove on me. Yet here I was, at long last, the gate that declared *Jedem Das Seine* shut behind me.

And what had brought me here? The stupid lampshade. A few weeks before I got on the plane to Berlin, Skip Henderson called me in his special kind of panic to tell me about a dream he'd had. It was the lampshade, hovering, against a black background. That was it, his entire dream. The shade never moved, just stayed there, blocking his view of anything else in life. This was when he realized something about the tassels, the little Hershey Kiss bobs everyone I'd talked to was certain had been added years, perhaps decades, after the construction of the shade itself. The guy from Sotheby's had told me: "Beaux arts, central European, midcentury, fringe added later." Hugo Ramirez, who owns a classy antique lighting shop on Fifty-ninth Street in Manhattan, had agreed: "Definitely central European, maybe thirties or forties; someone put those tassels on later."

"Take the thing out of the box," Skip demanded. "Look at the tassels."

"What about them?"

"They're Mardi Gras colors, aren't they?"

It is remarkable what you don't notice. Skip was right. The tassels were faded, not garish and plastic-bright like the beads the masked men throw at you from passing floats. But they were definitely green, gold, and purple. Green, gold, and purple, in that order, all the way around. So what did that mean? That the unknown individual, the surreptitious stitcher, the one who put the tassels on, had a really sick sense of humor? Who knew? If anything did seem certain, however, it was that Dave Dominici was right when he said the lampshade came "from the storm," that without Katrina it would have never come to light. It took the churn of Katrina's double, double, toil and trouble to dredge the Nazi lampshade up from the underground.

As I stared off into the Buchenwald fog, I felt a connection between this place of terror, where the lampshade supposedly had come from, and where it ended up, in the New Orleans flood. The lampshade had its secrets, things I needed to know. Perhaps Goethe, poet of the Wal-purgisnacht, would have had an answer. But even that was far from clear, as I knew from my copy of *Faust,* inside my shoulder bag even as I stood amid the murk on the *Appellplatz.* In the dedication, the poet, with "a shudder that shakes my frame" writes "the firm heart feels weakened and remote. What I possess, mine, seems so far away from me, and what is gone becomes reality."

PART 2

FIVE

Long before David delivered two hundred severed Philistine fore-skins as a dowry for Saul's daughter—the old king, in the midst of being driven crazy by God, had demanded only one hundred—the removal of large and strategic sections of skin from the human body already carried an extraordinary significance. The protective bound-ary between the inside and out, the skin is the largest organ and the most personal, the palette of individuality and free will. Without the skin, the rest of the body becomes a dripping pile of anonymous spare parts. Without the skin, the soul is nothing but a vaporous pres-ence on the hunt for a new host.

The skin's role as the keeper of the self is illustrated by the story of Marsyas. The satyr, finding an *aulos,* a flute that had been discarded by Athena, recklessly challenged Apollo, god of music and master of the lyre, to what the jazzmen call a cutting contest, to see which one of them was more adept on his instrument. The Muses were called to judge the match. The stakes were high: the winner would be free to do whatever he wanted with the loser. At first Marsyas outplayed Apollo, angering the deity. In response, Apollo turned his lyre upside down and repeated the same tune. Marsyas could not match this on his flute, so the Muses declared Apollo the winner. Punishing the satyr for having the temerity to confront a god, even one who cheated to win, Apollo decreed that Marsyas be flayed from head to toe.

Ovid retells the myth in *Metamorphoses*. "Why are you stripping me from myself?" the satyr screams. "A flute is not worth such pain." Marsyas's skin was hung from a pine tree near the Turkish frontier. Ovid says the satyr, his "sinews uncovered," his "trembling veins exposed," became "nothing unless a wound."

Throughout history people have skinned other people for the purpose of torture, execution, religious sacrifice, battle trophies, or sheer pleasure. Assyrians were known to have flayed their enemies and draped their skin over the walls of their cities as a warning to restive elements of conquered peoples. Michelangelo protested what he felt was Pope Julius's censoring of his work on the Sistine Chapel by painting his own face onto the flayed Saint Bartholomew in *The Last Judgment*. A 1661 entry in Samuel Pepys's diary describes his journey to the cathedral in Rochester, east of London, where "the great doors of the church are covered with the skins" of a Danish pirate who had supposedly plundered the place and was made to pay the price for his misdeeds. The Harvard Library owns a seventeenth-century English volume bearing the inscription "The bynding of this booke is all that remains of my deare friende Jonas Wright, who was flayed alive by the Wavuma on the Fourth Day of August, 1632. The King did give me the booke, it being one of poore Jonas chiefe possessions, together with ample of his skin to bynd it. *Requiescat in pace*."

Scalping—peeling away the skin on the top half of a vanquished enemy's skull with the hair still attached—is most recently associated with Native Americans but had been customary throughout the world for centuries. Herodotus reported that Scythian warriors, if they planned to share in the spoils of war, were required to deliver a number of enemy scalps to the king. Visigoths, Anglo-Saxons, and Franks also scalped victims, a practice that was brought to the New World by settlers who were just as likely to strip the skin from the skulls of Indian warriors as the other way around.

Various versions of skin removal, including the Semitic practice of circumcision, have been recorded in numerous cultures, but probably the most elaborate of such rituals is associated with the Aztec deity Xipe Totec, whose name means "Our Lord, the Flayed One." A late advent in the Aztec pantheon, not attaining widespread veneration until shortly before the arrival of Cortés's conquistadors, Xipe Totec, a.k.a. "the Night Drinker" and "the Red Smoking Mirror," was usually depicted wearing a coat of freshly severed human skin, symbolic of his status as a fertility god.

Celebrating the spring equinox, Xipe Totec ceremonies began with the sacrifice of several individuals on stone slabs near the Great Pyramid. Victims were slit open with obsidian knives, their skin carefully separated from the body to keep it in one single, uninterrupted piece. These skin suits were then dried in the sun and painted yellow to give them the aspect of sacred "golden clothes." Priests wore them for a twenty-day period during which they engaged in mock battles symbolizing Xipe Totec's ethos of change through conflict. When the ritual period ended, the priests took off the now decomposed skin suits, as a snake sheds his skin, to reveal a new body within. The rotting skins, seen as the sacred vehicle of change, were then sealed away in airtight jars in the temple.

While ritual flaying for religious reasons would now be considered the sign of a barbaric culture, the practice is still very much with us in the commercial, pseudoscience realm. Body Worlds is a traveling anatomy exhibition in which skinned human corpses are displayed engaged in various activities, including a number of sexual positions. Relying on an embalming technique called "plastination," which preserves human organs by the infusion of various silicons and epoxies, Body Worlds has been seen by more than thirty million people, many of them paying as much as forty dollars per admission. The brainchild of Dr. Gunther von Hagens, the son of an SS cook, who famously never appears in public without his trademark black fedora (he once performed a public autopsy in front of five hundred people while wearing the hat), Body Worlds is not without controversy. Questions have been raised about where those skinned bodies come from, and who gave permission for their use. Von Hagens has presented much documentation that his plastination shops in Dalian, China, and Kyrgyzstan are run according to local law, and that the remains were all donated with informed consent. That said, it is doubtful that any high school biology field trip visiting a Body Worlds show (or any of the similar, competing exhibitions) will see a skinless, epoxy-stuffed German, or any white European, exposing his insides while posed in the midst of kicking a brand-name soccer ball.

Perhaps the most influential flayer of human skin was not a bookbinder, shaman, plastinator, or organ dealer but rather one Ed Gein, a diminutive and seemingly unremarkable resident of windswept Plainfield, Wisconsin, population 889. Although he is often mentioned as the father of the modern serial killer, Gein (the name almost rhymes with "fiend") was charged in the death of only two people, which puts him at the extreme low end of the body count scale. Still, his notoriety—Gein's macabre deeds served as the basis for such resonant cultural touchstones as the Norman Bates character in *Psycho,* Buffalo Bill in *The Silence of the Lambs,* and Leatherface in *The Texas Chainsaw Massacre*—far outstrips the likes of Ted Bundy, Juan Corona, Wayne Williams, Dean Corll, Richard Speck, and many, many others. Much of Gein's infamy owes to the time and place of his deeds. Even with the Nazi camps and the mass death at Hiroshima fresh in the mind, it was still considered unthinkable that such insanity lurked in the American heartland. It was shocking to hear that a strange but supposedly harmless little man (as Anthony Perkins said, he "wouldn't hurt a fly") kept a supply of severed human noses purloined from graveyards in a water glass and ripped the skin from the dead to upholster the furniture in his sitting room. In Gein's case, the appalling thing was not the killing but the taxidermy.

There is no evidence that Gein had any knowledge of Xipe Totec when he murdered hardware store owner Bernice Worden, from whom he'd just purchased a gallon of antifreeze, disemboweled her, and began wearing her skin around his soon-to-be-infamous farmhouse. However, local police did find books on Nazi medical experiments, including those done at Buchenwald, along with the lampshade Gein made of human skin.

The Nazi lampshade entered the wider American mind-set in a Billy Wilder production, or at least Wilder gets the director credit.

A true citizen of the bygone century, the director was born in 1906 in Galicia, then part of the teetering Austro-Hungarian Empire. By the late 1920s he was in Berlin, where he made his first films. He fled with the rise of Hitler, arrived in the United States during the middle 1930s, and claimed to have learned English by listening to baseball games on the radio. While Wilder is known for the caustic world-view on display in movies like *Ace in the Hole, Double Indemnity,* and *Sunset Boulevard,* it is emblematic of his particular American immigrant experience that the murder of his mother, stepfather, and grandmother at Auschwitz did not keep him from winning six Academy Awards and racking up boffo box office with "madcap comedies" like *Some Like It Hot,* which featured Jack Lemmon and Tony Curtis playing cross-dressing jazz musicians.

Wilder's contribution to lampshade iconography came in the service of the United States War Department, for which he oversaw the editing of *Death Mills,* a documentary that utilized graphic footage shot inside the liberated camps. Along with other newsreel compilations like *Nazi Murder Mills,* Wilder's film played as a regularly scheduled feature at theaters throughout the United States.

"*Look!* Don't turn away!" narrator Ed Herlihy commanded from the soundtrack as the camp atrocities invaded the consciousness of the popcorn-munching masses. Much of this early footage was shot at Buchenwald, including a sequence recorded on April 16, 1945, five days after liberation, when the American high command marched some twelve hundred residents of Weimar up the Blood Road through Goethe's forest to see what their countrymen had wrought.

The march was endorsed by Supreme Allied Commander

Dwight D. Eisenhower and his hell-or-high-water four-star general, George S. Patton, whose Sixth Armored Division had been the first to reach the camp. After an April 12 visit to Ohrdruf, a Buchenwald "satellite" camp thirty-five miles to the west, a visibly shaken Eisenhower said, "The things I saw beggar description. The visual evidence and the verbal testimony of starvation, cruelty, and bestiality were so overpowering." In a much-quoted statement, the future president said he felt he had no choice but to see the camps personally, so as "to be in a position to give first-hand evidence of these things if ever, in the future, there develops a tendency to charge these allegations merely to 'propaganda.' " In contrast, despite such bluster as "We're not just going to shoot the bastards, we're going to cut out their living guts and use them to grease the treads of our tanks," General Patton (subject of Richard Nixon's favorite movie) declined to enter the camps. "He indicated that he would get sick if he did so," Eisenhower said.

A lampshade allegedly to have been constructed on the orders of Ilse Koch appears several times in the footage shot the day of the Weimar march. It is visible as part of what is described by the narrator as "the parchment display," an array of camp evidence Weimar residents were forced to view. Several views of the lampshade can be seen—a high-angle shot apparently from a rooftop and a number of fleeting close-ups. But the definitive shot is a still photo from that same day. Taken in front of the Buchenwald pathology lab, it shows three men, apparently newly freed prisoners, standing behind a table on which a number of gruesome objects are arranged as if part of a macabre show-and-tell exhibit. In the back row of specimens on what would come to be called the Buchenwald Table, or simply "the Table," are a number of glass jars in which human organs—lungs, a heart, a stomach—float in formaldehyde. According to the prisoners, these organs were all that was left of the victims of botched SS medical experiments.

In front of the jars, held down by rocks against the wind, sit several pieces of tattooed human skin. Among the tattoos are a cowboy wearing a ten-gallon hat, an Indian chief in a flowing headdress (images of the American frontier were popular in Germany), a pornographic picture of a woman with her legs spread apart, another of a bare-breasted woman sprouting large butterfly wings, and others in a similar mode.

On the Table's left-hand side sit a pair of shrunken heads. Set on small wooden pedestals, the heads, reduced to the size of a human fist and featuring long, flowing dark hair, were said to have been made from the remains of Polish workers hanged for engaging in racially forbidden intercourse with German women. According to a 1950 article in *Der Spiegel,* Ignatz Wegener, a prisoner in the Buchenwald medical ward, helped prepare the heads after reading about the process in a book about the South American Jivaro tribe. The heads were then displayed in the camp barracks as a cautionary note to inmates.

In December 1945 one of these shrunken heads would play a dramatic role at the Nuremberg trials. The American assistant prosecutor, Thomas J. Dodd (who became the U.S. senator from Connecticut, a position later filled by his son, Christopher), addressed the court: "We do not wish to dwell on this pathological phase of the Nazi culture but we do feel compelled to offer one additional exhibit." Then Dodd whisked away the white sheet covering United States Exhibit 254.

"A human head," Dodd intoned. "A human head with the skull bone removed, shrunken, stuffed, and preserved." It was, as Dodd said, echoing the words of Marlow upon visiting Kurtz's upriver camp, "a terrible ornament." If anyone still needed to be convinced of the barbarism that had seized the land of Goethe and Beethoven, here it was. In their malign, Faustian obsession with perfecting the human race, the Nazis had released the species' basest instincts. After all, who else but jungle tribes, dark-continent cannibals bereft of contact with a merciful God, would shrink a human head?

The presence of the shrunken head at Nuremberg served as a straightforward example of what was at stake in civilization's clash with Nazism. In the case of the lampshade, however, this argument is not so clear. Constructed to run on electricity, the lamp on the Buchenwald Table is a thoroughly modern object, something that might be found in any bourgeois home. Rather than "a terrible ornament" harkening back to a savage past, the lampshade is a glimpse of a far more brutal time to come. With their dream of a thousand-year Reich, the Nazis were nothing if not ardent futurists. The stiff-jointed Tomorrowland they envisioned depended on the eradication of Jews and other contaminated beings. This accomplished, it would only be wise state policy (the Nazis being one of the first "green" regimes) to recycle the translucent, warm-toned skins of decommissioned individuals into items like lampshades, in the manner that the hides of cows eventually become leather jackets.

When Jewish skin became too scarce to mass-produce, the shades would become value-added collector's items, relics of prehistory, exhibits to be gawked at by coming generations of Aryans, admonitory reminders of the times when Hebrews, insectlike carriers of society-destroying pestilence, still walked the earth.

Nuremberg prosecutor Thomas Dodd and a shrunken head

Indeed, Nuremberg might have been the last time someone like Thomas Dodd, a classic morally uplifted Yank, could realistically argue civilization's side against the forces of atavistic primitivism. With the carnage wreaked by modern weaponry during the war, it was becoming more difficult to consider human progress an unalloyed boon. Science and technology were now the tools of a dystopian world to come; mankind was beginning to be viewed as the planet's enemy rather than its salvation. (Even *1984* wasn't written until 1949.) As the innate righteousness of the species was called into question, the argument that one group might be guilty of crimes *against* humanity was losing credence to the idea that genocidal incidents were really crimes *of* humanity. In this context, the lampshade, harbinger of a bleaker yet unavoidable technological future, would have proved more philosophically problematic for Nuremberg prosecutors than a shrunken head. The situation never came up, however.

By the time the war crimes trial began, the lampshade on the Buchenwald Table, ballyhooed as the handiwork of Ilse Koch and her paramours, had disappeared.

Shortly before the second anniversary of Hurricane Katrina, Skip Henderson called to exercise his part-ownership rights (by this time I'd given him $17.50, which made us co-owners) to demand that the lampshade be donated to a Holocaust museum. The sooner the better.

"Since this thing appeared, it's like my face has been shoved into hell," Skip cried. He recounted an episode that had happened at St. Louis Cathedral in Jackson Square. He'd gone to mass, and while lighting a votive candle for his father, he was overcome.

"Suddenly I felt I was totally attached to everyone who had ever died in a horrible way. All the victims killed for no reason except they were who they were . . . every innocent, and maybe not-so-innocent person ever murdered on this earth. I started lighting candles. Candle after candle. All these people *deserved* candles, I thought. I must have lit, like, forty of them before this tourist standing there with his kids says, 'Hey, buddy, we got people to mourn, too.' I thought they were going to call the police. I had to go into the park and sit down."

This was what had convinced Skip that the time had come to turn the lampshade over to "the professionals."

Really, what else was there to do with it, short of flinging it out the window while doing sixty across the Huey P. Long Bridge? It wasn't as if you could place the thing on one of those Germania militaria Internet venues that played vintage recordings of "Deutschland über Alles" as web surfers clicked through the usual array of SS Totenkopf Death's Head Honor Rings, homoerotic Aryan gymnastics manuals, or the thousands of place settings of *AH* monogrammed flatware.

In Europe, you couldn't even show much of this stuff in public, much less sell it. Antique toy soldier dealers in Berlin had to blot the *Hakenkreuz* off the arms of each tiny Wehrmacht man before displaying it. The U.S. market for Nazi collectables, however, was holding "solid." According to a 2009 *New York Times* story, Nazi stuff was "recession proof." Even replica sales were booming. Quick sellers on sites like the Rapid City, South Dakota–based PzG.biz ("Your Third Reich HQ!") included "museum quality" copies of Zyklon B canisters marked "Konzentrationslager Auschwitz!—for display purposes only!"

People are often shocked to hear that many of the major collectors of Nazi "memorabilia" are Jews, some of them Holocaust survivors or their descendants. But this is not difficult to understand. If Hitler had purposely left Prague unbombed, with plans to make the city into a vast museum of "the extinct Jewish race," why shouldn't survivors collect relics of the extinct "master race"? Then again, one could explain the desire to amass Third Reich materials as simply as Lemmy, eternal guitar hero from the metal band Motörhead, did when he said, "Everyone knows the bad guys have the best uniforms."

Still, you weren't about to put a human skin lampshade on eBay, even if they allowed Nazi material or human remains, which they don't. For sure you didn't want to call up the venerable English Holocaust denier David Irving, who was running his own "Nazi eBay," offering items out of his "vaunted personal collection" like a lock of Hitler's hair, supposedly obtained by the Führer's barber by putting a piece of sticky tape on the bottom of his shoe. Irving also claimed to have a bone fragment from Hitler's ribs, which was going for a cool

$180,000. As for the veracity of his product, he said, "When people come to my website and see the name David Irving, they know they are buying an authentic item. It is the gold standard."

No, if you were going to entertain selling a human skin lampshade, you would have to reach deeper. You would have to dip into a world like the one depicted by the ever-reliable Don DeLillo in *Running Dog*, a story in which the writer's usual cast of oddly associated obsessives compete in a perverted *Maltese Falcon* hunt for a porno loop featuring Hitler and Eva Braun supposedly shot on that final night in the *Führerbunker.*

It was a sick little game, but in the interest of journalistic thoroughness, if a black market for Nazi lampshades existed, it would have to be checked out.

A couple of phone calls, arranged by a deep-sea diver I came to know while working on a story on the Miskito Coast of Nicaragua, led me to an alternately boastful and paranoidly surreptitious man named Steve. Reached at an undisclosed California locale, Steve, a purported Special Forces marine who claimed to have once ridden with Hells Angel Sonny Barger in the "five-keys-in-the-saddlebag days" and described himself as "a problem shooter" ("You hear of troubleshooting? I find a problem and I shoot it."), said he might possibly be able to "lay off" the lampshade for me, especially with a copy of the DNA test as corroboration.

The main problem would be deciding how much to ask for. That was always the case with what Steve called "one-of-a-kind specialties." Unlike the market for smuggled body parts, where costs were established over time and degree of desperation, a human skin lampshade was what Steve referred to as an "item of choice"; the price would depend only on how badly the buyer wanted the thing.

"How much did your friend pay for it?" Steve asked.

"Thirty-five dollars."

"Then that's the price," Steve said without inflection. But in reality there was no price. Not yet. This was why it was a good thing I'd called him. "This could be something, you know. Like a Holy Grail of evil. These things are pretty rare. At least I've never seen one. Not a real one." For his as-yet-undetermined 30 to 50 percent finder's fee, he would "put out the word" and try to get a couple of collectors bidding against each other.

For argument's sake I told Steve I didn't want to sell the lampshade to any neo-Nazi. There was no problem with that, he said. "Those jerkoffs are lucky if they have enough cash to buy a carton of cigarettes. They're not in the market. They read two pages of *Mein Kampf,* go on some websites, and are goose-stepping all over the place until the meth runs out."

Steve had another sort of person in mind. "He's, like, maybe sixty, loaded, lives in a big house south of Monterey. He comes in the room sweet as can be, wearing a sweater like Mr. Rogers, smoking a hand-carved pipe. His tobacco pouch is made out of a human breast. I know because my friend sold it to him. Some people are just that sick." The guy was "pretty creepy," Steve allowed, saying "he made me nervous, which is something because I'm the kind of individual who makes *everyone* nervous.

"Maybe I can get him bidding against Marilyn Manson," Steve conjectured with a laugh. The Goth rock star had a well-documented penchant for collecting what was euphemistically called "outsider art."

Steve stopped short. "But I'm really wasting my time here, ain't I?"

"What do you mean?"

"Because I can tell just from talking to you that you're never gonna sell this thing. I'm gonna get some people together and then you're gonna tell me you got cold feet or whatever. Some bullshit story. Then how am I gonna look? My ass out there on the line? That's bad for business, dude. So tell me, this ain't really for sale, am I right or am I wrong?"

I had to admit Steve was right. The lampshade was not really for sale, certainly not to Marilyn Manson or some Mr. Rogers impersonator who kept his tobacco in a human breast.

"Thought so, man," Steve said.

"Sorry."

"No worries. You're making the right choice. Take it from me, you don't need this kind of karma."

Donating the lampshade to a Holocaust museum was the "right thing" to do, Skip had said. But which Holocaust museum?

In the late 1940s a proposal to erect a modest monument commemorating the victims of the Nazi regime in Riverside Park on the Upper West Side of Manhattan, one of the most famous Jewish neighborhoods in the world, was rejected by the New York City Art Commission. Such a memorial would be "too tragic for a recreational park," the commission said. Several Jewish-American groups concurred, saying the proposed monument would be "detrimental to the best interests of Jewry since it would stand as a perpetual reminder" of the tragic recent history of the Hebrew people.

Sixty years later such mnemonic forbearance seems unthinkable. As of 2007 there were more than a hundred major institutions worldwide identifying themselves as Holocaust museums, study centers, or memorials, all dedicated to making sure the Shoah will never be forgotten. The majority of these institutions are in the United States, as befitting the so-called Americanization of the Holocaust. Now, besides the half dozen centers in New York and Los Angeles, Holocaust museums and memorials can be found in Denver, Tampa, Dallas, Miami, New Haven, and Atlanta, as well as the more unlikely locales of Albuquerque, New Mexico; Farmington Hills, Michigan; El Paso, Texas; Terre Haute, Indiana; Richmond, Virginia; and Tucson, Arizona. The most recent addition is the $45 million Illinois Holocaust and Education Center at Skokie, site of a neo-Nazi march in the late 1970s.

Given this plethora of options, it made sense to start at the top, the United States Holocaust Memorial Museum in Washington D.C. Opened in April 1993, a few months before the release of Steven Spielberg's watershed *Schindler's List* (Bill Clinton officially proclaimed

1993 to be "the Year of the Holocaust"), the USHMM, with its prime location near the National Mall, is second only to the Air and Space Museum as a Washington tourist attraction. More than 28 million people have visited the museum, an average of 5,000 a day. Its privately raised endowment of nearly $200 million augmented by federal funding, the museum has an annual operating budget nearing $80 million, more than 400 full-time employees aided by several hundred volunteers, and a membership of 175,000. Its archive includes testimonies of nearly 200,000 survivors and their descendants, 49 million written pages, 138 million images, and 13,000 objects and artworks.

Given its size, the USHMM has more or less set the template for a post–*Schindler's List* Holocaust museum experience. As if part of a solemn ritual, the visitor is taken through the forbidding, inexorable chronology. It is all here: the dramatization of Jewish life prior to the coming of the Nazis, the ominous run-up to National Socialism with recordings of Hitler's speeches gnawing through the acoustics, the documents of the Final Solution along with displays of identity cards and yellow stars pinned to tattered coats, the interactive boxcar where the visitor can imagine the nightmare journey, the pile of shoes of the dead, the audiovisual accounts of the survivors, and finally, the contemplative moment in the Hall of Remembrance—all adding up to the impossibly sad but fervent shout of "Never again!"

Some have found fault with the USHMM's representation of the Holocaust, charging that such institutional installations, especially ones aimed at a wider audience—the USHMM website takes pains to emphasize that 90 percent of the museum's visitors "are not Jewish"—are, by definition, emotionally manipulative. Much the same was said about *Schindler's List*, which film critic J. Hoberman memorably called "the ultimate feel-good movie about the ultimate feel-bad experience." But whatever the overall goal of places like the USHMM and its rival Yad Vashem in Jerusalem, there is no denying the visceral effectiveness of the assemblage, the sheer nonstop volume of it. In this onslaught of overwhelming heartbreak, however, one thing that will not be shown to the weeping visitor is the Buchenwald lampshade.

This doesn't mean the shade is not present. It makes a cameo appearance on one of the many video monitors set up around the USHMM, in the scenes of the Weimar residents filing past the Buchenwald Table. In one particular sequence, the photographer shoots from behind the Table, and the lampshade is visible through the crowd, dead center in the frame.

The lampshade dominates the image for a full three seconds. If you know what you are looking for, it pops right out at you. But chances are that, even though it is reasonable to assume that many of the USHMM's daily visitors pause to watch the video, few of them are aware they are seeing the famous Buchenwald lampshade. The museum makes no mention of it, either in the footage commentary or with a written explanation. Without context, reduced to an undefined rhomboid shape on the screen, it becomes nearly invisible.

In the Queens schoolyard of the 1950s, decades before the museums and *Schindler's List,* the lampshade *was* our Holocaust, the Shoah we knew. The lampshade and its succubus Bitch of Buchenwald enabler, Ilse Koch, were in the news every day, and deemed worthy of convening a special select committee of the United States Congress. Six decades later, having vanished from the Table at Buchenwald, missing at Nuremberg, never scientifically proven to be real, the lampshade had become an unmentionable ghost, a dybbuk, written out of the Holocaust.

"That is because it is a myth," said Diane Saltzman, the former head of collections at USHMM.

I was about halfway through an increasingly contentious conversation with Ms. Saltzman about the lampshade's disappearance from the neo-official version of the Holocaust narrative, and this was perhaps the tenth time she had used the word *myth* to describe the lampshade.

"Did you look at the DNA report?" I asked. At the request of the USHMM press guy, I'd sent the DNA report and several pictures of the lampshade to Washington.

"I did," Ms. Saltzman replied. "It was interesting. But inconclusive. Completely inconclusive. It proves *nothing.*"

Ms. Saltzman apparently had me pegged for something of a nut or, even worse, a reflexively sensationalistic journalist looking to make *National Enquirer*–style headlines with yet another hoary story about Nazi monsters, always a hardy perennial. Only the week before, one of the supermarket rags had a story about a "Nazi vampire" appearing in a subdivision outside Fresno, California.

I could understand Saltzman's trepidation. The lampshade had become the creaking flying saucer of the Holocaust, the domain of the huckster and the country bumpkin. People continued to find shades they imagined were made of human skin in attics or, as Skip Henderson did, at rummage sales. Positive of their authenticity, most of these people felt that these objects should be turned over to the Holocaust Museum. Many of these cases came across Diane Saltzman's desk.

Typical was a 2004 incident in the small town of Lovingston, Virginia. As reported in the *Charlottesville Daily Progress,* a suspicious-looking lampshade had been found in the voluminous collection of seventy-seven-year-old antique dealer Daniel Avery. "I think it's real because of what it looks like. It really looks like skin," said Doris Jones, a local antique shop owner who noted Avery was always coming up with "unusual things. He's very into snakes. He had snake rings, snake candlesticks." For his part, Avery, reportedly very ill, said he didn't want to part with the lampshade. He had a sentimental attachment to it since it was given to him by "my dear Mary," a barmaid he'd run into at a local saloon forty years earlier and hadn't seen since. It was Mary who told Avery the lampshade "was from human hide that came from the Germans."

Reached by the *Daily Progress,* Diane Saltzman dismissed the possibility that the Lovingston lampshade was made in a concentration camp. "None of the lampshades that have surfaced over the past fifty years have turned out to be real," she said. Daniel Avery disputed Saltzman's assessment. "That's what she thinks," he said.

As far as she was concerned, Ms. Saltzman told me, the lampshade was "like the soap, which is also unproven."

It would become a familiar refrain, this coupling of the lampshade with the story about how the Germans had engaged in the mass production of soap from Jewish bodies. Back in Queens, we all knew about the soap.

The "proof" supposedly came from many reported sightings of soap inscribed with the letters *RJF,* which was rumored to stand for *Reichs Juden Fett,* or "state Jewish fat." Many believed the story, including famed Nazi hunter Simon Wiesenthal, who in 1946 wrote, "The General Government [Poland] knew quite well what the 'RJF' soap meant. The civilized world may not believe the joy with which the Nazis and their women in the General Government thought of this soap. In each piece of soap they saw a Jew who had been magically put there, and had thus been prevented from growing into a second Freud, Ehrlich or Einstein." The idea that people could be made into soap carried such a stigma that when the first camp survivors emigrated to Palestine in the late 1940s, the established Zionist settlers, not enthralled to see the peasant newcomers, derogatorily referred to them as *sabon,* or soap. Later, however, it was pointed out that *RJF* was actually *RIF,* initials for *Reichsstelle für Industrielle Fett-versorgung,* or "National Center for Industrial Fat Provisioning." From there the soap story began to fade into the realm of folklore, a tale quite possibly left over from World War I, when British propagandists accused the Germans of using dead soldiers to make products for the war effort.

As it turned out, the Nazis did at least experiment with turning corpses into soap. According to testimony at Nuremberg and much subsequent research, in 1944 Professor Rudolf Spanner, the SS doctor in charge of the Danzig Anatomical Institute, was given the assignment to test the feasibility of such soap manufacturing. Reportedly writing letters to local town mayors urging them not to bury the dead but rather send the corpses to the Danzig Institute, Spanner devised a recipe for the process calling for five kilos of human fat to each ten liters of water along with five hundred grams of caustic soda. With the war going badly, however, there was little time or money for soap production. "It never reached the industrial stage, nothing close to the degree many believed," says Yehuda Bauer, preeminent Holocaust scholar at Yad Vashem.

It was exactly "distractions" like soap and lampshades that "created fodder" for the so-called Holocaust deniers, crazies for whom "no soap meant no Holocaust," Diane Saltzman said. This seemed a reasonable concern. The Internet had only further enabled the loonies claiming the "faking" of the Holocaust was responsible for everything from the establishment of the State of Israel to continued Jewish control of the planet, from Goldman Sachs on down. These maniacs had to be resisted on every level.

Yet what did that have to do with the lampshade Skip Henderson bought in New Orleans, the one that according to the Bode lab DNA report was real?

"You haven't presented enough evidence. This report is only one aspect of what must be done," Saltzman said. I should have examined the age of the thread used to stitch the panels of the shade together. I should have attempted to get a better sense of the age of the metal on the frame itself. "We are talking about specifics," she chided. "You don't provide them."

This was true. Beyond the DNA testing and showing the lampshade to a bevy of curators, I hadn't done much. But that's why I was calling her. The five grand I'd already laid out for the Bode report had maxed out the family budget for lampshade testing. My hope was that an organization like the USHMM, with its $200 million endowment, might be willing to share or, better yet, take over the financial burden.

Saltzman put an abrupt halt to that notion. "We wouldn't be interested in accepting such an object and we would never display it," she said. "We are an educational institution and this has no educational value whatsoever."

"You're saying even if it's real, it has no educational value?"

"This is a museum dealing with the Holocaust. This object cannot be proved to legitimately be part of the Holocaust, so we cannot treat it as such. Sixty-odd years of research and it has never been proved that a thing like this was Nazi policy or practice."

"What about all the stories about lampshades? Everyone knows about it; doesn't that make it at least worth talking about?"

"Not from the point of view of the museum." Diane Saltzman had about run out of patience. "What I'm saying is even if I could prove its reality, even if you could prove it was made out of the skin of a Buchenwald prisoner from 1943, *which you can't*—it would still not be part of the practice of the Holocaust. It would only be an isolated incident, the work of extreme individuals."

"The whole thing is pretty extreme, wouldn't you say?" Was Saltzman saying that if a lone lunatic SS man, some Ed Gein–style Nazi, had made a lampshade, that would fall under the heading of personal rather than institutional psychopathy and therefore not fall within the purview of august organizations like national museums? "Listen, all I'm trying to do is find out what it is."

"I already told you what it is. It is a myth," said the former head of collections. "Even if you could document it one hundred percent, it would still be a myth."

"What?"

She was getting ready to hang up.

"So what do you suggest I do with the thing? Just throw it out?"

Diane Saltzman gathered herself. This conversation had come to a close. "I wish you good luck."

SIX

It made no sense to me. Why would a top-level representative from the leading Holocaust center in the United States be so invested in maintaining that the lampshade was a myth? There had to be more to it than fielding incessant panicked phone calls from poor souls haunted by the specter of a paper shade in their attic.

To call the lampshade a myth was to place it in the class of objects like "the Spear of Destiny," aka "the Holy Lance," which John, in his gospel, says was used by the Roman soldier Longinus to pierce Christ's side as he hung on the cross. From this wound came "a sudden flow of blood and water," an anointment that, legend has it, imbued the weapon with vast mystical powers. According to the literature on the topic, the spear passed through the hands of many powerful men including the Persian king Khosrau II, Emperor Constantine, the Turkish sultan Bayezid II, along with a number of French kings and popes. It would later play a pivotal role in Wagner's *Parsifal*, which was almost certainly how the young Adolf Hitler became aware of it.

While living in Vienna, Hitler, then in his occultist Thule Society phase, saw the alleged spear on display at the Hofburg Treasure

House and wrote about it in *Mein Kampf.* "I knew with immediacy that this was an important moment in my life . . . I felt as though I myself had held it in my hands before in some earlier century of history, that I myself once claimed it as my talisman of power and held the destiny of the world in my hands." After the German-Austrian *Anschluss* in 1938, Hitler took possession of the spear and brought it to Berlin.

What happened after that is unclear. According to a series of books written by Howard A. Buechner, a New Orleans physician and longtime member of the faculty at both the Tulane and LSU medical schools (and also, by chance, one of the first Allied soldiers to enter the Dachau camp, where he witnessed the infamous Dachau Massacre of German guards by American GIs), Hitler, fearing the war was lost, ordered Himmler to dispatch a contingent of SS men to bury the Spear of Destiny in Antarctica. This was done to keep the spear from falling into the hands of General George Patton, who also coveted it. Patton writes of the spear in one of his many warrior poems, "Through a Glass, Darkly," in which he imagines himself as Longinus: "and I feel the rending spear. / Perhaps I stabbed our Savior / in His sacred helpless side." After the war the spear was returned to the Vienna museum, where it remains today, although Buechner claims the object is a fake, manufactured by the Nazis as a ruse. The real spear, the New Orleans doctor contends, remains buried under the Antarctic ice.

The lampshade was no Spear of Destiny. For one thing, the lampshade had witnesses, literally thousands of them. There was Ann Stringer, the UPI reporter who broke the story, who wrote that she could "see the pores and the tiny unquestionably human skin lines." There was the testimony of American soldiers. Harry Snodgrass, an enlisted man from Tennessee, said, "It was in the commander's office . . . lampshades made from the skins of Jews." Warren Priest, another enlisted man, said, "I saw lampshades made of human skin . . . the commandant of the post collected these as a hobby." Rudy Baum, of the Sixth Army, said he saw "lampshades and library book covers made from tanned human skin." Margaret Bourke-White, whose *Life* magazine photos established much of the visual record of the camp, said she saw "skins for lampshades." In a report dated April 27, 1945, Georges Vanier, the Canadian ambassador to France, wrote, "a lampshade was found—and this I saw—made from tattooed human skin." Beyond this is the statement of Adolf Martin Bormann, son of Martin Bormann, Hitler's private secretary, who many felt was running much of the Third Reich in the latter stages of the war. A longtime missionary, the younger Bormann recalled a visit to Himmler's house. "The furnishings were very strange," Bormann said. "There was a standard lamp, for example, with a lampshade made out of parchment. And this lampshade made out of parchment was made with human skin."

Were all these statements simply based on misidentification, propaganda, the effect of the shock of seeing what had happened at the camp, or a bout of collective hysteria?

"They won't take it," I told Skip Henderson, after my conversation with Diane Saltzman.

"Why not? Didn't you show them the DNA?"

"Of course I did. They don't think it is part of the Holocaust."

"What's that supposed to mean? Can't you call them back? I got to get this thing out of my life."

My conversation with Diane Saltzman continued to bug me. There were so many issues to discuss that I never got to. It went back to the DNA test, what could be found and what could not. This was a matter of "markers," as Bob Bever, the Bode lab vice president explained to me. The degraded lampshade samples yielded only so many genetic markers. There was enough information to certify the skin as human but not enough to determine what *kind* of human. The full genetic record, including the "ethnicity" of the poor soul who'd been turned into a lampshade, was not obtainable.

I called Bob Bever for some clarification. "You're telling me that there's not enough DNA to give a hint of who the person is? That it could as easily be some poor hitchhiker from Arkansas as a concentration camp victim?"

Bever was typically noncommittal. "We're bound by the results we get. So yes. As of now there's no way of telling the ethnicity of the lampshade material."

"So it could be *anyone*?"

"As far as these results indicate, the answer to that would be yes."

Asked what I should do next, Bever said, "Well, you can always keep on testing."

Yeah, sure. But would it be worth it? This stuff was hellaciously expensive. What were the real chances of a more complete finding? If our roles were reversed, what would he do?

"Don't ask me to advise you not to test," Bever said. "That wouldn't be good for business."

"Come on."

Bever took a breath. "If it were me I wouldn't do it. We worked a long time to squeeze out that little drop of DNA. What you have may be all you're going to get."

"That's it?"

"You never say never. But it is highly unlikely."

This was disappointing news, but the inconclusiveness did place the lampshade in a unique, and possibly illuminating, existential position. Here was an example of an object that, whatever Diane Saltzman said about it, had served as a most repellent symbol of Nazi racial terror, an icon of genocide. Yet it was not possible to know who had died and who had done the killing. Museums judge reality by provenance and dating. But beyond its apparent European origin and turning up in New Orleans after Katrina, the lampshade had no fixed provenance. Beyond its clear modernity, it came from no set time. The skin on the shade could have been made of anyone, come from anyplace.

The lampshade was an everyman, an every victim.

It is one of the oldest of Jewish philosophical arguments, the on-going dialectic between "particularism" and "universalism": do Jews have a unique existence and relationship with God, or is the true mission of a Jew to live in "the world" like everyone else? This is, above all, a discussion about the concept of "the chosen people." Does the "cho-senness" of the Jews, granted by the acceptance of God's Torah, entail an apartness, an eternal special-case condition? Or does it confer, as many liberal, cosmopolitan Jews believe, a unique obligation to reach out and fit in, to offer the not inconsiderable genius of the Jewish peo-ple to the larger society? With the Holocaust, the particular/universal dichotomy has been taken further, morphing into an overall theory of genocide itself. The main question from the Jewish perspective is whether the Holocaust was a wholly unique, distinct occurrence in the history of the world, or was it part of the larger circumstance of human nature? Put another way, did those people whose pictures I saw pasted to the walls at Tuol Sleng, or an Armenian killed by a Turk, or a Tutsi hacheted by a Hutu have anything in common with a Jew murdered at Auschwitz? Or is every instance of collective death a separate case, with its own particularized circumstances, discon-nected from the general trend of mass slaughter?

It was a dilemma. You had commentary from people like Anti-Defamation League president Abraham Foxman, that old reliable font of Hebraic exceptionalism, who in a 1994 edition of the ADL's *Frontline* publication said, "The Holocaust is something different. It is a singular event. It is not simply one example of genocide but a nearly successful attempt on the life of God's chosen children and thus on God himself."

This provincialism aside, there was a compelling truth to the par-ticularist position. Obviously the Nazis, the perpetrators, believed in the singularity of the Jews. Particularism was practical; it defined who was us and who was them; it circled the wagons; it was a way to survive. Universalism, on the other hand, was for simps. Universalism asked you to imagine yourself having as much in common with some Cambodian left facedown in a ditch as you did with your murdered uncle Max. It was a hard argument to swallow. Yet, being the sort of New York Jew I am, from the leafy workers' paradise of Flushing, Queens, I couldn't quite buy into being a particular kind of anyone. It wasn't the way I was brought up.

Perhaps it was a kind of romanticism, but I took the lampshade out of its Sugar Ray Robinson box that night, looked it over. Doña Argentina, the Union City spiritualist, had said it—*he*—wanted to stay with me. That he trusted me. It sounded insane then and it sounded insane now. But I had hopes, inchoate as they might be, that this purported symbol of racist lunacy, product of the worst humanity could conjure, might through its everyman DNA somehow stand as a tortured symbol of commonality.

It was just a thought.

Ken Kipperman, the world's best-known lampshade hunter, doesn't think much about concepts like particularism and universality.

"With my skills, I am not really much of a philosophy student, I'm afraid," he says in his self-effacing, preternaturally polite way. "It is easier for me to focus on one thing at a time."

He is a tall, youthful-seeming man in his early sixties, his longish salt-and-pepper hair combed in a semi-bouffant swoop. In the basement of his comfortable Maryland home, where he keeps two decades of research in neat piles on the pool table, Kipperman told me about the first time he became aware of the lampshade.

"I was about eight, after our family came to America," Kipperman said in the halting, almost disembodied inflection he falls into while reciting the events of his past. "We were living in Coney Island, in a neighborhood with a lot of war refugees like us, and I heard this angry, angry man on the television screaming in a language I didn't understand. I went to see what it was and I saw my mother and father spitting. They were spitting right at the TV screen! It made me afraid because I'd never seen them so upset. Later I found out it was Hitler on the television. But my parents never told me that. They wouldn't even speak his name.

"That's when I saw the Buchenwald Table for the first time. Of course I didn't know what it was. I didn't know anything. My parents didn't tell me about the Holocaust, any of it. But I knew there was something terrible on that TV screen. I asked, 'What is that?' but my mother told me that wasn't for me to know. That was how it always was: everything was a big secret.

"That was the first time I really ever thought about it, who I was and where I came from," said Kipperman, who was born in Poland in 1946 and spent his earliest years in a displaced persons' camp in Italy. "When you're a kid, you want to be like everyone else. But when I saw the Table, that was when I began to realize I wasn't. I didn't remember it at the time, the lampshade and tattooed skin, but it stayed with me, in the back of my mind."

Kipperman began hanging out at the Coney Island boardwalk freak show. "It kind of took me over, the idea that something had happened to these people that made them so weird. There'd be the snake lady, the fire-eaters, the guy who made himself into a pretzel. The barker said, 'You think this is beyond belief? Pay the extra money and come inside if you really want to see the horror of horrors.' That was me, I always wanted to pay the extra money."

For Kipperman the most fascinating freak was "the Illustrated Man," tattooed from head to toe. "It was like he was covered with a whole other language." Kipperman asked his parents if he could get some tattoos. The answer was "Absolutely not." It was against Jewish law; it said so right in the Torah, Leviticus 19:28, "Ye shall not make any cuttings in your flesh for the dead, nor print any marks upon you: I am the Lord." Get a tattoo and you won't be buried in a Jewish cemetery, you'll be shunned by your own people for eternity, his parents told him. This confused Kipperman, since during the summer when he went to the beach, he saw people he knew to be Jews, who went to shul every day, and they had tattoos on their arms. Why was that, he asked his parents, and they told him not to ask so many questions, to concentrate on being an American.

An indifferent student except for his budding talent as a *Mad* magazine–style caricaturist, Kipperman was expelled from Lincoln High School, then a storied bastion of NYC immigrant public education, for poor attendance. His life would change when he signed up for an engraving class. Showing unmistakable aptitude for intricate work, Kipperman was soon admitted to a ten-year apprenticeship sponsored by the U.S. Treasury Department for the training of stamp and currency artists.

For someone of self-described "incredible" absentmindedness (he got lost on the way to pick me up at the train station even though it is less than fifteen minutes from his house and he makes the trip all the time), Kipperman's prodigious ability to concentrate on one thing found a niche in the exacting practice of steel-plate engraving. "You have to have a lot of patience to do this kind of work," he says. "The details are so small, it can take months to make a small portrait. I'd sit down, start working, and when I looked up it would be tomorrow. There was something very satisfying about that."

By his early thirties, Kipperman was working for the Treasury Department's Bureau of Engraving and Printing, one of sixteen people in the country qualified to make the plates for U.S. currency. Every time you look at the picture of the immaculately handsome Alexander Hamilton on the ten-dollar bill, you're seeing the work of Ken Kipperman.

"It is a little thrilling," Kipperman says. "I see people buying groceries in the supermarket, handing over those pictures of Alexander Hamilton, and I think how lucky I am, because most artists can't get anything for their work."

When Kipperman finally became acquainted with the history of the Holocaust, "It came as a shock to me. I was so angry about not knowing. I screamed at my mother for keeping it from me. I screamed at God, who I thought was supposed to protect the Jewish people. It became an obsession," Kipperman says, describing a 1987 incident that would become his first of several encounters with the United States Holocaust Memorial Museum.

"It was very strange," Kipperman points out in his straightforward, nearly Aspergerian way, "because the Holocaust Museum didn't even exist at the time.

"I was surprised when they announced they were going to build the museum right across from my Bureau office on Fourteenth Street," Kipperman recalled. "There were these old brick buildings there, and in my mind, they looked like Auschwitz . . . kind of how I imagined Auschwitz would look. In a way, to me, they *were* Auschwitz. It seemed a good place to have a Holocaust museum. But then I heard the museum people say they needed more space. They were going to demolish the brick buildings to put up a modern one-hundred-sixty-million-dollar I. M. Pei Holocaust museum. This didn't seem right to me.

"It kind of surprised me one day when I came to work. They'd knocked down the buildings. There was nothing left but a chimney, a brick chimney. It reminded me of the chimneys at the camps. This is a holy kind of structure, terrible but holy. I thought I had to do something."

Saying he was an artist and wanted to sketch the chimney before it was gone, Kipperman convinced a construction worker to lift him up in a crane, whereupon he launched what he calls "my protest." He climbed into the chimney and refused to come out.

The police, thinking the sandwich in his paper lunch bag was a bomb, blocked off the entire area, stopping traffic for hours. "I was in there for what seemed like a long time," Kipperman recalls. "I could hear all the sirens, the helicopters overhead. And I'm thinking, you idiot, what did you get yourself into?" It was only when he peeked from the top of the chimney and saw a police marksman aiming a rifle at his head that he decided he had better come out. The next day a picture of Kipperman, his shirt ripped to shreds, being led away by two policemen was on the front page of the *Washington Post* Metro section.

Initially charged with a felony that could have locked him away for twenty years, Kipperman was given a battery of psychological tests that bore out his claim that he truly meant no harm. It was decided he was suffering from post-traumatic stress disorder from his involvement with the Holocaust, an event that, at least according to the calendar, was over before he was born.

Kipperman received a suspended sentence and was required to

perform one hundred hours of community service, helping administer art therapy to state prisoners. About a month later Kipperman came home to hear his wife, Paula, say, "You think we have trouble now, wait until the Bureau calls back." Shortly before the chimney episode, Kipperman, assigned to make a one-dollar stamp in honor of Yeshiva University president Bernard Revel as part of the Bureau's "Great Americans" series, had engraved a tiny Star of David within the scholar's beard.

"It was kind of a private thing. Lots of people at the Bureau have put these little personal marks into their work. Sort of an inside joke. I never thought anyone would notice, the star was so small," Kipperman says. "But they did." Over a million of the stamps had been printed before the star was discovered and the run stopped. Again reporters interviewed Kipperman's neighbors about how Ken was such a nice guy and how surprised they were that he'd ever be involved with something like that.

Amazingly enough—and evidence of how difficult it is to find engravers talented and focused enough to create U.S. currency—Kipperman was again not fired by the Treasury Department. There was some fallout however, as much stricter oversight was introduced at the Bureau, resulting in a long-term review of all projects and creating bad feelings throughout the office. When Kipperman returned to work, a message was taped to his desk. Written in a Hebraic-style font, the note said, "Fuck you very much in spades." Kipperman, ever the innocent, had to ask what "in spades" meant.

Six years later, in 1993, the chimney incident apparently sufficiently forgotten, Kipperman wrangled himself an invitation to the party celebrating the opening of the United States Holocaust Memorial Museum. While appalled by the display of wealth and privilege on the part of the well-heeled donors, Kipperman nonetheless got to see the exhibit on camp tattoos. Flashing back to the tattooed numbers he'd seen on his neighbors' arms in Coney Island, Kipperman started asking questions. There were technical things he needed to know. What kind of ink did the Nazis use, what type of needles?

Finding no one at the museum to provide him with the answers he sought, he turned his attention to the National Archives, where he met Robert Wolfe. A longtime archivist, Wolfe had only a moderate interest in Kipperman's tattooing inquiry, but he did, almost as an afterthought, mention that the Archives had a number of pieces of tattooed human skin in its collection.

"He said they had the skin and a piece of a lampshade. From Buchenwald," Kipperman reports. Wolfe believed the objects had come to the Archives following their use as exhibits during the Nuremberg trials.

"I was completely floored," said Kipperman, who asked to be allowed to see the objects. This permission was long in coming. "I kept calling and writing, asking for an appointment. They kept putting me off. Everyone was always on vacation." In the meantime Kipperman, his monomania fully engaged, began spending every nonworking hour in the library at the Holocaust museum and in the vast National Archives, compulsively xeroxing and re-xeroxing any and all material pertaining to World War II–era tattooed human skin. Eventually the Archives allowed him to see their holdings, which, contrary to what Robert Wolfe said, consisted of only one piece of tattooed skin, an image of a woman with butterfly wings. Kipperman took a picture of himself holding the mounted tattoo.

Later he traced more artifacts to the Archives' annex in College Park, Maryland. There he saw three more pieces of tattooed skin and a bisected shrunken head, all labeled as coming from the Buchenwald camp. On one of those long days at the Archives he came upon an oddly familiar picture.

"It was the Table. The Buchenwald Table. As soon as I saw it, I knew that this was the same thing I saw on TV back in my parents' house in Coney Island. The same picture that had been in my head all these years. The shrunken heads, the lampshade—all of it. After forty years, it came back to me, like a ghost."

The Buchenwald Table, April 16, 1945

From Kipperman's point of view, the truly horrible thing was that many of the objects on the Buchenwald Table had been in the United States all along, an hour's drive from his house. "I couldn't believe it, these awful, terrible things gathering dust right there in Washington D.C., no more than a few hundred feet from the Constitution, the greatest document of American freedom. It made me so upset, I couldn't think."

Soon after, Kipperman began his search for the lampshade. "I knew it was missing, that it had disappeared from the Table and had never been introduced in evidence at the war trials. But it had to be somewhere."

Kipperman found a clipping from the *St. Louis Post-Dispatch* headlined "Ex-Officer Has Human Skin from Ilse Koch's Home." The officer in question, the article said, was Major Lorenz C. Schmuhl, former commanding officer of post-liberation Buchenwald, who had taken home a number of "souvenirs" from the camp, including "most pieces of the famous lampshade."

Kipperman tried to make contact with Schmuhl, who was placed in charge of the camp on April 16, 1945, the same day the Table was set up to greet the people from Weimar. A World War I combat veteran, Schmuhl was a good choice to run a former concentration camp. He spoke German and had long been the deputy warden of the Michigan City, Indiana, penitentiary. Apparently he ran a tight ship. When John Dillinger, Schmuhl's most illustrious inmate, was incarcerated at Michigan City, the erstwhile public enemy number one was quoted as saying, "When I get out of here, I'll be the meanest bastard the world has ever seen."

"I knew Major Schmuhl had the lampshade from the Table, but had 'to prove it,'" Kipperman said as he pulled out a murky photo of Schmuhl's Buchenwald collection that had been published in a 1949 edition of the *Indianapolis Star.* "The picture's not too great, but what you see is that a piece was missing from the top of the lampshade in Schmuhl's house. In the footage from Buchenwald, the lampshade on the table was missing the same piece."

You had to admire Kipperman's legwork and wonder why the Nuremberg and Dachau trials prosecutors, Thomas Dodd included, hadn't been able to track down the lampshade, especially considering the enormous amount of publicity surrounding the object at the time. Might not someone have thought of asking Schmuhl, who lived in Ilse and Karl Koch's villa during his Buchenwald tenure, if he had any idea what happened to such a sensational piece of evidence? Also worth asking would have been why Schmuhl, after years in the law enforcement business (he would go back to his warden's job after the war and become the subject of a TV series called *The Man Behind the Badge*), removed a critical piece of evidence from what was essentially a vast crime scene, and why he didn't think to return it when the prosecution failed to produce the lampshade at the trials.

The picture in the newspaper was the closest Kipperman would get to the lampshade on the Table. By the middle 1990s, Schmuhl was long dead. Kipperman reached Henry Lange, author of the original *Indianapolis Star* piece, but the reporter knew nothing of what happened to the lampshade besides that Schmuhl had subsequently sold it to a collector who later disposed of it because "he couldn't stand to look at it anymore."

Kipperman pressed on, locating Schmuhl's son, Robert, then living in Annapolis, Maryland. Robert Schmuhl confirmed that pieces of the lampshade had indeed been in his father's house, that he'd seen them rolled up in a corner when he was growing up, along with a number of other souvenirs his father had brought home.

As for the lampshade, however, Robert Schmuhl, now deceased, could provide no information beyond what Kipperman had been told by Henry Lange. One day the thing was in his father's house, then it was gone.

His hunt for the Buchenwald tattooed skin brought Kipperman into another conflict with the U.S. Holocaust Memorial Museum. "They have no interest in these things," Kipperman said, inserting a VHS tape into a player. It was a copy of a ten-year-old local news show on which Kipperman appeared with Michael Berenbaum, who served as project director at the USHMM from 1988 to 1997, during which time he played a key role in the institution's creation and assembly of its permanent collection. With a curriculum vitae that included being a professor of Holocaust studies at Clark University, teaching positions at Yale, George Washington, and Wesleyan, in addition to serving as president of the Shoah Visual History Foundation and overseeing the editing of the twenty-two-volume *Encyclopædia Judaica*, Berenbaum evidenced no patience for Kipperman's claim that the Buchenwald human skin objects should be displayed at the Holocaust museum.

"Making lampshades out of human skin is another manifestation of evil," Berenbaum said. This didn't, however, mean that the lampshades had to seen, much in the way that one didn't need to put a corpse on public display because a murder has occurred. To show the artifacts of human skin in the way that Kipperman was advocating, Berenbaum said, was to run "the risk of almost being pornographic."

Nearly ten years later, the sound of the word still incensed Kipperman. *"Pornographic!* That's what they think. Does that mean it shouldn't be seen, that it should remain hidden? These officials, these big-shot know-it-alls, they think they can decide what can be shown and what cannot.

"That is wrong. I don't care what anyone says. The Holocaust cannot be censored."

A few months after first talking with Kipperman, I visited Berenbaum at his home in the Fairfax district of Los Angeles. No longer involved in what he called "the office politics" of the USHMM, he was now the director of the Sigi Ziering Institute, a board member of the Simon Wiesenthal Museum of Tolerance, and a rabbi at a Long Beach congregation. Of course he remembered Ken Kipperman, the man who tried to blow up the Holocaust museum even before it was built, Berenbaum said, with a shake of his head.

It wasn't as if he doubted Kipperman's passion or his sincerity, Berenbaum said, sitting in his tasteful living room. He could understand the impulse to show everything, to hold nothing back. But it wasn't that simple. The matter of human remains, Berenbaum said, was "a very problematic, a highly emotional area." It required a larger understanding of the factors at work. From the religious point of view, Berenbaum, ordained as an Orthodox rabbi when he was twenty-three, said there could be very little debate. All human remains of Jewish origin must be buried. Mosaic law was quite clear on that. It was in the social and political realm that "heated discussion" often arose.

"There was the issue of the hair," Berenbaum recalled, citing perhaps the most difficult of "representational" disputes at the USHMM: whether or not to exhibit the hair shorn from the heads of the camp victims and later used by the Nazis, in their utilitarian way, to stuff pillows and spin into yarn. Noting that two tons of hair is displayed at the Auschwitz museum, some of the USHMM planners felt that a similar exhibit would be an effective way of telling that part of the story. Others objected, pointing out that since Auschwitz was the scene of the crime, showing it there carried the weight of evidence. In America, however, in a museum geared for an American audience, such a display might seem gratuitous, "an exhibit out of place."

An early vote among the planners in favor of exhibiting the hair was overturned following a plea by a number of survivors who felt it would be disrespectful to the victims. "In the end this was what mattered most, the wishes of the survivors, whom it was felt had the weight of moral authority on their side," Berenbaum said. "No one wanted someone to come into the museum and think they might be looking at their mother's hair."

I told Berenbaum about my conversation with Diane Saltzman concerning the Katrina lampshade and asked him what he would do if he were still at the museum.

"I don't know if, in the presence of a DNA report, I would have said it was a myth. But I agree with Diane Saltzman, these types of objects are a distraction. They are a form of pornography because people focus on them to the exclusion of everything else."

"But if they exist, you can't ignore them, can you? What should be done about them?"

Berenbaum exhaled. It was Father's Day. He was looking forward to dinner with his family. This wasn't a conversation he wanted to have, not now, probably not ever.

Pressing the issue, I asked Berenbaum about a story I'd heard from E. Randol Schoenberg, the grandson of the composer Arnold Schoenberg. Randol's wife had coincidentally been a college friend of Skip Henderson's wife, Fontaine. A well-known Los Angeles attorney, Schoenberg successfully pursued the case in which five Gustav Klimt paintings stolen by the Nazis that ended up in the hands of the Austrian government were returned to their original owners.

Schoenberg told me he'd heard that Berenbaum had once purchased an object purported to be a human skin lampshade off "the black market" and had it destroyed "just so the thing wasn't out there anymore."

Asked if this was true, and if he'd bothered to test the lampshade before disposing of it, Berenbaum was noncommittal, saying only that "a lot of junk turns up on these right-wing websites."

Berenbaum peered across the coffee table and said, "Maybe this will help you. Maybe not. But when we were first making the museum, we acquired a number of canisters that had contained Zyklon B," he said, referring to the cyanide-based pesticide with which the SS gassed people in the camps.

"At the time I thought this would be no big deal, that it was just another distressing exhibit. But there was a problem. Someone thought the canisters were still dangerous; they called the EPA, who got all excited. These things were fifty-odd years old at the time, they'd been open, exposed to the air. They were harmless. But try convincing anyone of that. It was just the name . . . Zyklon B . . . the idea that the label was the same, that was enough. It was the symbol.

"No one wanted to be near these things. I was in charge, so I got stuck with them. They were delivered to me. I put them in my garage until we could have them tested to prove they weren't dangerous. And let me tell you . . . that night, the whole time those things were in my garage, that was a very long night. It was enough to send someone to psychotherapy."

Berenbaum looked at me. "How long have you had this lampshade?"

"Several months."

"Several months . . . and it is in your house?" Berenbaum rubbed his forehead.

"Here's some advice. You can take it or not. What I've found is that being around these kinds of things, thinking about them, can drive people out of their minds. I'd get as far away from it as I could." This was what he was trying to tell Ken Kipperman, Berenbaum said, and this was what he was telling me.

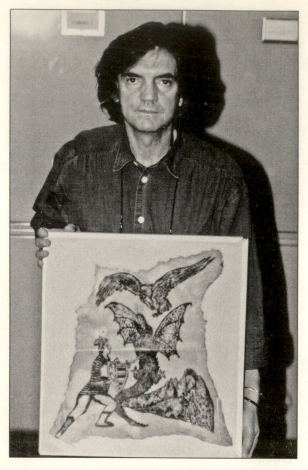

Ken Kipperman with Buchenwald tattooed skin

When I visited him in Maryland, Ken Kipperman was entering the second decade of his quest to call attention to the presence of the human skin artifacts at the National Archives and the National Museum of Health and Medicine. In the beginning Kipperman felt his campaign, which consisted of sending identical handwritten letters to newspapers, TV stations, well-known historians, and public figures asking for "respectful treatment for these victims" was having some success. In 2001 an article about him appeared in the *Washington Post* Style section. This led to a German documentary called *Shadows of Silence,* in which Kipperman comes off as an earnest if slightly touched Kafka character, attempting to do the right thing in an impossible situation. But the movie received little distribution, making it one more spectral, hard-to-find artifact. By the time I first spoke with him in 2007, Kipperman had all but abandoned his campaign, although not by choice. He had promised his wife he'd stop.

"That's why I didn't want you to come down here, so he'd get encouragement," Paula Kipperman told me in her lingering eastern European accent, as she prepared a deliciously copious lunch in the family kitchen. "I don't want him to start all this up again, because I can't take it anymore.

"I love Ken," said Paula, an upbeat, notably practical-minded daughter of Holocaust survivors who first met her husband when they were growing up in the refugee community in Brooklyn. "We have always been together. Childhood sweethearts. Ken is a very wonderful and talented man, a good husband, a good father, a good son, a great artist. Our daughter has three children. He is a wonderful grandfather. It is just on this one thing—*this thing!*—that he acts crazy. *Nuts!*

"I understand why he's done what he's done. But this has been difficult for me. I am a businesswoman. Before that protest about the Holocaust museum, I had a shoe business, a high-end shoe company. I had a lot of Jewish customers. After the protest, they wouldn't buy from me anymore. They said, Paula, we love you, but why did Ken have to do that? I had to close up. Then for years he was in the library. He was spending more time with Ilse Koch than he was with us! It is like an addiction. I made him promise that after the movie he'd stop being involved with this. *To let it go!* I was very serious. Maybe he heard me, for once."

As for her concern that her husband would be inspired to start up a new search after learning of the Katrina lampshade, Paula Kipperman did not have to worry.

Kipperman and I spent several hours together, during which time he described, as if by rote, the various aspects of his research, showing me the pictures of him with the shrunken heads, enumerating every step of his dogged search for the lampshade Major Schmuhl took from the Buchenwald Table. As for the New Orleans lampshade,

Kipperman listened to me tell my story, about Hurricane Katrina, and how Skip Henderson bought the thing from Dave Dominici, and how Shiya Ribowsky examined it and sent the samples to Bob Bever at Bode, and how the results came back positive, and how the Holocaust Museum said it was a myth. I was getting good at the story by then, having told it so many times.

Kipperman listened, looked at the pictures of the lampshade I had on my computer, glanced at the DNA report. He did all this with polite interest because Kipperman is nothing if not polite. He thanked me for bringing all this to his attention but asked few questions, expressed little wonderment.

Ken Kipperman knew what he was looking for, and this wasn't it.

SEVEN

If Ken Kipperman was frustrated by his inability to raise awareness about the fate of the Nazi human skin artifacts, there was at least one person who shared his fixation with the Buchenwald Table. This was Denier Bud, as in *Holocaust Denier* Bud.

I first became aware of Denier Bud, who also calls himself Mike Smith and lives somewhere in the San Francisco Bay Area, when I saw one of his web videos, *Nazi Shrunken Heads*. It sounded like one of those movies I used to see at the bottom half of Forty-second Street double bills, but it kept coming up on the search engine, so I clicked and there it was, the same footage of the Weimar people trudging up the Blood Road. That this was going to be a radically different take on the material was announced by Denier Bud's voice-over, the same lugubrious timbre that accompanies all his work.

"At the Buchenwald concentration camp in 1945, the Americans set up a display table to show Nazi atrocities," Denier Bud began miasmically as the camera panned over the familiar objects: "A lot of bogus items, tattooed skin supposedly taken off bodies, a supposedly human skin lampshade, which in reality is just a basic lampshade, but they really went over the edge of *dumb* when they put this on the table."

Pausing on a close shot of the shrunken heads, Denier Bud said that "they are being used to frame the Nazis as head-shrinkers. It's just so *dumb*."

Nazi Shrunken Heads then moved to the Nuremberg trials, where prosecutor Thomas Dodd, dramatically whisking the sheet off one of the heads, delivered his line: "The Nazis had one of their many victims decapitated, after having had him hanged, apparently for fraternizing with a German woman, and fashioned this terrible ornament from his head." This struck Denier Bud as *really dumb*.

In fact, it was evidence like this, Denier Bud said, that "might make you begin to understand why Holocaust deniers are Holocaust deniers."

It was through the use of "illusionary symbols" like shrunken heads and lampshades that events like the Holocaust are manipulated by the ruling class to further the unending militarism that inevitably benefits the rich and powerful, Denier Bud went on. The catalyst for these machinations, he said, is the unlimited capacity for human beings "to believe in evil." In the United States such gullibility "is related to TV, movies, and the Christian religion."

With a split-screen video image displaying a Bible on one side and a TV set on the other, Denier Bud explained, "Christianity, with its infantile *concept* of good and evil, and TV and movies, with their infantile *characterization* of good and evil, serve as the basis for most story lines. Add a dose of testosterone and you have gullible American men easily influenced to be pro-war. All the media has to do is portray someone as *evil*."

From there, as an example of how these "managed delusions" work, Denier Bud edited in a clip from the 1961 film *Judgment at Nuremberg*. Richard Widmark, in the Thomas Dodd role, is standing in front of the courtroom, showing the actual Buchenwald Table footage to the judges. As the camera moves over the Table, Widmark portentously ticks off the catalog of horrors: "A lampshade made from human skin; skin being used for paintings, many having an obscene nature; the heads of two Polish laborers, shrunken to one-fifth their normal size; a human pelvis, used as an ashtray."

Denier Bud stops the footage right there to say, "Let's compare dumb-dumb portrayals of evil which justify war."

He replayed Widmark intoning "A lampshade made from human skin," and then cut to a tape of George H. W. Bush giving a speech prior to the U.S. Senate vote on whether to attack Saddam Hussein in retaliation for his invasion of Kuwait in the Gulf War. "They had *kids in incubators!*" blurts the elder Bush in his spazzy, frat-party way. "And they were thrown out of the incubators! So that Kuwait could be systematically dismantled."

Watching this recalled a comment made by the late Raul Hilberg, author of *The Destruction of the European Jews* and the most magisterial of Holocaust scholars. Asked why he spent time monitoring the spoutings of Holocaust deniers, Hilberg said, "You never know, there's always the chance they might say something interesting." I wasn't sure if Denier Bud's work fit this criterion, but his rinky-dink DIY Power-Point videos and comic-book-nerd sensibility was a definite switch from the usual White Power rant.

A friendly if secretive sort, Denier Bud was "totally amped up" that a New York Jew, a member of the ever-suspect mainstream media, was interested in his videos. I was "just the kind of person" he felt he should be talking to because conversations with other Holocaust "revisionists" could get "kind of boring because some of these guys haven't had a new idea in decades." His web handle aside, Bud did not consider himself a "denier" in the strict sense but rather a "maker of Holocaust denial art."

Moreover, despite his frequent invocations of terms like *group evolutionary strategy,* a reference to the work of Cal State Long Beach psychology professor Kevin MacDonald, whose book *The Culture of Critique: An Evolutionary Analysis of Jewish Involvement in Twentieth-Century Intellectual and Political Movements* has become an upscale touchstone of the present-day ZOG/eugenics movement, Denier Bud wanted to make clear he was in no way "a raging anti-Semite or some skinhead." He knew a lot of "cool Jewish guys" and said that if Hitler walked up to him in the street, he'd "spit in his eye." Hitler was "a murderer," one more murderer in an age of murderers. An avowed pacifist, Denier Bud had nothing but contempt for the militarist side of Nazi ideology. All he was interested in was "the truth." To make sure there was no mistake about it, he inserted a flower-bedecked hippie peace symbol into the preamble of *Nazi Shrunken Heads,* over which he says he wishes "only good vibes" to the Jews of the world.

"It is my goal to lead the Holocaust denier movement away from the stench of anti-Semitism," Denier Bud proclaimed. "I don't think the Jews should be punished or suffer unduly for continuing to spread the lie of what happened to them during World War Two. They were a society under stress, so it is easy to sympathize with their motives. What I'm looking for is a Jew-friendly solution to the Holocaust hoax problem."

Despite this spirit of outreach, YouTube, in keeping with their policy against Holocaust denying, had banned *Nazi Shrunken Heads* and several of Bud's other videos. These included *One Third of the Holocaust,* a multi-hour attempt to explain away the well-documented history of the Aktion Reinhard camps—Treblinka, Sobibor, and Belzec—where nearly two million Jews were killed. *One Third of the Holocaust,* a tedious mélange of hokey computer graphics and half-baked arguments, captures none of the madcap offensiveness of *Nazi Shrunken Heads.* However, being a Jew of my particular stripe, I was outraged that YouTube, which seems to have no problem showing any manner of degrading imbecility and cruelty, refused to play it.

Denier Bud, who said he'd come to Holocaust denying in his early twenties in the aftermath of 9/11 when he began to realize "people will try to get you to believe anything if the stakes are high enough," had a far more sanguine attitude toward the YouTube ban of his work. Sure, he said nonchalantly, First Amendment rights should extend to Holocaust denying. But when you were an "outsider artist," getting banned was part of the deal, right? If it was good enough for Jean Genet, it was good enough for him. When you challenged "the consensus reality on the biggest taboo out there," you'd be a fool to expect fair treatment.

Far from deterred, Denier Bud said he had just put the finishing touches on what he considered to be his "best work" so far, a twenty-two-episode, two-hour-and-twenty-two-minute opus entitled *Buchenwald: A Dumb Dumb Portrayal of Evil*. The video contained "the most complete analysis" of the Buchenwald Table yet attempted, including "the real story" of Ilse Koch, whom he called "probably the most cruelly lied about woman of all time."

As far as Denier Bud was concerned, the saga of Ilse Koch and the lampshade story were so inexorably connected as to be "the same thing." He addresses the issue in episode 5 of *Buchenwald: A Dumb Dumb Portrayal of Evil,* entitled "The Ilse Koch Anachronistic Problem." Again showing the footage of the Weimar residents filing past the Buchenwald Table, this time with a British commentary referring to Ilse Koch as "a strapping redhead of ample proportions" whose "hobbies included the collecting of lampshades, book covers, and gloves made of tattooed human skin," Denier Bud disputes the Kommandeuse's involvement with the atrocities. By the time Americans liberated the camp, his video asserts, "Ilse Koch hadn't been at Buchenwald for at least a year and hadn't been in any position of power for much longer than that." Koch's absence stemmed in large part from the investigations of Konrad Morgen, the renowned "Bloodhound Judge of the SS," the supposed straight shooter in charge of rooting out corruption in the Nazi elite corps. It was Morgen who brought Karl Koch to trial and presided over his execution but turned up no evidence against Ilse Koch, acquitting her on all charges. As Denier Bud purports in his narration, "Morgen never found any objects like those shown on the Table."

So where did the lampshade and shrunken heads come from? Denier Bud asked me, rhetorically, when we spoke on the phone. "How did they suddenly appear the day of the Weimar forced march? Were they stored in some steamer trunk that only the Americans knew about? How convenient is that?

"What was needed was a show to help justify the war by making sure everyone knew, without a shadow of a doubt, that Nazis were completely evil," he went on. "Establishing the Nazi evil was important because the American powers—and in this I would include the Jewish elements of the American government and Zionists—knew the war wasn't really over. It would never be over. The Soviets were up next. You had to prepare for that. The idea was evil never sleeps, it just takes another form. You had to watch out, you had to keep the country on a war footing, which is what Eisenhower and John Foster Dulles wanted. That's why they got Billy Wilder and the other top talent to film the camps, to make it convincing. They did a great job but not a perfect job, because anyone looking at those pictures can see you can't take a lampshade that is supposedly made out of tattooed human skin and let the sun shine through it without revealing that it isn't a lampshade made of tattooed human skin. The lampshade on the Table doesn't have any tattoos on it. It is a totally normal lampshade! That's why it had to disappear after the psychological power of suggestion had created a myth about it.

"That's the lampshade's role. It is product placement and the product is dumb dumb evil, the kind of evil that can be manipulated for whatever its creator wants to use it for."

On a roll, Denier Bud continued: "Buchenwald is where things come together, where World War Two ends and the Cold War begins. It is a junction of history. This was the importance of the Buchenwald Table. It was a trial run in a new kind of American brainwashing; to paraphrase Noam Chomsky, an early model in the postwar manufacturing of evil because everyone knows killing six million people just because they're Jews is a terrible thing to do." The mechanisms of the mind game were right there, in *Buchenwald: A Dumb Dumb Portrayal of Evil*, for anyone who cared to have the scales fall from their deluded eyes.

The lampshade in newsreel footage of the Weimar march

The first and foremost thing to know, Denier Bud claimed, was that the Weimar forced march and the Buchenwald Table were an American intelligence operation run by the U.S. Army Psychological Warfare Division (PWD), the official propaganda unit attached to the Supreme Headquarters Allied Expeditionary Force (SHAEF) under the direct command of General Dwight D. Eisenhower. When Buchenwald was liberated, PWD men, a large percentage of them German-speaking Jewish Americans, were among the first of the U.S. forces to reach the camp. Their initial mission, according to Denier Bud, was to "plant" the stuff on the Table—the lampshade, the shrunken heads, all of it—to provide visceral images for the home front, thereby solidifying Eisenhower's position that would eventually lead to the presidency and forty-five years of Cold War.

If you knew whom to look for, you could see the architects of the deception at work, Denier Bud said. Episode eight of *Dumb Dumb Evil* focuses on two men seen in the Weimar march footage. One is a general, the star on his hat clearly visible, as he stands in the first row of the crowd mobbed around the Table. This individual, Denier Bud claims, "looks a lot like" Brigadier General Robert A. McClure, head of PWD. To the right of "McClure" is a bareheaded civilian standing in front of the Table holding up a human pelvis that SS officers had supposedly used as an ashtray. This man, Denier Bud claims, is C. D. Jackson, McClure's second in command.

It is hard to see why the presence of either McClure or Jackson at the scene is so damning, being that SHAEF and the PWD units were clearly, and publicly, running the show at Buchenwald at the time. It is also worth noting that the book *Psychological Warfare Against Nazi Germany: The Sykewar Campaign, D-Day to VE-Day* by Daniel Lerner, from where Denier Bud has cribbed most of his information, makes no mention of either man being present at the camp that day. Still, the name C. D. Jackson is enough to perk up the ears of even the most moderate Cold War conspiracy buff.

Born in 1902, a Princetonian, at age twenty-nine chief assistant to Time-Life head Henry Luce, founder of the Council for Democracy ("to combat all the nazi, fascist, communist, pacifist" antiwar groups in the United States), U.S. ambassador to Turkey, appointed managing director of Time-Life's international division in 1945, president of Radio Free Europe during the 1950s (including the period of the Hungarian revolt), Eisenhower's speechwriter during both his presidential runs, U.S. delegate to the United Nations in 1954, described by Carl Bernstein as "Henry Luce's personal emissary to the CIA," named publisher of *Life* in 1960, a position from which he would purchase the famous 8 mm Zapruder film of the Kennedy assassination but never show it, and buy the life rights of Marina Oswald but never publish anything—this is one hell of a résumé, and that doesn't even include setting up the American wing of the Bilderberg Conference.

For a paranoid of Denier Bud's particular persuasion, the notion that the same man who bought and suppressed the Zapruder film had, nineteen years earlier, presided over the Buchenwald Table and handled the famous lampshade was akin to orgasmic. The vast movements of history were drawn in invisible ink. What joy it was to connect the dots, Denier Bud said, to link two of the great plots of the benighted, unlamented twentieth century—the Holocaust and the murder of John Kennedy. Even if it wasn't C. D. Jackson standing beside the Buchenwald Table that day, the mere *suggestion* of the cold warrior's presence at this paradigm-shifting moment in the octopus-like spread of American/Zionist intelligence—and the role of the Holocaust as a justification of much of that policy—that was still news, or art, Denier Bud insisted.

No doubt Denier Bud displayed a manic talent for conspiracy, but what did that say about the lampshade, if anything?

Some light was shed by another video posted on Denier Bud's site, a tape of a 1994 *Phil Donahue Show*. With *Schindler's List* just out, the relentlessly topical Donahue invited Bradley Smith, a noted "historical revisionist" and founder of the Committee for Open Debate on the Holocaust (CODOH), to talk about a series of ads he'd been placing in college newspapers defying anyone to prove that a single Jew had died in a gas chamber during World War II. Arguing the other side was Michael Shermer, then a professor at Occidental College and executive director of the Skeptics Society, which takes on the claims of "fringe groups" like Holocaust deniers.

To place the discussion in its proper context, it is important to know that 1994 was the undisputed high-water mark of what is generally referred to as "scholarly historical revisionism," a phenomenon due in large part to the success of, and the resultant backlash to, *Schindler's List*. But Holocaust denying can be said to have begun back in the late 1940s with the first published works of the French writer Paul Rassinier.

An enigmatic figure, Rassinier was born in 1906 into a left-leaning family known for their pacifist views. Having joined the French Communist Party as early as 1922, Rassinier served in the Foreign Legion in Morocco, where he witnessed events that strengthened his pacifist and anticolonial outlook. With the Nazi invasion of France, Rassinier joined the Resistance, often risking his life helping Jews escape from German territory into Switzerland. He was captured by the Gestapo in 1944 and sent first to Buchenwald and then north to the satellite camp at Dora-Mittelbau in the Harz Mountains where he labored in the underground work camp manufacturing, among other things, the V-2 rockets Hitler hoped would save his war effort. Returning after the war to France, where he was awarded the Rosette of the Resistance by Charles de Gaulle, a severely disabled Rassinier served briefly as a Socialist Party representative to the French National Assembly and later worked with Jean Cocteau, André Breton, and Albert Camus on various left-leaning political projects. During this time, however, he found himself in sharp disagreement with what he took to be misinformed and exaggerated accounts about the way the Nazi camps were run. Reports of mass gassing of prisoners at Buchenwald especially irked Rassinier. After all, Rassinier said, he was there, he knew that for all the cruelties of the camp—like a winch-driven pulley system devised by the SS to hang large "groups of guilty men at a time"—there were no gas chambers.

Rassinier's first books, primarily *The Lie of Ulysses,* written in the early 1950s, established the basic "revisionist" canon: refuting the exterminationist gas chambers, questioning the widely cited death toll of six million, challenging the idea of German "intentionality," and blaming the so-called genocide myth on Communists (from whom Rassinier had become seriously estranged) and Zionists who would use "a false picture" of Jewish misery to sway public opinion in favor of the creation of the State of Israel.

These views gained wider currency in the late 1970s with the U.S. publication of a number of Rassinier's works, which were translated into English at the urging of Harry Elmer Barnes, a longtime Columbia history professor whose "America First" isolationist stance during the 1930s and '40s allied him with Charles Lindbergh and other Nazi apologists. In 1978, with the founding of the Institute for Historical Review (IHR) by Willis Carto, a former youth organizer for George Wallace's 1968 presidential campaign and would-be right-wing media mogul (he once owned the *American Mercury,* which years before had employed the journalistic hero and, alas, anti-Semite H. L. Mencken), Holocaust denying reached semi-think-tank status. A photo of an early IHR gathering showing twenty or so faux academics, some smoking pipes, might easily be mistaken for a still from a 1950s Madison Avenue adman convention or an early staff meeting at the *Paris Review* before the booze started flowing.

With funding provided by a reported $15 million endowment from Jean Farrel Edison, granddaughter of Thomas Edison, the organization's *Journal of Historical Review* published "scholarly" articles by well-known deniers like Robert Faurisson, a French literature professor known for challenging the authenticity of Anne Frank's diary. Other regular writers included the British historian David Irving, probably the best known of the revisionist academics owing to his widely publicized unsuccessful libel suit against American historian Deborah Lipstadt, author of *Denying the Holocaust: The Growing Assault on Truth and Memory.*

This was the background (Lipstadt's book had just come out) going into the aforementioned *Phil Donahue Show*. From the start, Bradley Smith, a former media spokesman for the Institute for Historical Review, tried to set the parameters of the discussion. A motorcycle-riding California libertarian of the old school, Smith wanted to talk only about the gas chamber issue, ignoring the rest of the Holocaust, as if these things could be separated. But Donahue, recognizing the public fervor surrounding the show—it was one of the very first appearances of someone who might be construed as a "Holocaust denier" on national TV—refused to restrict the debate. The topic was too emotional, too juicy to follow any set procedure. Another, younger, denier, David Cole, showed a tape "proving" that the gas chamber doors at Auschwitz opened out, not in, thereby supposedly showing that the victims could have escaped the room if they wanted. This "evidence" was unconvincing and boring to boot, but Cole offered the irresistible tabloid feature of being Jewish. Here was something to grab hold of, that whole self-hating trope, and Donahue pounced, asking, "Were you bar mitzvahed, David?"

Things went off the rails from there, as Smith, frustrated he hadn't been able to present his gas chamber case, took exception to the idea that most people thought the Holocaust involved "nobody but the Jews." Lots of people were killed in World War II, Smith said. Why did we have to spend so much time on this one particular segment of humanity? What about the Germans; weren't they victims, too? Not every German was a Nazi, yet they died, too, in the millions. Wasn't there "something vulgar about lying about Germans and thinking it is proper"? Smith said. "For example, it was a lie that Germans cooked Jews to make soap out of them. It was a lie—"

Shermer, the skeptic, interrupted at this point. "No, not a lie. It's a mistake."

It was an honest if inelegant attempt on Shermer's part to set the record straight. By 1994, much of the soap research was in. You could understand why victims believed it; sitting in a hellish camp, surrounded by so much death, anything seemed possible. But it wasn't so. Scholars were very much in agreement on that. History was not the product of a snap judgment, Shermer contended, but rather an ongoing process of discovery. The fact that mistakes could be made did not change the overall picture. There were some questions that might never be answered.

Had this situation been unfolding in a university seminar, Shermer might have been able to carry through on discussing the problems of understanding the past. But this was not a classroom and there was no time, because right then, one Judith Berg, an Auschwitz survivor sitting in the front row of the studio audience, rose to say, "*It was true!* They made lampshades and they cooked soap! That's true."

Shermer turned toward Judith Berg. "Excuse me," he said, defending rationalism, "but historians make mistakes. Everyone makes mistakes." He attempted to make his case about "refining our knowledge," but Smith, a raconteur of such moments, saw his opening.

"Ask why they're doing this to this woman," Smith demanded. "Why have they taught this woman to believe that Germans cooked and skinned—"

Judith Berg jumped out of her chair. "I was seven months in Auschwitz! I lived near to the crematorium as far as I am from you. I smelled—you would never eat roast chicken if you were there— I smelled—"

"Let's get to the bottom of one thing," Smith interjected. "She says soap and lampshades. The professor says that's mistaken. Which is it?"

"Even the Germans admit it," Berg shouted, rolling up her sleeve to reveal her camp tattoo. *"They admit they had lampshades!"*

Trying to regain control of his show, Donahue turned to Smith with plaintive accusation. "Do you have any empathy at all? Are you concerned with the pain that you cause this woman?"

"Me?" Smith replied, with an innocent look.

It went on like this for a few more moments, Smith pleading the case of unfairly maligned SS men, Berg screaming that she was told not to use the soap "because it could be your mother." Finally, mercifully, Donahue broke for a commercial.

Trying to make sense of the incident in a book he wrote with Alex Grobman, *Denying History,* Shermer says, "So much for the reliability of Holocaust survivors' composure on national television."

Given the venue and the cast of characters, however, what could anyone expect? The event was all emotion, and that is why things like the soap and the lampshade never leave the discourse. The lampshade is more a feeling than a fact: it is stitched into the heart, not the mind. Once it came into the conversation, any pretense of rationality went out the window. Diane Saltzman said the object sitting inside my Brooklyn closet was a myth; Michael Berenbaum said the wishes of the survivors must always be paramount.

But what if the lampshade is a myth that lives inside the survivors? How do you manage that?

It was sometime after watching *Buchenwald: A Dumb Dumb Portrayal of Evil* that I finally mentioned the existence of the Katrina lampshade to Denier Bud. Maybe it wasn't fair, to have withheld the information until now, but I had feared it would muddy the conversation. Revealing I had a real lampshade in my possession might have given Denier Bud the idea that I questioned his conclusions. Like every scummy journalist, I needed his trust.

"You know, I have this lampshade," I told Denier Bud. "The DNA test says it is made out of human skin."

Denier Bud's reaction was similar to Ken Kipperman's when I told him the same thing. He said, "Far out," and little else. I told him the story, as I'd told it to Kipperman, but little of it appeared to register. In fact, Denier Bud seemed more interested in Ken Kipperman than he was in any Mardi Gras–tasseled lampshade found in an abandoned building by Dave Dominici.

Something told me it was a mistake to mention Kipperman to Denier Bud, but it seemed unavoidable, what with their mutual fascination with the Buchenwald Table.

"I can't believe I missed this guy," Denier Bud said when he called me back a few days after our previous talk. He'd found the article about Kipperman in the *Washington Post* and was blown away.

"It is so odd, Kipperman and me," Denier Bud exclaimed, "the two of us kind of being on the opposite end of things. But I really feel I can understand what he was going through. To be searching for the truth, and to feel you can't quite grasp it. We have so much in common."

Denier Bud wanted to contact Kipperman. "The guy has been tricked like so many others. He's suffering. I think I can help him. If I could only have a couple of conversations with him, it might really clear up a few things. I could be his knight in shining armor, his rabbi."

This was a nice gesture, I told Bud, offering to explain his "Jew-friendly" version of Holocaust denying to Ken Kipperman. But I didn't think Ken Kipperman would see it that way.

EIGHT

Denier Bud told me about Albert G. Rosenberg. He said it was Rosenberg, commander of a small group of German-speaking American soldiers attached to the Psychological Warfare Division of SHAEF, who'd been a chief architect in creating the lampshade myth. According to Denier Bud, Rosenberg had been largely responsible for setting up the Buchenwald Table, personally supplying the pair of shrunken heads, which, according to Denier Bud, the soldier had obtained while manning an Army weather station in Natal, on the northeastern Brazilian coast.

"Rosenberg has the Midas touch, but instead of gold he finds shrunken heads," Denier Bud chortled.

When I reached him on the phone at home in El Paso, Rosenberg, nearly ninety, remembered speaking with Denier Bud.

"He called up one morning out of the blue and said he wanted to talk about Buchenwald," said Rosenberg in his faint German accent. "He seemed like a nice fellow and was very knowledgeable about the period. I thought he was working on a college paper of some type. But then he started speaking of these shrunken heads, asking me if I'd brought them to the camp. I was flabbergasted. That I should have carried shrunken heads from Natal, Brazil, taken them across the ocean, and then kept them in my rucksack through Europe in the middle of World War Two for the express purpose of framing the SS for brutality! As if they needed me for that. *What an idea!*

"Then he told me he was a Holocaust denier. I told him twenty-eight members of my family died in this thing you say never happened and hung up. It was a very strange conversation."

I knew a few things about Rosenberg, mostly gleaned from the introduction of *The Buchenwald Report,* an account of life at the camp he had compiled from a series of interviews in the weeks following liberation. The report contained testimony from 104 prisoners and was a key source for the prosecution at both the Nuremberg and Dachau war crimes proceedings, including the trial of Ilse Koch. It was Rosenberg who chose the Buchenwald inmate Eugen Kogon to write the main overview of camp life that Kogon would later expand into *The Theory and Practice of Hell.*

After the war, the original report dropped out of sight. The two copies given to SHAEF disappeared ("Lost in the fog of the intelligence departments," Rosenberg said). Kogon's copy was destroyed in a flood. Rosenberg, however, had kept a carbon copy. He always assumed the government would eventually release the original report but after waiting forty years, he decided to try to donate his copy to several Holocaust museums, including the Yad Vashem memorial in Jerusalem.

"I couldn't get anywhere with them. They told me they were swamped with work and I should send the report to a post office box and they'd look it over in due time. I didn't think it should be sent to a post office box.

"You see, there were problems with the report. Right from the start it was perceived as being too much the product of the Communist groups at the camp, which was true to a large extent," said Rosenberg, adding that he hadn't thought all that much about what color triangle was worn by the people who contributed to the document. "It was my job to get the thing done. The Communists had battled it out with the criminals and were on the top of the heap among *Häftlingsführung,* the system of kapos that the SS depended on to run the place. They were the best-educated people in the camp; they knew the most. Besides, in 1945, the Soviets were supposed to be our allies. Of course, we knew not to believe everything we were told. The Communist kapos were guilty of a lot of crimes. Sometimes they were worse than the Nazis themselves. It was a complicated situation, obviously. But then the Cold War was on, and suddenly no one was supposed to listen to anything a Communist said, right or wrong. I guess they decided the report was too troublesome, so they did what authorities do, which was hide it in a drawer. But I said to myself, I've got the thing. How can I die without telling someone about it?"

Rosenberg made contact with publisher Frederick Praeger, whose father, Max Praeger, a noted Viennese bookseller, had been imprisoned at Buchenwald from 1939 to 1945. The younger Praeger, an intelligence officer in Patton's army, arrived at the camp only to find that his father, like most of the Jewish prisoners, had only days before been shipped to Auschwitz, where he was murdered. Praeger told Rosenberg that he would publish the report but that it needed to be translated and edited.

"This wasn't a task I felt capable of doing," said Rosenberg, then a professor of social work at the University of Texas at El Paso. "So I gathered up the pages, some of them in pretty bad shape, and walked down the hall to the office of my colleague David Hackett, who was a history professor with an interest in the Third Reich. Hackett was a bright guy and a perfect German speaker, plus I liked the idea that I could keep an eye on him. It was pretty much on the spur of the moment, quite unannounced. I think David was somewhat startled when I dumped this massive stack of pages on his desk, told him what it was, and asked him if he was interested in working on it. After he got over the shock, he said yes.

"That was 1987, I think. Five years later, Hackett finished," Rosenberg told me during our first phone conversation, adding that

Fred Praeger had a stroke and died only moments after writing the foreword to the report. "That was like a Greek play, Fred dying like that."

I was somewhat leery of telling Rosenberg about the Katrina lampshade, fearful that he'd think I was one more loony. But he was interested. "It was tested and found to be human? That's remarkable. Well, if you want to know about lampshades, you've come to the right place," Rosenberg said.

"When we first came to the camp—and we were among the very first Americans there—I had a lot of paperwork to do. There was always a lot of paperwork with SHAEF. I needed a place to work and sat down at a desk of what I thought was probably some high-up SS man. I couldn't have been sitting there very long when a French prisoner came and started shouting at me, saying I was no better than the Germans. That I had no shame. Didn't I know the light I was using to write my reports had a lampshade made of human skin? How could I use this awful light for mere bureaucratic scribbles? I found another place to do my work. There was plenty of talk about the Nazis and human skin. I saw wallets and gloves and asked, are these skin? The answer was almost always yes."

Rosenberg was fascinated that a lampshade that might be from Buchenwald would turn up in post-Katrina New Orleans, especially since he himself had once lived in the Crescent City. Family members living in New Orleans's Jewish community had helped him escape Germany in 1937 after he was almost beaten to death by storm troopers in his hometown of Göttingen.

"It was very terrible," Rosenberg said. "These heavy boots thudding against my body, over and over again. My non-Jewish friends chased the thugs away. They saved my life. My jaw was broken, my spine wrecked. The pain from those injuries has been with me, on and off, ever since that day, but luckily, these people in New Orleans got me out."

"Those were some of the best years of my life," said Rosenberg of his time in New Orleans. He lived "on Johnson Street out by Tulane" and loved to take the streetcar along St. Charles Avenue. The memory of the swoosh of the trolley wheels over the rails along the grassy neutral ground, the branches of the trees making a canopy overhead, always made him smile.

"I spent a long time doing social work at the Desire Projects," he recalled. "My job was to get people jobs, sign them up for government benefits, work out whatever problems I could. But it wasn't easy; a lot of the time you'd set up appointments and no one would show up. It was hard to win trust. Everyone simply assumed anyone walking around with a badge or a clipboard was some kind of cop. You felt there was a lot of graft. One weekend I think seven people were murdered at Desire alone. But I must say I enjoyed the place, in spite of everything."

New Orleans was "full of serendipity, good and bad," Rosenberg said, remembering the days when he'd leave his office on Camp Street and see "this skinny, somewhat bedraggled figure handing out these leaflets. 'Fair play for Cuba!' he'd shout. Then, when Kennedy was shot, I knew right away, it was him—Oswald!—right there, on my lunch hour.

"When the hurricane hit, we were in the middle of a drought here," Rosenberg recalled. "It hadn't rained in I don't know how long. The Rio Grande was drying up to a trickle. I'd watch the drought story on TV, and then they'd show New Orleans and I could see the places I'd enjoyed so much—Canal Street, Napoleon Avenue—completely underwater. Those poor people, on the rooftops. I truly felt like crying. And now you're telling me about a lampshade made of human skin, from Buchenwald, washed up in the flood. My God!"

I told Rosenberg that I was likely to be in Albuquerque, New Mexico, five hours or so up the interstate from El Paso, within the next few weeks. Would it be all right if I stopped in for a chat?

"Absolutely!" Rosenberg said, there was a very nice Howard Johnson Express just a few blocks from his house if I wanted to stay over. Then he asked me if I knew a book titled *Literature or Life,* by Jorge Semprún.

"No," I said, though Semprún's name rang a dim, unidentified bell.

"You might find it interesting," Rosenberg said.

Jorge Semprún was the grandson of Antonio Maura, a five-time prime minister of Spain. At the start of the Spanish Civil War, Semprún, a young teenager, was out of the country with his father. Refusing to return to Spain after Franco's Nationalists took over, Semprún, a philosophy student, settled in France and later joined the Resistance. In 1943, the twenty-year-old Semprún was captured by the Gestapo and sent to Buchenwald, where he spent the rest of the war. In the years that followed, he wrote a number of books and screenplays, including *Z*, the celebrated Costa-Gavras film about the overthrow of the democratic government in Greece, which won two Academy Awards. He also wrote a number of films for Alain Resnais, maker of both *Night and Fog* and *Hiroshima Mon Amour*. In 1994 Semprún published the memoir *Literature or Life*, devoting a full chapter to his encounter with a man he calls Lieutenant Walter Rosenfeld but who is quite clearly Albert G. Rosenberg.

Semprún first sees "Lieutenant Rosenfeld" the day of the Weimar forced march. "In the crematory yard," Semprún writes, an American lieutenant, speaking German, addressed several dozen Weimar residents, most of them women "wearing spring dresses in bright colors. The officer spoke in a neutral, implacable voice.

" 'Your pretty town,' he told them, 'so clean, so neat, brimming with cultural memories, the heart of classical and enlightened Germany, seems not to have had the slightest qualm about living in the smoke of the Nazi crematoria!' "

Two days later, Semprún writes, he found himself sitting opposite Rosenfeld in one of the SS command's former offices. Semprún knew the Americans had decided to prepare "a comprehensive report on life and death in Buchenwald" and were especially interested in interviewing prisoners who'd participated in "the internal administration" of the camp. They included Semprún, who'd spent time working in the *Arbeitsstatistik* office, a plum assignment secured by his Communist connections, keeping track of inmate labor assignments. The two young men—Rosenfeld was twenty-six, Semprún twenty-one—hit it off and began a short-lived but highly resonant friendship.

As Semprún tells it, over the next week, Rosenfeld and Semprún, liberator and liberated, spend several hours in what Semprún calls "Goethe's landscape." Walking through the Ettersberg woods and hearing the birds in the trees, Semprún is "intoxicated" by "their songs, their trills, their warbles." He tells Rosenfeld that for two years he rarely heard any birds; the smoke from the crematorium kept them away. They make their way along the Ilm River, to visit Goethe's forest cottage, the country retreat where the master enjoyed "the twin delights of refreshing coolness and solitude." Another day they drive in Rosenfeld's jeep through the bombed-out streets of Weimar to see Goethe's house, where an old watchman tells them no one is allowed into the great poet's house without "special permission from the authorities."

"I am the authority," Rosenfeld tells the old man. "Authority with a capital *A*, all the authority imaginable." When the watchman continues to protest, praising Hitler, saying how wonderful it was the last time the Führer had come to Weimar and stayed at the Elephant Hotel, Rosenfeld grabs the old Nazi by the collar, drags him over to a closet, and locks him inside, allowing the two friends to "complete our visit in peace, out of range of his despairing and malevolent voice."

Mostly, Semprún and Rosenfeld discuss literature and philosophy. Rosenfeld mentions people like Theodor Adorno, Max Horkheimer, Herbert Marcuse, the Frankfurt School, names new to Semprún. Rosenfeld also speaks enthusiastically about the German exiles Bertolt Brecht, Hermann Broch, author of *The Sleepwalkers,* and Robert Musil, who wrote *The Man without Qualities.* In return, Semprún describes his admiration for Camus, Heinrich Heine, and the "poisonous beauty" of Pola Negri, whose films the SS would sometimes show the Buchenwald prisoners on Sunday afternoons. He mentions to Rosenfeld that he had been looking forward to seeing Jean Giraudoux's play *Sodome et Gomorrhe* the evening a Gestapo officer smashed open his scalp with the butt of an automatic pistol, beginning his long journey to Buchenwald.

Semprún writes that it was in one of these conversations that Rosenfeld first told him that Martin Heidegger had been a National Socialist as far back as 1933. Rosenfeld revealed that the philosopher hadn't lifted a finger to help when his revered teacher, Edmund Husserl, was barred from the university for being a Jew. As a schoolboy, Semprún had spent "long, austere" winter evenings oppressed by Heidegger's dense prose, hacking his way through "torturing pseudo-etymologies," "purely rhetorical resonance," and "assonance." Completing his assignments, the young Semprún had wondered: did these ideas mean anything in any language other than German? It was almost a relief to hear that Heidegger was a Nazi; in retrospect, this was the only part of the man's work that made any sense.

Although he never quite comes out and says it, Semprún's chapter on Lieutenant Rosenfeld is an extended thank-you note. In the measured way the American liberator dismisses the self-serving obliviousness of the people from Weimar, in his manhandling of the old Hitler supporter at Goethe's house, and most of all in his open-handed intellectuality, it is Rosenfeld who pulls Semprún from what he calls "the whirlwind of nothingness, the nebulous void."

In *Literature or Life,* Semprún says it is only when he sees Allied soldiers gazing at him with a kind of morbid curiosity that he begins to realize he is indeed alive and again responsible for all that breathing and thinking entails. Until then he was somewhere in between, which, he says, puts the lie to the statement by Ludwig Wittgenstein (whom Semprún calls "this idiot") that "death is not an event of life. Death cannot be lived." To be in the camp was to be in both, to "cross through death," like the forty-nine-day *bardo* described in the Tibetan Book of the Dead. Returning to life is no simple journey, Semprún says. "Many people who will come out of this place will not be sur-vivors, they'll be ghosts, revenants." It is Lieutenant Rosenfeld, this German Jew returned "to fight against his own country," this tough-guy spouter of poetry and philosophy who has arrived, like Charon rowing against the current, to deposit Semprún back on the shore of the living.

The two men spend a lot of time discussing Rosenfeld's Bu-chenwald project. To tell the story of the camp, and do it in three weeks, is an impossible assignment, Semprún says. How to speak of these things in a way that both satisfies the moral parameters of the situation and translates it into the crabbed language demanded by SHAEF? Where should the story start? With Goethe? With the birds driven away by the smoke? It is difficult to know, says Semprún, who will spend much of his life looking for a way to tell his own version of the story.

One thing is certain, however, Semprún tells Rosenfeld: the sim-ple chronology, the facts and figures, are insufficient. You could re-count the story of "any day at all, from reveille at four-thirty . . . the fatiguing labor, the constant hunger, the chronic lack of sleep, the persecution by the *Kapos,* the latrine duty, the floggings from the SS, the assembly-line work in munitions factories, the crematory smoke, the public executions . . . the death of friends," and never compile a true history of Buchenwald.

"What's essential," Semprún says, "is the experience of Evil . . . You don't need concentration camps to know Evil. But here, this ex-perience will turn out to have been crucial, and massive, invading everywhere, devouring everything . . . It's the experience of radical Evil."

Hearing this, Lieutenant Rosenfeld looks at his young compatriot "sharply." *"Das radikal Böse,"* he says.

Semprún looks back at Rosenfeld, in amazement. So this man who has pulled him back to the living knows Kant as well?

"Of course," Rosenfeld says.

Albert Rosenberg in El Paso

"Das radikal Böse . . . ," murmured Albert G. Rosenberg, as he sat in the living room of his apartment in El Paso, repeating the famous phrase from Immanuel Kant's 1793 treatise *Religion within the Limits of Reason Alone*. It was sixty-three years since he had discussed these matters with Jorge Semprún inside an SS office at Buchenwald. Now Rosenberg lived a few miles from the Mexican border with his wife of thirty years, Lourdes, in a modest two-bedroom apartment in a hillside subdivision.

He said, *"Radical evil* was Kant's term to explain what happens when evil, which he believed was an inherent human trait, is unchallenged by the exercise of free will. Free will, coupled with certain maxims of the good, keeps evil at bay. It is on the state level, such as in the totalitarian, dictatorial society in which the free will of the people is completely oppressed, that evil becomes dominant. It becomes the way of things—*das radikal Böse."*

Then, his blue eyes suddenly infused with a mischievous glint, Rosenberg laughed. As sharp as ever, he was nonetheless tickled that he still remembered something about Kant, whom he hadn't thought about "for decades." But there was the German educational system for you. Even with the Nazis coming to power, the gymnasium wasn't the paltry sort of thing that passes for learning in the United States. Drummed into the brain, a German education had staying power.

Who knew how Kant might have chosen to define the word *radikal* had he been writing in 1945 rather than 1793, but the Prussian philosopher had "come pretty close" to predicting the way the Third Reich worked, Rosenberg thought. This didn't make Kant clairvoyant, he said. Rather it was that "the dark side of German character was there a long, long time before Hitler came on the scene."

"Radical evil—total destruction of opposing will, wiping it out, sending it up the smokestack—that was what the camps were," said Rosenberg, who said he never felt sadder than the day he took his SHAEF jeep and drove to Bergen-Belsen, the camp in Saxony where he'd heard that several of his relatives had been sent by the Nazis.

"I drove through the camp, through that horrible death, people lying there staring into space, shouting on my U.S. Army bullhorn, screaming out to see if anyone knew the Rosenberg family from Göttingen. I found no one. Later I met one of my relatives, my cousin Henry, one of the few who survived—twenty-eight died—and he told me he heard me. He heard me shouting! But he could barely move. He couldn't answer my call."

Literature or Life took him by surprise, Rosenberg said. He vaguely remembered Jorge Semprún, the twenty-one-year-old partisan and philosophy student, and had no idea that Semprún, whom he had not seen or spoken to since those days in the Ettersberg woods, would remember him so vividly.

"When I first picked up the book and saw that chapter 'Lieutenant Rosenfeld' and began reading it, I thought, who could have dreamed this? Who could have imagined my life like this? But it wasn't a dream. It happened. To me, and him." That said, even though he thinks *Literature or Life* is "a masterpiece," there are things in it that he did not recall happening quite the way Jorge Semprún did.

Semprún described the tone of his speech to the people from Weimar as "neutral" and that was good, Rosenberg said. "But I didn't feel neutral. I was seething. Göttingen, where I grew up, was not all that different than Weimar. A shitty, right-wing town. Full of fascists. They tried to kill me in Göttingen, but it could have just as easily been Weimar. For all the lovely history and poetry, it was that kind of place. Those people from Weimar—I took them around, showed them the crematorium, the places where the medical experiments took place, where the Nazis ripped off the prisoners' skin and made the lampshades . . . I might have sounded neutral, because that is the way a soldier is supposed to conduct himself. My father was a soldier. He fought for Germany in the First World War. Fought for these same people! The same people who fifteen years later would follow Hitler!

"To me, that is one of the great ironies of it, an irony I understood very well at Buchenwald. SHAEF was very smart to give me the job of tour guide that day. They couldn't have gotten anyone better. Those people claimed to be innocent, but I knew they weren't. I knew that because I knew them. They said they were crying because they didn't know. But that was a lie. They were crying because they *did* know. They were hoping their tears would absolve them, as if someone would pat them on the head and say, don't worry, it's going to be all right. But they had the wrong guy for that. The trains ran to Buchenwald every day. People from Weimar worked at the Gustloff factory next to the camp. Guards lived in the town. So don't say you didn't know, because you did. *You knew.*"

Eating taco chips, we sat at Rosenberg's dining room table looking over some of his "souvenirs." He had "stacks of stuff" from the war, which he kept in the "magic closet" where he once stored the remaining copy of *The Buchenwald Report.*

He had his "SHAEF pass," which he referred to as "the ultimate Eisenhower get-out-of-jail ticket, a 007 James Bond license to kill that let us do basically whatever the hell we wanted." Dated 18 February 1945, the pass said in bold capital letters, "THE BEARER OF THIS CARD WILL NOT BE INTERFERED WITH IN THE

PERFORMANCE OF HIS DUTY BY THE MILITARY POLICE
OR ANY OTHER MILITARY ORGANIZATION BY COMMAND
OF GENERAL EISENHOWER."

He had his "intelligence officer's identity card" with a picture of
him as a young man with horn-rimmed glasses and a far-off gaze that
made him seem more like a young Arthur Miller than a spy or a soldier. He had copies of old Nazi newspapers, photographs from the
camps, and a translated letter dated November 29, 1941, sent from
Gestapo chief Reinhard Heydrich to SS Gruppenführer Otto Hof-
mann of the Reich Race and Settlement Main Office inviting him
to a meeting at Wannsee "in regard to organizational, practical, and
material measures requisite for the total solution of the Jewish question in Europe."

He had a prayer book given to him by a relative. "It was the prayer book of my favorite uncle," Rosenberg said. "He kept a diary day to day, separated by years, 1937, 1938, 1939, 1940, 1941, 1942, 1943. Then nothing. Nothing."

It was quite a collection, but not all that it once was, Rosenberg said matter-of-factly. For years he had a piece of tattooed human skin that he had taken from the Buchenwald Table, just as Major Schmuhl, whom Rosenberg remembered as a "heavy-set sort of man," had taken the lampshade.

"It was a tattoo of a woman, with a hat on her head. It came from a man's chest because you could see the nipple alongside the girl's head."

Asked why he took the piece of skin, Rosenberg shook his head. "I have asked myself that same thing many times. In the beginning it seemed like no big deal. At the time there seemed to be many such objects at the camp. The pathology block was a veritable factory of human skin products. Ilse Koch was supposed to have had gloves of human skin, purses of human skin, a whole Paris collection. There was no reason not to believe any of these stories. You heard them over and over again. Everyone said pretty much the same thing . . . We had entered hell, so there was no surprise to see hellish things. To me the skin was just one more incredible item. It was years before I came to the conscious realization that that curled-up little piece of tanning had once been part of some poor soul's hide.

"Then I couldn't stand to have the thing near me anymore. I was having so many terrible dreams—I still do—and the tattoo had so many associations. The Nazis had perpetrated the worst crimes in the history of the world and here I had this little knickknack. God!

"I asked myself, why do I keep this awful thing? I was ashamed to have had it for so long. But I couldn't quite part with it. It was some kind of pathology perhaps. I went to psychotherapy for years and still couldn't figure it out. It was like it was part of me. I locked it up in a safe-deposit box at the bank, but it still haunted me. I sent it to a friend in Chicago. I told him to give it to Yad Vashem, do whatever you want. I never found out what finally happened with it and don't want to know."

Rosenberg sat there for a moment, looking out the window. It was midafternoon now and the winter sun was sinking behind the jagged peaks visible over the fence behind his apartment.

"What did you say that fellow called his movie? The one who thinks I brought the shrunken heads from Brazil? *Buchenwald, Stupid Evil?*"

"No. *Dumb. Buchenwald: A Dumb Dumb Portrayal of Evil.*"

"Dumb Dumb." Rosenberg smiled wearily. "Well, that's not a half-bad title, when you think about it. Evil is dumb. That is why it is evil. There are so many stupid people in the world willing to believe stupid things; put them all together and they can be very, very stupid. A stupid, dangerous crowd out for blood. To me, that's what the Nazis were, one gigantic lynch mob."

As for Denier Bud's assertion that the PWD set up the Buchenwald Table, Rosenberg could only roll his eyes. The idea that Psychological Warfare did political propaganda was no great insight. "We were in the political propaganda business, for chrissakes," Rosenberg said, with a cagey smile that seemed to indicate that once an intelligence man, always an intelligence man. Rosenberg supposed he could have "gone into the spy business." The PWD was an easy, entry-level step to the OSS and the CIA beyond. One of the young men in his unit, called "Kampfgruppe Rosenberg," was Michael Josselson, then an international buyer for Gimbels but soon to be the head of the CIA-run Congress for Cultural Freedom that would fight the intellectual Cold War in Europe. Among Josselson's many projects was *Encounter* magazine, which was edited by Stephen Spender and Irving Kristol and published the work of such people as Arthur Koestler, James T. Farrell, Ignazio Silone, Bertrand Russell, and Sidney Hook. These career pathways were open, Rosenberg said, for the right sort of person.

But as for C. D. Jackson holding up a human pelvis that day at Buchenwald, Rosenberg said this was news to him. As far as he knew, there was no way the Buchenwald Table, with the lampshade sitting on it, was a PWD operation.

"The Table was set up by the prisoners themselves, the Communists. Those kapos! Who knows how many people they killed! They had their own agenda. Obviously the lampshade had propaganda value, but it wasn't *our* propaganda."

Rosenberg's wife, Lourdes, was home now. A cheerful woman who looked to be at least twenty-five years younger than her husband, Lourdes met Rosenberg when he was teaching at the University of Texas at El Paso. They fell in love and married.

"That's the worst thing about being so damn old," Rosenberg said, "Lourdes having to take care of me all the time. She deserves better."

Lourdes, who sets up school programs in both El Paso and across the border in teeming Ciudad Juárez, thought this was ridiculous. "You take care of yourself," Lourdes said. "Besides, Albert has been very good for me. Once I was a poor Mexican girl. Now, thanks to Albert, I am a great European intellectual," she joked.

Later Lourdes told me, "Albert suffers, you know. He likes to joke. He has a dark sense of humor. I think he does it to protect himself, because he has those dreams. Sometimes I'd wake up and he'd be banging against the wall or throwing the pillows around, in his sleep. Sometimes he'd throw *me* around in his sleep. He has so much he can't talk about. So many people he knew were killed."

For now, Lourdes looked at the picture of the lampshade with a sense of duty. "Is this like the one you saw at the camp, Albert?"

"*Cuál?*"

Lourdes shot Rosenberg a stern glance. "The one on the desk of the commandant."

"Could be. It is very similar. It is not unattractive, I think. Maybe we could use an extra fixture."

Lourdes had had enough of this and excused herself, giving Rosenberg a peck on the top of his bald head.

"She'll probably ask the Virgin to forgive me now," Rosenberg said.

"I don't know why she's mad. She must have dozens of relics of the saints lying around. Catholics love their ossuaries, you know. Bones, bones, and more bones. I know she'd like to convert me but I'm holding out. I have never been very observant, but what else could I be with a life like mine but a Jew?"

Rosenberg sighed. Fate was so consigning. Not that there weren't times when he had felt "totally free, out of the shadow of who I was." When he first came to the United States, after being beaten in Göttingen, he lived for a time with relatives in Jackson Heights, Queens. He got a job working as a junior hotel detective at what was then called the Park Central Hotel on Seventh Avenue in Manhattan.

"I was a real junior G-man, fantasized myself as a kid gumshoe. Mostly I was supposed to chase out the prostitutes who hadn't paid off the right people. But I didn't care. Being there was such a perfect introduction to the kind of America I wanted America to be: fun and seedy, like a black-and-white Hollywood movie. Arnold Rothstein, the gangster, once lived at the hotel. Room 307. I was told to hold my breath when I passed the room because Rothstein was supposed to be the smartest man who ever lived. He fixed the World Series, they said. I didn't even know what the World Series was, but after Göttingen I thought if a man named Rothstein could fix it, America had to be the greatest country in the world."

Asked how he'd wound up in El Paso, Rosenberg said he'd been living in Dayton, Ohio, where he wasn't fond of the weather. He and his son had a car and they started driving. "We went through everywhere, saw the country. This was the 1960s, a different time." One day they reached El Paso and the temperature felt right. Rosenberg liked that it was on the edge of the country, as far as you could go. He got a job at the college, met Lourdes, and that was it, he said.

"A place to hide, I told myself," Rosenberg related. "But eventually you realize there's no escaping, no matter how far you go." Only a few months after we first talked, Rosenberg was reading a *New Yorker* article about a recently discovered cache of photos taken at Auschwitz during the war. In one of the photos Rosenberg saw his cousin Aleeza, who would be murdered at the camp, standing on the selection ramp watched by the notorious SS man Emmerich Hoecker.

In El Paso it was the same. Every day, it seemed, the paper had another story about the murders right across the border in Juárez. The place was insane. In 1970 twenty thousand people lived there; now it was over two million with more pouring in every day. One of the most violent cities in the world, the murder rate was triple that of Detroit. The drug wars were so endemic that local officials had petitioned the United Nations to send peacekeepers. It was the *feminicidios* (femicides) that most upset Rosenberg. Dozens of women were being killed each year, their often mutilated bodies found behind the maquiladora factories that have sprung up since NAFTA, in garbage dumps, or simply dumped in the desert. Lourdes often went to Juárez and Rosenberg was worried about her, but it was more than that.

"So many of these murders aren't simply murders," Rosenberg said. "Women are killed and have their organs removed. They're left hollowed-out corpses. Some women are killed when they're eight months pregnant, ready to give birth. They're left to die and the baby is taken away. They say it's the drug cartels, or some cult that uses the body parts. The police can't stop it, even if they wanted to. They're part of it. Over and over the same thing happens. It frightens me, the lawlessness of it. It is so familiar. So horribly familiar. Evil, radical evil—everywhere you go, there it is."

Sometimes he thought this was the true story of his life, Rosenberg said: trying to outrun evil, trying to stay one step ahead. Even though he'd lived to be ninety, he couldn't say he'd succeeded. His legs were nearly useless to him much of the time. He was convinced this was due to having been stomped by Nazi thugs back in Göttingen.

"It might sound silly, that a ninety-year-old man would be dying from the effects of a beating that took place in 1937, but it is true, both physiologically and metaphorically. This pain has been inside me since that day."

The sun had nearly sunk behind the mesa outside Rosenberg's

window, and he was tired. "So what are you going to do with this lampshade?" he asked me.

"I don't know yet," I told him. "What would you do?"

"I'd toss it in a Dumpster. But I'm not you." Rosenberg smiled. "I'm sure you'll figure it out."

"Right."

I asked Rosenberg what it was like being in a place like El Paso, Texas, being the only one like him, the only person with memories like his.

"You mean to end up here, after all that?" Rosenberg looked out at the fading light on the reddish hillside. "Surreal, isn't it?"

NINE

I first met Dani Dominici Babineaux, Dave Dominici's sister, in front of her brother's ramshackle house. A vivacious, good-natured woman a few years older than her brother, Dani was walking across heavily potholed Royal Street in high heels, wearing a pale blue dress, and carrying a huge armful of long-stemmed red roses, maybe five dozen altogether.

An events manager, Dani was organizing a convention dinner that night and was in a rush to get to the venue to oversee the arrangement of the tables. She wanted to make sure everything was "perfect, down to the last possible detail" because with visitors fitfully beginning to return to New Orleans in the wake of the storm, it was important that the conventioneers have a really good time and go home bearing the happy message that the Big Easy, the Birthplace of Jazz, home of Bourbon Street and Mardi Gras was "back up running and open for business."

Dani tossed the roses into her van and turned back to her brother, who was standing in the doorway of his house wearing nothing but a pair of droopy gym shorts.

"Is it possible for you not to screw me up one damn time?" Dani screamed at Dave, and drove away.

To characterize Dani's relationship with her younger brother as "difficult" would be something of an understatement, says Dani's husband, Alvin Babineaux. "I'd call it more like tortured. Dave's the torturer and Dani is the torturee." Alvin is an outgoing, friendly guy in his fifties who was born in the border town of McAllen, Texas. A professional musician, Alvin has been employed at Pat O'Brien's, the always mobbed tourist joint in the French Quarter, for the past forty years.

"I play the tray," Alvin says. He stands on a small stage between two piano players (Alvin's mother was a Pat O'Brien's piano player) and provides the one-man rhythm section to the Billy Joel/Elton John songs by beating on the bottom side of a metal bar tray with his fingertips, on which he wears a variety of thimbles, each producing a different sound. Often attired in wild, sequined costumes worn to celebrate ultra-drinking days like Saint Paddy's or Mardi Gras, gyrating his body like a genial belly dancer and mugging rubbery features until the cows come home, Alvin is what is usually called "an institution" in the French Quarter. Indeed, since the death of Eddie Gabriel, the original New Orleans tray player, Alvin is probably the only living practitioner of the form. A few years ago Dani helped him patent his tray and thimble setup. "It ain't Buddy Rich but it pays the rent," Alvin says of his gig.

Alvin and Dani have been totally devoted lovebirds for several years now, but Dave remains a sore point in their relationship. "I like Dave, but he's done nothing except give us a pain in the butt," says Alvin of his brother-in-law. "One time I went over to that mess of a house of his and he's got, like, thirty-five bicycles in the kitchen. Now, why is someone going to have thirty-five bicycles in their kitchen? Next time I go over there all the bicycles are gone down to the last one. I don't have to ask where the money goes. All I know is every time there's a water bill coming due, who pays? Me and Dani. Every time a light bill comes due, who pays? Me and Dani."

Dani says, "I love my brother. I want to make that clear: I love my brother. But it isn't easy. It has never been easy."

Dani told a story about the day she and Alvin were married. "This is the biggest day of my life. The day I always dreamed about. Before the ceremony David says, 'Hey, Dani, your car is dirty. You can't go on over there like that. It's your wedding day. You have to come in like a princess. Let me go get it washed for you. Make it nice. It'll only take a minute.'

"Made me feel good, you know. Because I thought David realized what all this meant to me and he was trying to be a good brother, for once. I should have known.

"So now it is time to go. They're calling from the church, and David still hasn't come back. I was in a panic. I wound up having to almost hitch a ride to my own wedding. It was very embarrassing. Then, just as the service is about to begin, David comes roaring up in the car at, like, a hundred miles an hour. The car wasn't washed. It was dirtier than it was before. I didn't even want to know where he claimed to have been."

Dani says that even though she would never do it, there have been times she thought about never talking to her brother again. "But that would break my mother's heart."

This is true, says Patsy Dominici, a marvelously brassy woman in the New Orleans style who has "been through the trials" of being Dave Dominici's mother for more than fifty years. Sitting in her "temporary house" near the Kenner border while she waits for her Road Home settlement to rebuild her St. Bernard Parish home that was "washed away whole," she says, "I know what the other kids think, that I pay more attention to David than I do to the rest of them. I love all my children, but David, he *needs* more. He was the most difficult of my deliveries. I had to go back to the hospital three times before he came out, they had to induce labor, then he got stuck in the birth canal. That boy just didn't want to be born.

"David took it hardest when my husband, Mr. Dominici, died. He was sixteen, and no one could get him to leave the coffin. People say I'm blind when it comes to the boy, because I've given him so much money, tried to get him out of so many jams. But when it comes down to it, maybe that's just the way mothers are: blind. God made them that way. David is my cross to bear. He's like I was: a free spirit."

Dani says that the cemetery thefts were "the worst. Dave was on the front page of the paper every day, and people were looking at me like, 'Isn't that your brother?'" She has attempted to take Dave's questionable life choices in stride. She did, however, sound upset when she called me on the phone shortly before the second anniversary of Hurricane Katrina.

"They've got David locked up over there at the OPP," Dani said, using the local shorthand for the Orleans Parish Prison, New Orleans's infamously overcrowded and violence-ridden city jail. In New Orleans just about every arrestee, from murderers to parking ticket delinquents, sooner or later winds up in the OPP. Years ago Johnny Cash made a record about the place, "Orleans Parish Prison," easily his worst prison song, which kind of fits.

Dominici had been in and out of various lockups since his teens. The difference this time was, Dani explained, "they got him on the tenth floor, in the psych ward. They're going to give him a Lunacy Hearing."

It was another of those New Orleans things, not simply the way Dani pronounced the word *loo-na-cee* in her sweet Chalmette accent, but also the fact that this was the official name for a state-sanctioned practice, the way a term like *psychological review* might be employed in other places.

"David doesn't need a Lunacy Hearing," Dani went on. "He might be a lot of things. He might not take his medicine like he is supposed to. But he's not crazy. He doesn't belong with those maniacs they have up there. My mother is sick out of her mind worrying about this—"

Then, without warning, Dani interrupted herself. "Do you know something about a lamp?"

"Lamp? You mean the lampshade?"

"Yeah, lamp*shade*. David keeps talking about some crazy lamp-shade. He said you knew about it, that's why I'm calling you. Look, I don't know what David told them over at the courthouse, but would you mind writing a letter to the judge telling him you're a reporter from New York and you know about this lampshade, because they think David just dreamed the whole thing up. That's why they're giving him the Lunacy Hearing, because of that lampshade."

Over the next few weeks the story would become clearer. Actually I knew a good portion of it already. Apparently, around the time that he scavenged the lampshade, Dominici had also "found" many other objects to his liking. "Believe me," Dominici told me one evening, "if you have a discerning eye, you can find some very fashionable things." Sometimes, Dominici said, if he wasn't crazy about what he was wearing at the moment and he ran across some garments that were generally clean and his size, he'd change clothes right then and there. "I'd leave my stuff there, in trade.

"One night I found this nice pair of Wrangler jeans, folded and broken in, and I'm driving back to Piety Street in my little old Amigo pickup. It didn't have any headlights or windshield. But it's New Orleans after the storm, so who the fuck cares about a couple of headlights? The National Guard didn't give a shit. But the N-O-*fucking*-P-D, they're all concerned. Running without headlights is just the kind of crime they figure they can handle. So they stop me because of the lights. They want to see my license but of course I don't have my license. I gave them some other shit with my name on it for ID. I see them looking at it with flashlights. Then I hear them laughing. They're saying, 'Look who we got here, Mr. David Domi-nici. Step out of the car, Mr. David Dominici!'

"Those guys were always pulling me over. The same cop stopped me seventeen times. Since the cemetery bandit thing I'm like Brad

Pitt to them. So they're giving me the star treatment, in between a little knee in the stomach. One of them pats me down, then he reaches into the pocket. 'Look what Mr. Dominici has, fellas,' he yells.

"The cop has this little white pellet in his hands, the size of half a raisin. They're saying it is crack cocaine. I told them it wasn't mine, that I don't use crack. They're saying, 'Oh, yeah, then how did it wind up in your pocket?' Well, I couldn't tell them that I just boosted the pants, could I? Is that some kind of fucked-up luck or what?"

Telling the story got Dominici riled up about it again. "I paid my debt to society. All I want to do is live my life as a normal citizen, get my credit straight, fix up my house. And they're harassing me, popping me for this stupid shit. Look at the way they filled out the arrest report."

Dominici handed me the report, pointing to a series of little boxes in the middle of the page where the arresting officer is asked to indicate various characteristics describing the suspect. In the category labeled "Race," the box indicating "black" was checked. Under "Teeth," someone had ticked the "gold" box.

"They think I'm a black guy with gold teeth!" Dominici thundered. "What kind of crap is that? It's bullshit!"

I had to agree. At best, this was some very sloppy paperwork on the part of the NOPD. "Dave," I said, "you're a white guy with hardly any teeth. They can't get away with that. You're going to beat this case."

"You think so?" Dominici answered. "That's great."

The New Orleans courts being as they are, it took several months before Dominici's case appeared on the calendar. During this period a number of things had happened. Dominici and Gaynielle Dupree broke up and got back together at least two times. Plus he received a check from the State of Louisiana Road Home program, giving him a tidy settlement for the damage Katrina had done to his house.

"I didn't want that Check For Zero," Dominici said of the payment, referring to the dread "Check For Zero" that many homeowners had received from the state. The Check For Zero came in a windowed envelope, with the "Pay to the order of" part visible, leading many desperate residents to think that finally their relief money had arrived and they might begin to rebuild their lives. Yet upon opening the envelope, the embattled homeowner would find a State of Louisiana check for $000,000.

"I thought it was one of those," Dominici recounted. "But then I saw that little number one in there and I was proud to be an American." One of the best things about it, Dave said, was that the check came on his birthday. "How great was that? Gaynielle got me a card that played the theme song from *Law & Order*."

Perhaps it was this long break since the original arrest that made Dominici forget that his court date was coming up soon. It was this oversight that, he told me, caused him to get high with some friends even though there was a near certainty that his appearance would include a drug test. Caught off guard, Dominici became enraged by the whole process and, in the company of a number of court officers, declared that there was nothing Orleans Parish, or any other law enforcement agency, could do to him.

"You can't do anything to me," the wide-eyed Dominici reportedly declared. "You can't do anything to me because I'm the one who found the Nazi lampshade. I'm the one who found the Nazi lampshade and the *New York Times* is coming down here to make a movie of my life. So screw you." Apparently Dominici made this assertion a number of times.

It was then, Dani Dominici Babineaux said, that the authorities began thinking of giving her brother a Lunacy Hearing.

A few weeks later I visited Dave Dominici at the OPP and asked him if he really made those statements concerning the lampshade in the presence of Orleans Parish officials. Sitting on the other side of a two-inch-thick piece of Plexiglas and talking into an old-style black telephone receiver, Dominici gave a sheepish look and said, "Perhaps."

Dominici takes pride as someone who "jails well." In Angola, he recalls, "they had me pulling out these huge eight-foot-around tree stumps with a tiny little shovel. You had a partner with you, digging all day long. When you finally get the stump out, you have to fill in the giant twelve-foot-deep holes. Ten hours a day, pulling stumps. That's Angola. You could tell the place used to be a slave plantation, you can just smell it."

The OPP was another kind of clink. Before the storm, there had been as many as sixty-five hundred prisoners (90 percent of them African-American) locked up in the place, which made it the ninth-largest jail in the country. It was a massive operation, a multistructure complex with an annual budget of $75 million, employing twelve hundred people including the kitchen workers who served eighteen thousand meals a day. With the city paying the sheriff's office $22.39 per day per prisoner, jailing people in New Orleans was a lucrative business.

Katrina put a serious crimp in the OPP operation. With several of the complexes severely damaged, many prisoners were transferred to other facilities around the state. By the time Dave Dominici got to the OPP psych ward, the place felt all but deserted, with most of the inmates consolidated within the decrepit House of Detention (the sign outside says, simply, House of D) with its skeleton crew of guards and a lone metal detector.

Being cooped up on the tenth floor was giving Dave Dominici the creeps. The problem was more than just the usual mumblers, starers, and guys who'd rip out your lungs if they got half a chance. Every prison had those people. Even the suicide rate, one of the highest in the country, didn't faze Dominici. Nor did the fact that many OPP prisoners had been in the facility for months without seeing a lawyer or even knowing the precise charges against them.

What was driving Dominici around the bend was the ghosts. It sounded pathetic, Dominici said, the illustrious cemetery bandit being freaked out by ghosts. But these weren't the tourist poltergeists that Quarter barkers hustled on "haunted New Orleans" tours. They weren't the dead-and-buried ones, fifty years stone-cold in a Lake

Lawn mausoleum. These ghosts were fresh and desperate, searching and hungry, screeching in pain.

Dominici knew "bits and pieces" of how bad it had been in the OPP during Katrina, but it wasn't until he got locked up that he heard "the whole bad thing." It was a nightmare to be sure: with everyone in the city running for their lives, many of the prisoners were left in their cells, without food or drinking water. First thing, the power went out, followed by the emergency generators, so you had thousands of men, the usual hair-raising array of OPP offenders, many of them still handcuffed, sealed into the fetid pitch dark by jailers who'd deserted their posts. And all the while the floodwaters were rising, to as much as eight and nine feet on the lower floors. There were awful, awful stories, tales of prisoners who tried to swim through the waters to safety, only to get ripped to shreds by the submerged razor coil wire.

The city fathers, from Ray Nagin on down, were denying the whole thing. Sheriff Marlin Gusman, Nagin's close associate, who had never run a prison before taking over the OPP, told the press that stories about what had happened at the OPP were the fantasies of "crackheads, cowards, criminals . . . and disgruntled former employees." But no one believed that, certainly not Dave Dominici. He was from New Orleans, he was a convicted felon, and as such he was of the opinion that nothing any local official ever said in a time of stress could possibly be true, especially when it came to what happened in the jails. People had died at the OPP, Dominici had heard. They had died horribly, either drowned or stomped, or by heart attack, which didn't make it any less a murder. Since he'd been checked into the psych ward, that's all he'd heard about, the madness of those days, the way the fleeing deputies had sprayed the wards with machine gun fire to push the prisoners back into their cells.

"They say guys are buried in the walls," Dominici said, recounting stories about panicked inmates who had supposedly tried to break through the walls to escape the stench-filled water and had gotten trapped. Dominici didn't believe these wilder tales, but as he said, "they prey on your mind."

Dominici pushed his head against the Plexiglas, let it rest there for half a minute or so before speaking again.

There were a lot of things he'd done in his life that could have been better, he finally said, confessionally. He could have been a better brother to Dani, to his other sister, Dawn, and to Ralph Jr. He could have been a better son to his mom; Patsy was "a saint." He despaired over the times he'd made her bail him out, the time he wrecked his car on the railroad tracks, all the embarrassment he put her through. He could have been a better son to his father, too, or at least to his memory, even if his Pops had been a hard sort, the kind who'd give you a slap if you talked when Lawrence Welk was on the television.

It was the same with Gaynielle. She was his "soul mate," they were made for each other, but there were times when he treated her poorly, when they didn't allow themselves to express the love they felt for each other. Then there were his children. One of his daughters lived with Patsy. She was doing fine, too, had a good job, was going to college, going to make something of herself, yet when you mentioned her father, she narrowed her eyes and said, with equal parts disdain and regret, "Oh, my father. Let's not talk about my father."

That was his fault, Dominici said. No one else's. He had been given great gifts throughout his life and had squandered every one.

And for what? Being a dope fiend. How could being a dope fiend be worth losing the love and trust of so many good people? So many times in who knew how many court-ordered treatment program meetings, Dominici had said he'd tried to "open his heart to Jesus Christ." But even if he'd been an altar boy, the Jesus thing had never worked for him and it never would, at least not with the kind of Christ the priests tried to shove down your throat.

"It's like I told you, from the beginning Albert Einstein made more sense to me than Holy Communion. Good luck with that in St. Bernard Parish! The fact is I'm not like the rest of these people. I got ideas. I told you about the Thermo-Squat, right?" Yes, Dominici had told me about the Thermo-Squat, his idea for a remote-controlled heating system for toilet seats. He'd told me more than once, but there was a special urgency to the sales pitch this time, as if a prewarmed toilet seat was the singular innovation upon which the continued spin of the planet depended.

"I'm not a bad person. I never did anything that hurt anybody. Not really. That's why they shouldn't have done to me what they did."

We were close to the nub of it all now, the specter of the future that had increasingly come to haunt Dominici since being locked up with the ghosts of the OPP. It was part of his sentence in the cemetery bandit case, he claimed. He was barred from every cemetery in Orleans, Jefferson, or St. Bernard Parish.

"Dead or alive! I can't set foot in a cemetery dead or alive. I can't be buried in my home ground."

This was the first I'd heard of it. If true, the sentence was breathtaking, both unmistakably appropriate and shockingly cruel, a punishment beyond day-to-day jurisprudence, almost tribal in nature.

It was the kind of retribution one might expect to find in a far-off place like the venerable Varanasi, the Indian city most loved by the world-destroying Shiva. Devout Hindus came to die in Varanasi, to have their bodies burned on massive woodpiles, the ashes flung into Mother Ganges. Piles of the dead, wrapped in gauze, were everywhere. Varanasi was municipality as death cult, but wasn't that also true of New Orleans, another decaying former colonial metropolis set on the banks of a primal waterway. Dave Dominici had broken one of New Orleans's inviolate taboos, had carelessly trampled, as dope fiends tend to do, upon sacred rules. So what other choice did the court have but to deny him the final splendor of earthly presence down here, the moment when the fellas yell, "Cut him loose!" and the band begins to play?

"That supposed to be fair?" Dominici wailed. "They don't do that to murderers. They don't do that to rapers. They'd only do it to someone like me. Someone from the other side of the tracks. A despised person like me."

Dominici again rested his brow on the Plexiglas, as if the full weight of fate was upon him. Then, as if ejected from a crashing fighter plane, he jumped from his chair, straight up into the rank jail air.

"They don't have the right! Throw me in here all you want, but no court has say over eternity. I'm from New Orleans. New Orleans is my home. I should be buried in New Orleans!"

A moment passed before Dominici said, "You know what's going to happen to me? I'm going to be like that lampshade! Just like that fuck-ing lampshade! All these years, since Hitler, and there's no rest. From hand to hand. Wandering . . . *The wandering Jew!* No place to lay its head. That's going to be me."

TEN

It was a typical late summer afternoon at the intersection of Tulane and Broad, east of the OPP. Rain was beginning to fall, but vertically, always a relief during hurricane season. Since Katrina, the tempests had stayed away. Ernesto petered out over the Atlantic, Dean hit Mexico, but nothing big, nothing "named," made it into the upper Gulf. The bit of moisture beating down today would quickly drain, leaving only soggy shoes and perhaps a couple more customers for the fungicide guys who put up the 888-MOLD signs on telephone poles in Treme and St. Roch, not that any of these treatments could be considered surefire. The problem was deeper than that.

In the middle of the last century, Tulane Avenue had been a decent sort of commercial thoroughfare, no Canal Street but a place to buy a couch and eat a reasonable bowl of gumbo at a restaurant with or without a tablecloth. The Katrina tide had been ten feet high here, and now, with the *Times-Picayune* running stories saying more than one-third of the residential structures in the city were uninhabited or "fatally blighted," the avenue was half wasteland, with few cars and even fewer pedestrians. Many of the buildings were still boarded up, marked with fading "TFW" (Took Flood Water) National Guard marks. A spray-painted "U Steal, We Get Real" sign, barely visible, covered a piece of plywood nailed to the front of a former store that, in the idiosyncratic black southern tradition, had once doubled as an outlet for both tuxedo rentals and po' boy sandwiches. The plywood was about all that was upright about the place; the remainder of the building had caved in behind it.

The only commercial establishments that could be said to be flourishing were bail bondsmen. There was the Free Me BailBond, the Abra-Ca-Da-Bra BailBond, the 1, 2, 3 Rollout Bailbond, and half a dozen more. This owed, of course, to the real business of Tulane and Broad, the meting out of justice at the massive Criminal Courts building that has dominated the intersection since it was built by Jim Crow labor in 1929.

Jurisprudence has often been a catch-as-catch-can thing at Tulane and Broad, no more so than since the end of the thirty-year reign of District Attorney Harry Connick Sr., father of the singer. Connick's successor, Eddie Jordan, the first African American to be elected Orleans Parish DA, was on the verge of resignation. Known as "the Hat" thanks to his affectation of wearing an expensive derby, Jordan had just lost a $3.7 million civil action filed by several former DA office employees who claimed he'd systematically fired them for no other reason than that they were white. Of the fifty-six white employees fired, all but one was replaced with a worker of color, the suit charged. Claiming he was only trying to do "what was best for the city," the Hat denied that his actions were motivated by race.

Whatever the merits of the suit, there could be no arguing the dismal performance of the DA's office. In 2003 and 2004, with New Orleans in contention as the most crime-ridden city in the country, fewer than 12 percent of all homicide and attempted homicide cases resulted in conviction. Since Katrina, with the courts and police department in disarray, that number had decreased even further. In 2006 Jordan's office, operating under Louisiana's much-lambasted "701" law, which required the release of prisoners not indicted within sixty days of their arrest, managed to bring only 7 percent of *all* felony cases to trial.

These numbers were a disaster, nothing that should ever happen in a major city. But then again, could anyone really claim that New Orleans was a major city? Barely three hundred thousand residents lived in the town, half the 1950 population. It wasn't even the biggest city in Louisiana anymore; Baton Rouge, that former governmental backwater of frat houses and Taco Bells, had more people. As of 2007, New Orleans was listed as the fifty-ninth-highest population center in the country, right behind Aurora, Colorado, wherever that was. The mystery was how so many of the remaining inhabitants still found such large numbers of other people to shoot and kill.

The chronicling of the nearly daily deaths became an obsessional pastime for the city's bloggers. In the weeks before I visited Dave Dominici at the OPP, one Internet site, the New Orleans Murder Blog, provided the following content: On August 12, "A man and a woman were shot to death Saturday morning in the Village de l'Est neighborhood of eastern New Orleans, police reported." On August 14, "Two people were shot fatally and a third wounded at North Villere and St. Philip streets, near Armstrong Park in the Treme neighborhood, New Orleans, police said." On August 15, "A man shot multiple times in the 7700 block of Chef Menteur Highway, Garry Flot, an information officer for New Orleans police, said." On August 16, "A New Orleans woman was critically injured Wednesday night when a man entered a Mid-City bar and slashed her throat, police said."

A few days later the Murder Blog carried the following account of an apparent murder in the Seventh Ward: "The deceased was a 25-year-old light-complexioned African-American with a gold tooth had the following tattoos 'Ms. Coco,' on the left thigh; a drawing of a naked woman on the left inner forearm; 'Big Mike,' on the outer left upper arm; 'Fatt' or 'Fatty,' on the left arm; 'Darryl,' on the left wrist; 'Belinda,' on the left hand; a butterfly on the back of the left shoulder; 'B,' in the middle of the back; and 'Queen,' on one buttock, and

'B@#$HV,' or 'B@#$HY,' on the other buttock. He wore a long blond wig, makeup, a short blue skirt, three tanktops and gold shoes."

Mayor Ray Nagin's commentary on the steady drumbeat of doom proved less than helpful. In response to the shooting death of two brothers who themselves had been implicated in fourteen murders, the mayor said the killings were "not good for us, but it also keeps the New Orleans brand out there."

"I wouldn't say that the whole city is trying to kill itself, but sometimes it sure does seem that way," the Orleans Parish coroner Frank Minyard told me. Dressed in his customary white lab coat, a patrician shock of silver hair rakishly combed atop a highball-red face, Minyard is about as close to a Walker Percy character as you can find in the Crescent City these days.

Once a highly paid uptown gynecologist, Minyard, seeking "something with more meaning to it," first became coroner in 1974. He has been reelected eight times, always using the same campaign poster, a shot of a fortyish version of himself dressed in a white linen suit blowing his beloved cornet on a Mississippi River levee. It is this image, along with unimpeachable homeboy credentials like residence papers from Charity Hospital and a penchant for volunteering remarks like "As a medical man I thought the efficacy of Viagra might wear out when nearing eighty, but I'm happy to report this is not the case" that have made Minyard a favorite of New Orleans local color writers.

One of Minyard's NPR interviews, given shortly after Katrina, stands out. Speaking from St. Gabriel, Louisiana, where the feds had belatedly set up a massive high-tech morgue, Minyard was asked if he could foresee an end to all the suffering.

"I don't think so," Minyard said in his loping, smooth-syllabled drawl. "You see, these are my people, every one of them. I get emotional about it. I get emotional about the people, I get emotional about the city, I get emotional about the music. You know, I play trumpet. I have a band. A couple of weeks ago—I hadn't practiced or played because of the hurricane—I took out my trumpet in the quiet place of my trailer, and I played 'Do You Know What It Means to Miss New Orleans?'. And I started crying. The devastation not only of the place but of the people and our lives—none of us will ever be the same."

It was an overworked trope by then, singing and playing "Do You Know What It Means to Miss New Orleans?", which was written by Eddie DeLange and Louis Alter in 1946 for a Hollywood musical called *New Orleans* that featured Billie Holiday playing a domestic. Louis Armstrong's version was classic, true, but hearing the tune every time an out-of-town newsman appeared in a windswept yellow slicker could drive you crazy. Minyard's a cappella version, however, just the first two lines, "Do you know what it means to miss New Orleans / I miss it each night and day," sung by the doctor of the dead from inside a government-issue trailer parked in a postmodern morgue, returned to the sublime.

"Great song," Minyard said to finish the interview.

I'd come over to talk to Minyard about the lampshade, which, after all, had been found within his jurisdiction. Sitting at his makeshift desk in the lobby of the funeral home on Martin Luther King Boulevard—his old office at Tulane and Broad had been flooded in the storm, trapping him for three days—Minyard looked through the pictures of the lampshade I had stored on my computer.

"You say it was the guy from the cemetery case that had it?" Minyard inquired. A Louis Prima fan, Minyard remembered the mausoleum looting well. Dave Dominici's involvement with something like the lampshade was "a heck of a coincidence," the coroner said.

I asked him how he might have handled the lampshade case. "You mean, if I was responsible for finding out what it was?" he replied, thinking a moment. "That would be tough because, from our point of view, you'd have to prove that a crime had been committed. If it is really sixty years old, from the war, then what can you do here in New Orleans? I don't think it would be illegal just to have it."

Minyard called in Alvaro Hunt, his chief forensic pathologist. Hunt, a sweet-faced man who has worked with Minyard on and off for thirty-five years, stared at the lampshade photos awhile. "It looks like it's been tanned. Definitely tanned," Hunt said. He thought he saw a particular skin pattern but it was impossible to say anything definitive from looking at a photo.

"He's got some DNA on the thing," Minyard said, handing Hunt the printout of the Bode lab findings. Hunt looked the report over before saying, "They could only get the mitochondrial, huh? That makes sense; the sample had to be very degraded. This sort of work is way beyond us right now."

This was because more than two years after the storm, Orleans Parish still didn't have an operational crime lab. Much of the work was being sent to LSU in Baton Rouge. Minyard took another look at the lampshade picture. Like Shiya Ribowsky, who'd seen so many shattered parts of former humanity after 9/11, the coroner of New Orleans, the Murder Capital, shook his head.

"Incredible what people will do," he said. "What can you say? It is one of those unthinkable sort of things."

Minyard leaned back in his chair. "I've thought about it, what it might have been like to have done this work at a concentration camp, at a place like Auschwitz, when you're looking at so many bodies. Taken one by one I don't think determining the cause of death would be that difficult. You'd have asphyxiation, choking, circulatory collapse, pulmonary edema, gunshot wounds, blows to the head. You could put the reports together in a nice, neat pile. But 'the why'— the why of it—that would be another thing altogether. Forensics are never going to answer that, why people would do something like that to other people."

Minyard took another look at the photo of the lampshade. "That's a sad thing you have there," he said.

Asked if he saw any reason why, out of all places, a lampshade identified with Nazi concentration camps would turn up in New Orleans in the aftermath of Katrina, Minyard said that if you didn't count the obvious answers, "like it was brought back by some vet," this was a troubling mystery. Katrina had turned everything upside down, "shaken things loose." There had been many times since the storm, Minyard said, when he had felt truly lost, that the world he grew up in was "off its compass."

"There's a warehouse downtown where we have as many as one hundred bodies of people killed in the storm. We're just storing them there. Some of the corpses are unidentified, but we know who a lot of them are. But when we notified someone and said, 'We've got your uncle Fred here,' they said, 'Why don't you just keep him?' " The unclaimed bodies kept turning up. "We've found thirty-five bodies since we stopped looking for bodies, so what can I assume?"

It bothered Minyard, "this kind of disregard," the namelessness of it all. "You know, the records from our potter's field were washed away in the storm. It is almost like dying twice and still nobody knows you. The murders are just more of it. We had two shootings here yesterday. We might have two today. Two more tomorrow. The police can't stop it. They can put a dent in it, but they can't stop it. Maybe no one can stop it, not the politicians, not the pastors. I'd like to think God can, but he hasn't seen fit to do that. Not yet."

If a human skin lampshade was going to turn up somewhere, perhaps New Orleans after the storm was as likely a place as any, Minyard said. "We're no different than anyplace else when you come down to it. We're the product of history and human nature. Prisoners of it, you might say. And, as you know, we have a tragic history here in New Orleans."

By the time I got to Lee Circle I was dripping wet. Robert E. Lee was there, or rather a bronze twelve-foot-tall likeness of the Confederate general, built in 1884. Perched atop a sixty-foot stone column, Lee stood ramrod straight in the downpour, arms crossed, left foot forward, water pouring off the brim of his hat.

It has never been easy to get used to these monuments found throughout the American South celebrating those who fought and died to preserve the "peculiar institution" of slavery. In New Orleans, onetime home to the nation's largest slave market, an ornate tribute to Confederate president Jefferson Davis sits at the intersection of Canal Street and the Jefferson Davis Parkway. Over by City Park, on a horse, is General P. G. T. Beauregard (from St. Bernard Parish), who ordered the first shots on Fort Sumter that started the war.

Statue of Robert E. Lee, Lee Circle, New Orleans

But Lee Circle is the focal point. The St. Charles Avenue cable car circumnavigates the circle at the beginning and end of its run past the genteel mansions of the uptown rich and powerful. Almost all the old-line Mardi Gras parades, from Comus on, have passed by here, where bleachers are set up to accommodate the cheering crowds. The fact that New Orleans fell without much resistance to a Union naval assault in April 1863 and that the Virginian Lee never set foot in the city during his time as commander of the Confederate forces does little to tarnish the general's status as the first son of what is often called the Cult of the Lost Cause.

Standing there looking at the statue, I wondered what present-day New Orleans would look like to the man who said that slavery was "a greater evil to the white than to the colored race. While my feelings are strongly enlisted in behalf of the latter, my sympathies are more deeply engaged for the former. The blacks are immeasurably better off here than in Africa, morally, physically, and socially. The painful discipline they are undergoing is necessary for their further instruction as a race, and will prepare them, I hope, for better things. How long their servitude may be necessary is known and ordered by a merciful Providence."

In keeping with the southern bromide that a man of honor should never turn his back on a Yankee, Lee faces northeast, which, during Katrina would have afforded him an excellent vista of the flooded Central Business District. A glance to the left and he could have seen the Superdome. A turn to the right would have given him a view of the nearby Crescent City Connection, the bridge across the Mississippi River to the Westbank Jefferson Parish communities of Gretna and Terrytown. Following World War II, the Westbank became an early "white flight" refuge for those who could no longer tolerate living in New Orleans with its rapidly increasing black population. Half a century later, in one of the most distressing of Katrina incidents, hundreds of stranded, desperate New Orleans residents attempted to cross the bridge in the days after the hurricane only to be turned back by cops under the command of the general's namesake (albeit the Chinese version), Jefferson Parish sheriff Harry Lee. To show they meant business, the police fired a volley over the heads of the crowd, vowing to shoot whoever set foot on their side of the river.

One hundred and forty years after his surrender at Appomattox, what would the general in chief of the Confederacy think of that? This was a question I began asking around town. The responses were remarkably consistent. Several people quoted a bumper sticker seen on pickup trucks lined up at the frozen-daiquiri-to-go spots, at least the ones catering to whites: when it came to black people and their continued presence in the city, We Should Have Picked Our Own Cotton.

Elaborating on this theme was Dr. Raynard Sanders, a former public school principal who now spends his time steadfastly trying to save what's left of the system in the city. "Robert E. Lee, oh, Robert E. Lee. Robert E. Lee would have watched what happened after Katrina and thought, well, things never change, do they? He would have seen another example of how the North will always desert the South when it is in need, and in that he'd be right, of course. As for what was happening to people trying to cross the bridge, Lee wouldn't have cared about that, and not because he was so hard-hearted or hated black people. However, if those people were running away from a plantation, that would have been a different story altogether because then they would have had a business function. They'd be property, a means of production, worth something. What were those people on the bridge worth? Who did they belong to, what was their economic value in the society? No, they'd be invisible to Robert E. Lee."

These conjectures about Lee's opinions were interesting, but I found myself wanting more from the commander who ordered Pickett's charge at Gettysburg, a military blunder that did much to seal the South's fate. I wanted to know if Lee, the legendary gentleman, felt any regret or pain over the decisions he'd made, the side he'd chosen. I wanted to know if standing there at the center of his circle for 120 years, he had sometimes felt like shrieking, *"Enough!"* so loud that even the soused loungers inside the Circle Bar could hear. Or would he shout, like Marlon Brando's Kurtz raging, "Kill them! Kill them all."

It would be fascinating to hear the general's views, because when it came to the issue of race, he'd seen the Beast in action, right there at Lee Circle.

•   •   •

New Orleans has had its share of race riots. In 1866 a group of former Confederates attacked a meeting of Radical Republicans who were protesting the state legislature's refusal to allow freed blacks to vote. Thirty-eight people were killed. In 1874, at the so-called Battle of Liberty Place, thirty-five hundred armed members of the "White League" seeking to overthrow the "carpetbagger" government and the rule of "the insolent and barbarous African" faced off against a like number of mostly black local militia troops under the command of "turncoat" ex–Confederate general James Longstreet. The White Leaguers overran the poorly equipped blacks, driving the forever disgraced Longstreet into the river. Dozens more were killed.

Race relations in New Orleans and the country at large entered a new stage in 1892 when Homer Plessy, a twenty-nine-year-old light-skinned Creole man from the Treme district challenged the recently passed Louisiana "separate car" law by boarding the "whites only" section of an East Louisiana Railroad train at the Press and Royal Street station in the Bywater. Plessy challenged his arrest, leading to the 1896 "separate but equal" Supreme Court ruling that legalized the Jim Crow codes throughout the South.

Racial discrimination had also acquired a new vocabulary, as evidenced by a story in the *New Orleans Times-Democrat* of July 17, 1900, in which Dr. Gustav Keitz, a German-born Canal Street physician with a passion for eugenics, wrote that the number of Negroes could be reduced through "asexualization, a measure which should be practiced at the earliest possible period of life." Less than a month later, this relatively modest proposal was eclipsed by an editorial written by Henry J. Hearsey, a former Confederate major and editor/publisher of the *New Orleans Daily States*, the official journal of city government and leading afternoon paper in Louisiana. More than forty years before the Nazis used the phrase at the Wannsee Conference, Hearsey wrote of "The Negro Problem and Its Final Solution," declaring that if blacks should continue to "by word or deed listen to the screeds of agitators in the North," the South would have no choice but to engage in a full-scale race war. Hearsey regretted that "whites would suffer some casualties in the conflict," but there would be a major consolation: "The Negro Problem in Louisiana at least will be solved—and that by extermination."

Hearsey's editorial was responding to the just concluded "Robert Charles Riots." The incident had begun on the evening of July 23, 1900, as Robert Charles, a thirty-five-year-old black railway worker, sat on the stoop of a house in the 2800 block of Dryades Street, then in the middle of New Orleans's Jewish neighborhood. Approached by a trio of New Orleans police officers, Charles was told to run along. Son of illiterate Mississippi sharecroppers and a self-educated follower of the fledgling International Migration Society, one of the first groups to advocate that former slaves repatriate themselves to Africa, Charles declined, telling the cops he was waiting for his girlfriend, Virginia Banks, and her roommate Ernestine Goldstein. The fact that Charles was something of a dandy, decked out in clothing purchased from Hyman Levy's clothing store on Poydras Street (Levy would later describe Charles, with whom he had a friendly relationship, as "a stylish negro, above the average darkey in intelligence"), probably didn't help matters. At some point in the conversation, one of the cops knocked Charles's snazzy brimmed hat from his head. Told to leave the hat on the ground, Charles refused, and committed what the police report described as "an aggressive act." A struggle ensued, the police discharging their weapons in Charles's direction. In possession of a small handgun, Charles returned fire, wounding one of the policemen. Shot in the leg, Charles was cornered several hours later in a house on Fourth Street, a few blocks away. This time Charles shot a police captain through the heart and, shouting "I will give you all some!", sent another bullet through a second policeman's head and fled.

Thus commenced the largest manhunt in New Orleans history. The fully mobilized 315-man NOPD was quickly joined by a rapidly swelling army of vigilantes. The black journalist Ida B. Wells-Barnett described the development in a pamphlet entitled *Mob Rule in New Orleans: Robert Charles and His Fight to Death, The Story of His Life, Burning Human Beings Alive, Other Lynching Statistics.* "Wednesday New Orleans was in the hands of the mob . . . ," Wells-Barnett writes. "Unable to vent its vindictiveness and bloodthirsty vengeance upon Charles, the mob turned its attention to other colored men who happened to get in the path of its fury . . . The reign of absolute lawlessness began about 8 o'clock Wednesday night. The mob gathered at the Lee statue . . ."

Wells quotes at length from the account that was published in the *New Orleans Times-Democrat* the next morning. The Lee Circle gathering of about seven hundred was addressed by a man introducing himself as the mayor of nearby Kenner, who said, "'I have killed a Negro before and in revenge of the wrong wrought upon you and yours, I am willing to kill again. The only way that you can teach these Niggers a lesson and put them in their place is to go out and lynch a few of them . . . String up a few of them, and the others will trouble you no more.'"

Two days later, his hideout at 1208 South Saratoga Street revealed by a paid police informer, Charles was besieged by a crowd wildly estimated at anywhere between one and twenty thousand. Fighting alone, using homemade bullets made from a lead pipe melted down over a charcoal stove, Charles held off the mob, the NOPD, and the Gatling gun–wielding state militia for several hours, shooting twenty-one of his attackers. He was routed only when the house was set on fire, whereupon he was shot, burned, and beaten beyond recognition, then dumped into a potter's field grave.

Thirty-eight years later, Jelly Roll Morton, one of the earliest New Orleans jazz geniuses, the brilliant Storyville piano player and noted braggart (he claimed to have invented jazz single-handedly in 1902, when he would have been twelve years old), recorded a number of interviews with Alan Lomax for the Library of Congress. One of these sessions included a segment entitled *The Story of the 1900 New*

Orleans Riot and the Song of Robert Charles. As Charles was well on his way to being completely forgotten by this time, no one was checking Morton's veracity, which was spotty.

Playing chords at the piano as he speaks, a weary-sounding Jelly Roll (his career in tatters, he would be dead within three years), begins the Charles story with a burst of bluster. Claiming to have "been there when it all happened and been there when it all stopped," Morton says that "Robert Charles must've been a marksman . . . because every time he would raise his rifle, when a policeman was in sight, there'd be a policeman dead. It was never learned how many policemens [*sic*] were killed. Some said thirty-two, some said eighteen, and so forth and so on." (The actual number was seven.) After reporting that "anyplace a white man seen a colored man, there was a fight, or a colored man seen a white man, there was a fight" and laying in a little tourist hoodoo about Charles possibly still walking the streets at night, Morton seems to tire of the topic. Fending off the eager Lomax, Morton says he can't recall any of the "bad man" songs inspired by Charles's act save a lyric about how "the police wouldn't let him get his hat" and soon drifts into talking about some obscure blues singers.

This is too bad because Jelly Roll does allude, briefly, to "this one killing that arose Robert Charles to fury, a killing that haunted Robert Charles and started the great New Orleans Riot." As mentioned in the accounts of both Ida B. Wells-Barnett and William Ivy Hair, whose *Carnival of Fury* is the accepted basic source on the Charles Riots, the "killing" was very likely the 1899 lynching of Sam Hose in Georgia. Charles was apparently obsessed by the incident.

In one of the grisliest post-Reconstruction episodes, Hose, a farmworker, was accused of murdering his employer, Alfred Cranford, raping Cranford's wife, and maiming their child. Hose's protests that he'd killed Cranford with an ax in self-defense after the boss drew a gun during a dispute over wages (Hose denied the other charges) fell on deaf ears. He was tried two weeks after the killing and sentenced to death. His execution brought out a crowd of two thousand (two trains full of gawkers came from Atlanta), people craning their necks to get a better view as Hose was systematically tortured, his ears, fingers, and genitals severed from his body, the skin sliced away from his face and torso. Then, doused in kerosene, he was burned alive before being hung from a tree.

The local paper, the *Newnan Herald and Advertiser,* devoted the entire front page to the event. "The expected has happened," the account began somberly. "Sam Holt [*sic*], the black fiend . . . has been caught and made to pay the penalty for his crime . . . Overtaken by the wrath of an outraged community, burned at the stake, his very ashes scattered to the winds, there is nothing to remind us that such a monster in human form ever had existence save the bitter recollection of his infamous career while on earth."

As horrific as Hose's death was, what most affected Robert Charles, according to Hair's book, was that many viewers had approached the ravaged corpse to cut off pieces of his skin to take home as souvenirs. Later Hose's heart, knuckles, and facial skin were displayed in local store windows and offered for sale.

Seven decades after Robert Charles made his last stand at 1208 South Saratoga Street (now a bottle-strewn vacant lot in the Central City murder zone west of the I-10), another black man took on a fully deployed New Orleans police department. In an eerie reprise of the Charles incident, Mark Essex, an AWOL Navy man, entered the Downtown Howard Johnson on January 7, 1973, and began firing. Running past a frightened black hotel maid with a .44 carbine, Essex reportedly said, "Don't worry, honey, I'm only killing whites today, no black people." By the next morning, Essex, whom Stokely Carmichael praised for "carrying our struggle to the next quantitative level, the level of science," had shot twenty-two people, killing nine, including six policemen. When he was finally stopped on the hotel roof in a hail of NOPD fire, Essex's body had been hit over two hundred times. His right leg and tongue were severed from his body and found on the other side of the roof, several yards away. Like 1208 South Saratoga Street, the Howard Johnson, now a Holiday Inn with a jaunty painting of a clarinet on the side, is only a few blocks from Lee Circle.

• • •

Standing beside the general's monument, I wondered if there was ever to be an end to this. One of the things people said about Katrina was that it pulled the covers off the question of race in America. Maybe for out-of-towners it did. But few in the Crescent City needed Kanye West to tell them that George Bush didn't care about black people. That had been apparent once again only days before, on the second anniversary of the day Katrina made landfall. There was supposed to be a march from the spot in the Lower Ninth Ward where the Industrial Canal levee broke, down St. Claude Avenue, over to the Morial Convention Center, where thousands of storm victims had been stranded for days without food, water, or power. Skip Henderson and I decided to go over to the Lower Ninth to check things out. "They'll get twenty people, if they're lucky," Skip said, as we made our way over the St. Claude bridge.

Much to our surprise, the trash-bound streets on the other side of the canal were packed with cops. Helicopters hovered above. There'd never been so many cops in the Lower Ninth in the history of the city.

"What's going on?" inquired Skip.

"Bush!" replied one overweight white cop from behind the visor of his riot helmet. "Bush is in there," the cop said, pointing to the Martin Luther King Jr. Charter School for Science and Technology at the corner of North Robertson and Caffin Avenue.

The president was in there talking about everything his administration was doing to aid New Orleans's recovery. As White House spokesman Gordon Johndroe told reporters, the MLK speech was Bush's "fifteenth visit" to the region since he'd first viewed the devastation from the window of the low-flying Air Force One. Inside the charter school, just about the only building in the entire neighborhood that was back up and running, the president greeted the children in his best *Pet Goat* style, before making a speech in which he reminded restive locals that U.S. citizens had already "paid out one hundred fourteen billion dollars in tax money—*their money*—to help folks down here" and that instead of complaining, people should look at the storm as "a great opportunity to really jump-start the re-form efforts in New Orleans." He finished up by saying how happy he was to once again be "in this part of the world," as if giving a nod to Henry Stanley and other great profiteer explorers who had the temer-ity to venture to remote corners of the planet.

The unannounced speech was closed to the general public. Still, a cluster of neighborhood people, perhaps fifteen in all, had gathered in a sudden downpour at the corner of Poland Avenue to make their feelings known to a heedless man in a speeding bulletproof limousine.

Moments later, preceded by a long line of NOPD cruisers running full lights and sirens, the president's car appeared on the rise of the heavily rusted Claiborne Avenue Bridge. However, to the consterna-tion of the group, who had taken refuge from the rain under the porch of an abandoned home, they never got to see Bush. They'd picked the wrong side of the street. All that could be seen was a fleeting, anti-climactic glimpse of a smiling, waving Laura Bush. She was there for a moment, then gone, tailed by a phalanx of NOPD motorcyclists.

That's when he came into view: an enormous reddish brown man, three hundred pounds if he was an ounce, Beach ball–like shaven head mounted recklessly atop a much bigger but equally round pro-truding belly gave him the aspect of a dark snowman or a fat, stern Buddha. Attired in nothing but flip-flops and a pair of soaked-through maroon shorts clumped about his genitals, the guy, who looked to be in his mid-thirties, was standing on the opposite side of Claiborne, fleshy arms raised above his head, both middle fingers extending up-ward in a double fuck-you. If Bush had been looking out the window, waving like Laura, there was no way he could have missed him.

"Okay. Show's over," said the NOPD officers as they got in their cruisers and drove off. People began trudging down Claiborne, but the man in the maroon shorts did not move. Rain pelting off his brown skin, he held his stance, middle fingers raised. The way he stood there, his giant stomach hanging over his shorts, accusing fin-gers pointed to the roiling sky on the anniversary of the disaster, he was like an angry prophet confronting God.

Two lynchings: Masha Bruskina and an anonymous black man

• • •

I was convinced there was a link between the terror of Buchenwald, where the story of the lampshade began, and this sad, beaten-down New Orleans, where the most recent incarnation of the icon had turned up. But I couldn't quite put it together. There was something missing, some piece that could not be supplied by a professor or scientist. So it was a good thing to run into Mac Rebennack, aka Dr. John the Night Tripper, author of the unbeatable acid voodoo record *Gris-Gris* and always my favorite New Orleans musician, at least among the white guys.

Just the night before, I'd seen the Doctor playing at Lincoln Center along with Wynton Marsalis, another, albeit far more kempt, New Orleans refugee. Now, the next morning, we were booked on the same flight from LaGuardia to Armstrong Airport. The plane was delayed, and since at the previous night's gig the Doctor had played "Witchy Red," a composition about a "conjure woman" who carried "a mojo satchel made of human skin," this seemed as good a time as any to provide Rebennack with a short version of the lampshade saga.

"That's a weird story," said the Doctor, who was attired in a blue silk jacket with an NOPD patch and gold-buckled blue suede shoes. "But there are a lot of weird stories in New Orleans, especially since the storm. Things are off the hook, out of whack. You see all kinds of birds hanging with birds that they never hung with before. They got these giant watermelons growing out in St. Bernard Parish. Botanists from LSU are studying them with stethoscopes. The whole balance of nature is backwards. Every time I fly into the city, I look out the window to see what's there and what's not."

The Doctor was enraged over what had happened during the storm and since. He'd cut a number of songs protesting the wetlands destruction and appeared at benefit concerts to aid the displaced. "All my life I heard people saying they was just trying to live through the Long dynasty," he said. "Now I'm just hoping my coonass gets through the Bush dynasty."

I asked the Doctor if, in his long interface with the hyped-up New Orleans voodoo tradition and its attendant sub-rosa spiritual arts, he'd ever heard of anyone who dabbled with human skin, someone who might have knowledge of something like the lampshade.

"Not off the top of my head," he replied. "But I've been out of town." As far as he knew, outside of Sallie Ann Glassman, the Bywater Jewish voodoo priestess, all the decent practitioners had left town after the storm. But he said he'd think about it. In case anything came to him, I gave him my number, thinking that would be the end of it.

A few weeks later the phone rang sometime after midnight. "This is Mac," the Doctor said. "Can't get that lampshade off my mind. It's haunting me. I got some Jewish on various sides of family, you know. There's everything else, but there's Jewish, too. I got this uncle who parachuted behind Nazi lines during D-day, and another uncle who was fighting in the Spanish Civil War against the fascist fuckers. When World War Two started up, he tried to enlist on the German side. My father couldn't hack that. They had to put that uncle of mine away, on account of his imbalance. War is like that, I suppose. It puts you over the line.

"But whatever it is, I don't think I can leave this lampshade shit alone. I remembered a guy who messed with that sort of human skin thing. He hung around the Saturn Bar on St. Claude. Can't recall his name right now, but it'll come to me. When it does, I'll call you back."

Over the next few months I received a scattered series of late-night calls from Rebennack. Sometimes he'd be barely intelligible. Other nights he'd rage eloquently about conditions down in New Orleans.

"I have been radicalized," the Doctor declared. "You know in New Orleans there's all kinds of evil. There's the fake evil, for the tourists. Hoodoo, voodoo, bullshit-doo. That's the kind of evil that's fun, the kind when you step out a bit. I've done that. I got a whole Ph.D. in the breaking of totally reasonable rules. The silly evil is the stuff you go with to make a little money and to take your mind off the real evil, which is out there in the streets at the end of a rusty knife. The bullet in the head. The body in the river with the arms and legs pulled off. That's why you make up the fake evil, to keep you from thinking about the real evil. But I can deal with that. What I cannot deal with is the institutional evil. Slavery was an institutional evil. What happened down here with Katrina is like that, the way the wetlands were eaten away, the way the city's run, the way the private armies moved in, what you had with Bush. A whole way of life being swept away. That's the institutional evil. *Nazi evil.* That's what you got to fight. *What you was put on this earth to fight!* What you got to go down fighting to fight, if need be."

Then one night Rebennack called and said the name of the man by the Saturn Bar who messed with human skin had come back to him.

"It's Cheeky," he croaked. "Cheeky Felix. *Felix. F-E-L-I-X.* Like the cat. But it could be Felice. Creole guy. He used to mess with human skin. Made masks of human skin. Slip them right over your head, give yourself a whole new face. He's probably a bit older than me. So he might be alive. He might not. But that's his name."

I put the word out, but no one knew a Cheeky Felix. Trips to the tumbledown Saturn Bar were equally fruitless. Back in the day the Saturn was run by one of the old-time characters, O'Neil Broyard. The first time I had gone by there, the place seemed open, never a sure thing, but the door could not be budged. It turned out that O'Neil was inside, asleep, his head propped up against the front door like a pillow. But now O'Neil was dead, and the Saturn Bar had moved in the video poker machine, so there was no help there.

News that no one seemed to remember Cheeky Felix bugged Dr. John. "Before the storm, you would have found someone," he said. "Definitely." The interruption of the chain of oral history was one more tragedy. "No one can remember nothing. It's like the storm blew the memories right out of their head."

I got a lead from Andy Antippas, who owns Barrister's Gallery on St. Claude Avenue only a few blocks from Skip Henderson's house. Antippas, a sinewy chain-smoker from the Bronx and one-time

English literature professor, has one of the best collections of African art in the country. He also runs a gallery where he favors what he calls "the transgressive and biological." In his front yard he had an eight-foot statue of the Bahamut, an Arabian-influenced manifestation of the devil, constructed wholly from a pile of bones Antippas purchased from a Freemason temple that had fallen on hard times. It was this sort of "unusual" taste, Antippas allowed, that almost got him locked up in the Dave Dominici cemetery case.

"The cemetery robbers came by here offering these stolen statues," Antippas said in his fast-paced way as he sat in his living room surrounded by large Yoruban sculptures. "It wasn't Dominici but some of the other guys working with him. They had this marble angel, a really nice piece, and were very, very apologetic because they must have broken one of the wings off when they threw it in the van. They still had the wing, which they set down very carefully beside the angel. They were going on and on about they'd lower the price on account of the damage. It wasn't even worth it to try and explain that an angel with a broken wing was far more exciting than a regular angel. So I just told them I wasn't interested. I just didn't want to get mixed up with that.

"What got me in trouble was when the cops came over. They were looking at every dealer in town. They come banging on the door and right off they see the African stuff. They're asking me where I got it. The statues were freaking them out. Then they go into the next room, where I had this piece I was working on, *The Helmet*. I got the idea from a story about a Knight Templar who had gone off to Jerusalem to fight in the Second Crusade. The knight was a great fighter. The pope had personally bedecked his helmet with relics of the saints. But the knight ran afoul of the Muslim defenders and had his head chopped off by Saladin himself. It occurred to me that if a lot of the collections of Western museums are essentially trophy art taken from conquered peoples, then what might it be like if the tables were turned and the Muslims decided to exhibit this dead Knight Templar's head, with his relic helmet still on, in the main museum of Baghdad or Constantinople. It gave me the idea for the piece.

"I wanted to make it realistic, so I called up some of these people I know who deal with the aftermath of autopsies. This one guy from Cincinnati sent a bunch of eyes with the retinas removed. I incorporated them into the piece. But now the cops are there and they're going nuts.

" 'These are eyeballs!' they're yelling. 'You got human eyeballs! It is illegal to have eyeballs.' They thought they'd found, like, the castle of Dr. Frankenstein or something. I'm screaming back at them, 'They only *used* to be eyeballs! Now they're trash. Organic trash! Organic trash from Cincinnati! With the retinas removed.'

" 'The retinas removed?' one of the cops screams. 'Who removed them? You?'

"It got out of control from there. I had cut up these lamb skin Forex condoms to simulate skin. Now they're fixated on that, saying I skinned people to make the piece. I told them, 'These are condoms, man, condoms!' They're not listening to a thing I'm saying. They're fixated on the condoms. 'What's this?' they're shouting.

" 'That's symbolic of the Virgin,' I said, which was the truth because what is the central idea of Christianity anyway? Belief in the Virgin birth was the reason these Crusaders are in Jerusalem to begin with.

" '*What?*' the cops are screaming. And all of a sudden I'm handcuffed to the wall in my own house. The cops are ripping the place apart, going, 'Look at this, look at this.' It was like everything I owned was conspiring against me."

It eventually got worked out, Antippas said, slouching in his chair as if exhausted by the memory of the events.

I asked Antippas if he knew of any African tribe brought to America during the slave trade that might have used human skin in their rituals. Antippas said the only group that came to mind were the Ekoi, a warlike culture from Nigeria known for painting large, flowery murals and making giant masks, often from human skin. Antippas had none of the original masks but did have some pictures, which were simultaneously hauntingly beautiful and creepy.

Around that time I became aware of the Afro-Louisiana History and Genealogy project, a database created by Rutgers University professor Gwendolyn Midlo Hall on captives who may have passed through New Orleans slave auction houses from 1719 to 1820. Most of the information came from the logs of the French slavers, who were easily the match of the Nazis when it came to record keeping. On a whim I entered "Orleans" into the search engine as "Plantation Location" and "Ekoi" for group of African origin.

Only two names came up. One was Felix.

The Felix in question was listed in the database as a black female who first disembarked from the slave ships at age twenty-two in 1792. Her master (recorded as deceased) was named Landry, owner of the plantation Chapitoulas. Her "selling value" was set down as $430. At the bottom of the sheet was noted "woman is pregnant."

Was this really the record of the Ekoi ancestor of Cheeky Felix, who Dr. John said hung around the Saturn Bar and knew about making things out of human skin? If it was, who would that make the pregnant woman? Cheeky Felix's ten-times-great-great-grandmother?

I called Dr. John to tell him the news. He was touring somewhere in Colorado, bitching about the altitude. "Cheeky Felix from 1792, that's far out." Then he said, if I wanted to keep looking I should talk to Cyril Neville. "Cyril knows things."

Coincidentally the Neville Brothers, one of New Orleans's greatest family acts, were due to play at Brooklyn's Prospect Park band shell, a block and a half from my house, a couple of days later, so talking to Cyril Neville seemed the thing to do. Dr. John said he'd give Neville a heads-up.

"Look," the Doctor said. "I'm helping you because there's no time in the world that anyone should be made into a lampshade. I don't care who it is. No one. You need to get to the bottom of it. So go do it."

Cyril Neville, then fifty-eight years old and the youngest of the four Neville brothers, didn't exactly know why Dr. John insisted I talk to him. He said he didn't know what was happening in New Orleans. He'd left the city after the storm, moved to Austin, Texas, and had no plans to return.

"What for?" Cyril demanded to know. "There's nothing there. All that tradition and history, and the truth is a musician can't make a living there. Now you can't even live there, period. Maybe some fish can, not me."

Cyril's brother, the nonpareil Aaron Neville, a large, faintly scary-looking tattooed man with maybe the sweetest voice in the world, sat on the other side of the room eating a sandwich. "We're scattered to the four winds," he said.

I gave Cyril the short version of the lampshade story and he was interested but again insisted he had little to add. "Well," he finally allowed, "there was the Gown Man. If our mother wanted to keep us home, she'd tell us about the Gown Man. He was this big white guy in a hospital gown, and he'd snatch you off the street, put you under his arm, and take you over to the dissection room at Tulane University medical school. They'd pull off your skin and you'd get chopped up by medical students, practicing their autopsies."

"They had the Needle Man, too. Supposed to shove a six-inch needle in your eye, suck out your brain out right from the socket," Aaron Neville chimed in.

Showtime was approaching and Cyril looked about ready to say good-bye when he said, "There *is* this one thing. Don't know if it helps you or not, but when we were kids our parents used to send us to this Boy Scout camp by the Lake. We'd play ball and that, but on Wednesdays we went to the movies because that's the day they set aside for black people to go to the movies.

"They always showed these horror movies, like *Attack of the Crab Monsters. Creature from the Black Lagoon.* The usual shit, trying to scare us, but the movies were so corny, we'd just laugh. Then there was this one time the movie came on and you could tell from the first second this wasn't going to be the same old thing. The film was all messed-up-looking, with these scratches in it. At first you didn't see anything. It looked overexposed. Then you saw these people coming out of what looked like a giant hole. These skinny, skinny people, their eyes sunk deep inside their head. They were wearing what looked like striped pajamas. They showed these dead bodies, stacked up. And right away, I was scared. We were all scared. Because we knew this wasn't something fake. It was real. Remember that, Aaron?"

He nodded.

"Then they had these other people, marching by. And I think I saw that thing you're talking about—a lampshade they said was made of human skin. That was *really* scary."

"You're talking about footage from Buchenwald. The Buchenwald concentration camp," I said.

"Some concentration camp, that was for sure," Cyril answered. "Long as I live I'll never forget those pictures. Gives me the chills thinking about it even now. Because there's two things about seeing that movie that have always stayed with me.

"First of all, I couldn't believe white people would do that to other white people. But even more than that was the question about why they picked that particular Wednesday to show that particular movie to us—the kind of message they were trying to send."

ELEVEN

Herr Wolfgang Röll put on his white cotton gloves, turned the key in the gray metal door, and opened the cabinet. The main museum at Buchenwald was several hundred yards away, down the hill from the *Appellplatz*. But these objects, kept in the temperature-controlled cabinet inside the former SS barracks that now served as the administration offices of the Buchenwald Memorial, were "separate." They were "not for public view," Herr Röll told me as he carefully placed the items on the table between us. There was a cardboard box of tapered vials from the Serum Institute, part of the Department of Epidemic Typhus and Virus Research run by Waffen-SS doctors in camp blocks 46 and 50. In one research experiment, twenty-one of the thirty-nine prisoners tested died, which added up to, as dutifully noted in the final report, 55.5 percent of "the control group." There were also some human body parts floating in formaldehyde, a shrunken head, and a lampshade.

The lampshade was small, probably a third the size of the object found in New Orleans, and it was crudely made, the diminutive panels stitched together with thick rawhide on a metal frame. It was grayish in color, with darker blemishes in a scattershot pattern.

It was thick and bumpy to the touch. It felt inert, without animation.

"This is a fake," I told Herr Röll.

Röll smiled. "Yes," he said.

"It is plastic or some laminated paper."

"Yes. Quite fake." Röll smiled again, a knowing but somehow inscrutable smile. "But it wasn't *always* fake. Once it was real. Or at least that's what was said. In the GDR times, *much* was said about lampshades and everything else."

Herr Röll's cabinet

A few nights earlier, in Berlin, I'd been out to dinner with some friends who had grown up in the German Democratic Republic, aka GDR, or East Germany. They told me about the lampshade in Herr Röll's cabinet.

"It was something they always showed you when you went on school field trips," recalled Anetta Kahane, who was born in East Berlin in the early 1950s into an illustrious German Jewish family. Her

father, Max Kahane, fought in the Spanish Civil War on the loyal-
ist side, which was considered the gold standard of heroism in the
stridently antifascist cosmology of the GDR state. Max later became
head of the official GDR news service. Anetta's mother, Doris, a well-
known state-sponsored painter, was the niece of Victor Klemperer,
author of the famous diaries detailing his day-to-day life in Berlin and
Dresden during the Third Reich. Doris Kahane is buried in Berlin,
in the same cemetery as Bertolt Brecht, in a grave alongside Herbert
Marcuse. "It is the family joke," Anetta said. "They sit there playing
cards, all those old Commies.

"We were the elite, we lived in Pankow, which is where all the
Party members lived, the big shots," said Anetta, who at fifty-six still
sports a wild mane of orange red hair. She is the head of the Amadeu
Antonio Foundation, a group that keeps track of right-wing violence
in the former East Germany (Amadeu Antonio was a young Angolan
immigrant murdered by neo-Nazis in 1990). "Being one of the elites
you felt a special kind of pressure. Even when I was little I felt it. The
Wall had just gone up, not to keep people in, but, as we were told, to
keep the fascists from the West out. All the Nazis were over there, in
control of the government, doing the bidding of their new American
masters. The Wall was put in place to protect us, to enable the growth
of the antifascist *Nazi frei* East German state.

"I wanted to be a good Communist girl. A perfect model of East
German youth, especially at Buchenwald. In the GDR, Buchenwald
was a sacred place, where the heroes of antifascist resistance rose up
against the SS. My idol was Olga Benário, who was a great spy and
fighter against the fascists from her teenage years. She traveled to
Brazil to try to spread workers' revolution and smoked cigarettes in
a most romantic way. She was betrayed to the Gestapo and gassed
in 1942, defiant to the end. To me the heroes at Buchenwald were
like Olga. They seemed so impossibly brave and good. This was how
I wanted to be, ten years old and totally fearless.

"Instead, when they took us to Buchenwald the very first time and
I saw the lampshade, I got so upset. We were supposed to think that

even though the fascists were willing to stoop to such a level that they would make lampshades out of people, this did not deter the heroes in the antifascist struggle. They battled on to victory. We were expected to follow in their footsteps. Our resolve to oppose the West was supposed to be stiffened by seeing such a miserable thing as the lampshade. Except I couldn't stop crying.

"It was awful because I was supposed to be setting an example. We were in the vanguard. And here I was crying because I saw a stupid lampshade. The teacher had to lead me away. It was so embarrassing. I felt as if I'd let everyone down, my classmates, my family, the state, the entire glorious future of the German workers' Utopia. My weakness had betrayed everything.

"Of course, there was this extra added factor, something I didn't really consider at the time: being Jewish. I mean, I *knew* I was Jewish, but as a member of the elite, a good little Communist girl, it wasn't something that was considered a factor. My mother and father rarely talked about it. Good commies didn't. Why would they? In the GDR there was really no such thing as being Jewish. Judaism was a religion, not a cultural or ethnic designation, and there being no religion in the GDR meant there were no Jews. When we learned about the camps, Jews were not mentioned. Persecution of Poles, yes, Hungarians, yes. Not Jews. It was a shadow existence. Besides, there were so few Jews left in Berlin. They were all dead.

"But that day they showed us the lampshade—*the fake lampshade*—I think I remembered who I was, a Jew in Germany. Because none of the other children were crying, not the way I was."

To make sense of the lampshade inside Herr Röll's cabinet, my friends in Berlin told me, it was essential to understand Buchenwald's pivotal position in the "foundation myth" of the late GDR, how in the East German version of events, the camp was not freed by Patton's army but rather "self-liberated" by the prisoners themselves under the command of the red kapos, the Communist leadership of the inmate underground. It was these men, people like Ernst Busse, the "camp senior number two" in charge of the infirmary; Robert Siewert, head of the construction detachment; and Hans Eiden from the prison clothing department, guided by the inspiration of the murdered Ernst Thälmann, leader of Kommunistische Partei Deutschlands (KPD), who drove the fleeing SS from the camp on April 11, 1945, at precisely 3:15 in the afternoon, the time memorialized to this day by the stopped clock on the camp gatehouse. The Americans may have been around but played no part in the liberation.

More than fifty thousand people died at Buchenwald between 1937 and 1945, but in the GDR the camp was not a symbol of inhuman behavior, but rather a scene of triumphant struggle, a crucible of fire from which emerged a wholly new Germany. The Hitler years were spoken of as a catastrophe that had engulfed the unblemished People like a plague of unknown origin. That any individual of the steadfastly antifascist multitudes living in the East might have taken part in Third Reich activities was considered an impossibility.

"This was the kind of thinking that we grew up with in the GDR," said Harry Stein, a lank-haired, sober, fiftyish man who has been the official historian at the camp since the early 1980s. "But we have learned, very much the hard way, that the truth is a good deal more complicated than that.

"The GDR was not what could be called a real country in the traditional sense," Stein explained in his office down the hall from Herr Röll's cabinet. "It was a product of political negotiation, a construction. We were different than the other East Bloc states under Soviet control. Poland, Hungary, Czechoslovakia, and the others were existing countries, with a distinct culture and history of their own before the war. This was the bedrock of the country over which Communism was placed.

"But what was the foundation of the GDR? Of course we had the German culture. The great German culture. But look where it had led us—to National Socialism. This was an unacceptable past, painful and self-incriminating. Something else had to be worked out." What needed to be done, Stein said, was to make another Germany, a phoenixlike place that might rise from the ashes as a wholly new thing. But a nation cannot come from nothing. So "the myth of the heroic red kapos was invented, right here at Buchenwald," Stein said.

While never less than polite, Stein ran through his thoughts on the lampshade with a dutiful brusqueness. It was his conclusion that lampshades of human skin were indeed made at Buchenwald, although in far fewer number than often talked about. Proof was far from conclusive, Stein said, but he believed that Ilse Koch had given her husband, Karl, such a lampshade, constructed in the pathology block, for his birthday in 1939.

"This was something of a fad among the SS wives," Stein said. "They were very intrigued with the research Dr. Wagner was doing on the tattooed men." As for Ilse Koch actively selecting individuals to be skinned, however, Stein was dubious. "What must be understood was that Buchenwald was run like a kingdom under the Koch family. Karl was the king and his wife was the queen. People like to please the queen. The queen doesn't necessarily have to be an active participant. But it seems, according to the witnesses, as if Ilse Koch did give a human skin lampshade to Karl Koch and everyone applauded because it was such a wonderful gift." As a caveat, Stein added that Karl Koch's reputation for cruelty and corruption was widespread, "so wherever Koch went, stories like the lampshade came up."

This did not mean that the lampshade was an insignificant item, Stein said. "As a symbol it had great power, and as you are telling me, it still does." The Allied forces were certainly well aware of its value. There were reports of an American soldier who had "gone through the entire camp" looking for lampshades to ship back to the States, but no record was kept of what he found and what might have happened to the objects. Stein wondered if perhaps the shade found in New Orleans could be one of those.

In any event, Stein admitted with apologies that he found it difficult to focus on items like the lampshade. He was in the midst of compiling a complete list of all those who had met their death at Buchenwald. In the past several months he'd assembled as much information as possible on over forty thousand people. There were several thousand to go.

"I am so up to my neck in death, if you came and put that lampshade from New Orleans on my desk, it would hardly register."

This was a response I'd heard several times before. In New York, one survivor said, "I have a head full of terror and what do you show me? A lampshade. I have more miserable memories in my pinkie finger than a hundred lampshades."

Yet when it came to discussing the lampshade in Herr Röll's cabinet and the circumstances surrounding it, Harry Stein sighed distressed. As "a GDR boy," he'd taken those field trips to Buchenwald, been shown the lampshade and the shrunken heads, and never once had it occurred to him that they were not real.

"Perhaps a historian, even a young historian, should be more skeptical," Stein said. He then explained how his faith in the GDR version of the Buchenwald story began to unravel.

"When I first came here during the 1980s, I was a firm believer in the official version. I revered the red kapos and came to know several of them personally. To me they were the old lions. Wonderful, wonderful men. I respected them tremendously."

Yet as he began to research the camp history, especially with the fall of the Wall, the inconsistencies became too pronounced to ignore. Stories of how several of the red kapos had been accused of collaborating with the SS to maintain their positions of power inside the camp structure, charges long suppressed by GDR authorities, began to surface. In writing his guide to the permanent historical exhibition, certainly the most complete, and corrective, update of Eugen Kogon's *The Theory and Practice of Hell,* Stein was dismayed to find that founding "heroes" like Ernst Busse, Walter Bartel, Harry Kuhn, and others had exercised their kapo powers over their fellow prisoners in ruthless and corrupt ways, often convicting "real or alleged traitors" in kangaroo courts or, in Busse's case, wielding "power over life and death" in the inmates' infirmary.

"I found these revelations difficult to accept at first," Stein said. "But that is a historian's job, isn't it? To shatter illusions, even if they are your own."

So it was with the lampshade Stein and so many other GDR children had been shown as evidence of Nazi brutality. Shortly after the Wall came down, the shade was sent to Frankfurt for testing. It didn't take long for the scientists to determine that it was fake. "Another false symbol," Stein said, sourly.

Nothing, however, affected him as much during this period as "the confrontation with the bones."

In 1989, one of the camp workmen came to see him. "He said, 'If you care so much about the dead, why don't you do something about those bodies in the woods beyond the storage house?' This was news to me. I never heard of any bodies out in the woods, so we went out there to look. That's when we found the bones."

In a small booklet entitled *Buchenwald: A Tour of the Memorial Site* that he wrote with his wife, archivist Sabine Stein, is a description of what came to be called Special Camp No. 2, one of several internment facilities maintained by Soviet forces in Germany during the aftermath of the war. It was "hardly four weeks after the last survivors" left the camp that Buchenwald once again "became a place of isolation and death for another four and a half years."

Noting that the "anti-Nazi policy" of the Soviets was "put in practice in a Stalinist way and distorted the process of denazification," the Steins write that even though many interned in the special camp had "worked on low and intermediate levels of the NSDAP . . . a larger number of the persons came to the camp because they had been denounced, taken for somebody else or arrested in an arbitrary way." Of the estimated 28,000 people who would suffer "from overcrowding, vermin, and cold in the barracks" at Special Camp No. 2 from 1945 to 1950, 7,113 would die there, their bodies tossed into mass graves without notification to their families.

"During the GDR it was a tremendous taboo to talk about such things, so the existence of these graves was unknown. There were rumors, but I didn't believe them. I never imagined the Soviets would do a thing like that."

Then the historian who dealt with so much death on a daily basis rubbed his brow. He was choked up, close to tears.

"I remember the day I went out there, to where the bodies were. The ground was soft from all the leaves that had fallen from the trees and rotted away. You didn't have to dig very deep to find what was left. That is when it truly struck me, as I stood in the forest confronting the bones . . . I was a historian, writing essays, attempting to be authoritative, complete. And right here, no more than a few hundred meters from my office, was this, all this new horrible history. A completely other chapter of cruelty. It was death on top of death, layers of fear and terror.

"I realized I would have to go back to the beginning again. To check everything again. To check and *recheck* . . ."

It was past six o'clock and already dark and cold, a German dark and cold, when I took the number 6 bus down the Blood Road away from Buchenwald. I didn't feel like going back into the hotel, shutting myself away in that little room quite yet, so I walked down Schopenhauerstrasse, past the Bahnhof, to the Internet café near Ernst-Thalmannstrasse. There were a couple of emails waiting for me from Skip Henderson: more photos of houses on top of cars, pleas for more bottles of Manhattan Special espresso soda, and a rant about how the fools in Hazelhurst, Mississippi, *still* refused to allow the unveiling of the tombstone of Tommy Johnson, avatar of the highways 49 and 61 crossroads, even though Bonnie Raitt, a bona fide white person, had paid for it. Amended to that was further news of the Bus and Skip's unending quest to find jobs for America's Least Wanted.

"Sometimes you just have to shake your head," Skip wrote. "The other day I got the Bus parked out by the mission near St. Charles and this kid, like 17 or something, comes in with 'fuck bitches' tattooed on his face. The 'fuck' is under one eyebrow and 'bitches' under the other. I took one look at him and said, 'now why you want to make my life harder like that?' The kid kind of hung his head. I guess he had some second thoughts about the ink. He said that sometimes he'd walk into a store about to ask for a job and wouldn't even get to open his mouth before they said, 'no.' Nothing else. Just no.

"I told him not to worry because I was going to get him a job. I would get him a damn job if it was the last thing I did. 'This is our city' I told him, 'we got to work together on this thing.' The kid looked at me like I was one more crazy white man, so I tried to break it down for him. I told him to look at himself, with the 'fuck bitches' and the white T-shirt, and the Yankee cap on his head. Didn't that look like someone who needed to have a little money in his pocket? He nodded, sure, everyone needs a little money in their pocket. So I asked him question two: didn't he look like someone who if he couldn't get that money by working a nice, safe job would instead be out in the street trying to get that money some other way? He didn't get that part of it, so I asked him, 'who would you rather meet in a dark alley, me, or you?' The kid said, if I put it that way, he could see my point. He didn't want to rob and steal, he was trying to be a good citizen and build a better New Orleans. So I sent him out on some jobs in the back of the house of some restaurants, where the public doesn't see you. I got him signed up for cooking school. I told him to forget about the 'fuck bitches,' to wear sunglasses."

That Skip, I thought, he was a great New Orleanian, a great American, always trying to raise the level of hope among the hopeless. His second email, however, was not so uplifting.

Dated a day later it began, "Mark. What the hell are you doing with that lampshade? You have got to get rid of it. Now! It is driving me insane." Skip detailed another dream he'd had. He'd woken up after the storm to find himself on top of the A-frame roof of a house. "It was just me on top of the roof," Skip wrote. "I knew the water was coming up. But it wasn't water. It was lampshades! A sea of lampshades bobbing up and down like shark fins. Circling, closing in! So save me, brother. Save me!"

This email pissed me off. Skip lays the lampshade on me and now I'm supposed to exorcise his guilty dreams? But I knew what he meant. The tide was rising, inside my mind.

Leaving the Internet place, walking around Weimar, I thought Harry Stein was right. When it came to Buchenwald, it was best not to make assumptions. Just because seven thousand bodies were found dumped into a mass grave didn't mean there weren't more, maybe thousands more, a hundred feet away. The hand of malevolence was on the place, it could never be redeemed, if that's what the GDR history makers were trying to do. The truth would never be found here. In the early 1950s, when the Soviets handed the place over to the GDR, the idea was to make Buchenwald into "a place of solemn memory." To that end, the first thing they did was knock down most of the camp, save the crematorium, the SS barracks, and the pathology blocks. Several years later, many of the old barracks were reconstructed to serve as a set for the state-produced film *Naked Among Wolves (Nackt unter Wölfen)*, the story of how heroic red kapos banded together to hide and protect a young boy smuggled into the camp by his father. *Naked Among Wolves* was originally written as a novel by former Buchenwald inmate Bruno Apitz. The movie version, mandatory viewing for all citizens, was presented as fact. The use of the rebuilt camp, it was said, added to the story's "authenticity."

Weimar itself has been renovated. Left to decay under the GDR, a cash influx of over $700 million had since transformed the town into a classical fantasyland, and it was while strolling from Puschkinstrasse back toward Lisztstrasse behind the Bauhaus Museum that I ran into the Nazis. I couldn't say I hadn't been warned. "World Heritage Site" or not, Weimar was a "brown" (as in "Nazi") town. Always had been, maybe always will be. Neo-Nazis lived in the old East German housing blocks and out in the suburbs, places like Apolda and Magdala. Garages where Trabants, the old East German–made, underpowered, smoke-belching sedans, once sat are often filled with the music of bands like Kommando Freisler, who sing children's folksongs with lyrics about how "in Belsen" we hang them by the neck, and how *Judenhaut* is only good for *Lampenschirme, fidiralala, fidiralala, fidiralala*. There have been hundreds of documented violent incidents involving neo-Nazis and other far-right groups in Thuringia since reunification.

This was what happens, people in Berlin said, when twelve years of National Socialism is immediately followed by forty years of neo-Stalinist clampdown with Stasi microphones under every pillow, when phony socialist Utopia abruptly gives way to grim post-industrial, capitalist reality. In the West they had six decades of post-Nazi *Vergangenheitsbewältigung,* another of those ingenious German word-phrases meaning roughly "working one's way through the past." In the East there was no such process. Here there was only the stolid cult of the New Man and polluted rivers. The past was off-limits, left to fester like a piece of cheese ripening under glass for forty-five years. When the lid came off the Pandoran nastiness, it was best to stand back.

Not that the Nazis—there were four of them, tramping up Lisztstrasse right toward me—were immediately identifiable as such.

Only a few blocks from here, on January 15, 1933, days before becoming chancellor, Hitler addressed ten thousand cheering people in the Marktplatz in front of the Hotel Elephant. Those were the Nazis I knew, chinstrap-straight Aryans in the thrall of their master's voice. Also recognizable would have been those twenty-two skinheads and their fraus who, on July 24, 1994, according to an Associated Press account, attacked the Buchenwald camp "shouting 'Sieg Heil,' giving the stiff-armed Hitler salute, and threatening to burn 'with their own hands' a woman who works at the camp."

But as for the young men in front of me, it was hard to tell. Sometimes present-day Nazis announce themselves with brand loyalty to their preferred *gegen,* or fighting apparel. Favorites are Thor Steinar and Lonsdale—the latter a familiar soccer club T-shirt logo that, with a jacket worn over it, can be arranged so only the letters *N, S,* and *D* show, for *Nationalsozialistische Deutsche.* On Lisztstrasse, however, these self-signifiers were nowhere in sight. Under the streetlights the Nazis presented as merely generic-looking punks, black hoodies pulled down over the brims of baseball hats, low-slung jeans, Chuck Taylor Converse sneakers. At this distance it was nearly impossible to distinguish them from the "antifa," or "antifascist" left-wing youth, who also wear black hoodies, low-slung jeans, and Converse.

"This is because there is the antifa and the *anti*-antifa, two sides of a coin," I would later be told by a man who chose to call himself Hans, which he said was "a perfect German name, straight from the earth, dripping with blood, soil, and beer."

Raised in "a big, soft-with-money Nazi family" in West Germany, as a teenager Hans found himself more at home with the disgruntled youth in the shabby outlying neo-Stalinist housing projects in East Berlin "Ossie" suburbs like Marzahn and Lichtenberg.

"It started with the music," Hans said. "Real good hard-core fuck-the-world music. I wanted to know how they felt, to be at the bottom of the barrel, unloved and wondering why. I saw how it worked with these people. Their parents filled their heads with the commie bullshit. At school was the reunification bullshit. The TV had the American buy-this, buy-that bullshit. But over there, in the corner, was Grandpa. He was an old man now, sick. No one paid much attention to him. But he once was a Wehrmacht soldier, a defender of the Reich. Smart in his uniform on the bloody front. And when he talked about those days, it was not bullshit. It was about another time, when there was something to believe in, when the world was there for the taking.

"I felt, this makes sense," said Hans, who joined up with a variety of hard-right groups. "I stayed with them for years but could not continue. Maybe I wasn't desperate enough, maybe it became clear that the right wing politicians were as corrupt as anyone else. Maybe I met some of those people I was supposed to hate, even Jews, and I found they weren't all the same like I'd thought. I even liked some of them. But mostly it was the violence. I didn't want to walk into a room blind drunk and be helpless to stop my finger from pulling a trigger as I shouted, *'Heil Hitler.'* "

Now entering his thirties, long frizzed mullet grown onto his formerly shaved skull, Hans said it was the "stupidity of the state" that gave the right-wing anti-antifa no choice but to dress in the exact same way as the left-wing antifa.

"The *Hakenkreuz* and everything else are banned," Hans explained. "If you are seen with a swastika, you are put in jail. So it is best to go out dressed plainly." At first many of the right-wing youth resented this curtailment of their so-called self-expression, but they soon realized this "plain dress" annoyed the left-wing youth.

"When we heard the antifa were in their bars and squats, angry that we were supposed to be copying them, that was great. Anything that made them mad, the stupid arrogant fuckers. If the antifa made a decal saying, 'Good Night, White Pride,' with cartoons in the middle, the anti-antifa made the same thing with 'Good Night, Left Side' and Mario from Donkey Kong in the middle."

It made sense, Hans said, because when it came to the most militant members of the antifa and the anti-antifa, there wasn't all that much difference between the two. "They all hate capitalism, say they will do anything to save the planet from big business and pollution, and want Israel blown off the map. They might have completely different reasons, but this is what they want. But what they *really* want to do is fight. Punch each other in the head."

There was one sure way to tell the difference between the antifa and anti-antifa, Hans said, pulling up the sleeves of his sweatshirt. "You look at the skin. Then you know."

He was covered with tats, had at least twenty, he said. On his arms was some of the typical Nazi stuff, a Celtic cross along with other runic geometry, and a bunch of gothic-lettered tributes to black metal bands including "an old one" honoring Absurd, whose leader, Hendrik Möbus, was jailed following a pilgrimage to West Virginia, where he was photographed exchanging Hitler salutes with late white nationalist William Pierce, author of the apocalyptic Nazi novel *The Turner Diaries*. On his back, Hans said, he had a six-inch-wide swastika and the head of Geronimo, owing to his longtime infatuation with Native Americans, whom he regarded as more legitimate pagan souls than the greasy-bearded Wotanists revered by most neo-Nazis. Running his hand over the black sun imprinted on his forearm, Hans said it was a problem, what to do with these things once you stopped believing in them.

Talk of tattoos got us onto the lampshade. Hans said lampshades were something of a coming thing in the German right-wing underground. He still had contacts around the black metal music scene, where "you hear people go on about lampshades, getting their hands on one. Buying one or even making them." Not that Hans believed this was anything more than "big talk." Personally he'd never seen a lampshade, even a fake, and that was okay since the whole idea gave him "the creeps."

"Maybe that's what we're all doing," Hans allowed with a shrug, pulling down his sleeves. "Preparing ourselves to be made into lampshades."

As for the Nazis in Weimar, I need not have worried about them, Hans said. "They wouldn't have known you in a thousand years."

This was true. After all, my nose is big, a definite honker, but it isn't *that* big; it doesn't quite hook like the Shylock beaks in Goebbels's Expressionist propaganda posters. Nor was I hunched over like an insect under a soiled prayer shawl. I held no visible puppet strings by which I controlled the reins of international capital. In 1937 the race scientists at nearby Jena University might have applied their phrenological calipers to my cranium, so as to suss out my dirty secret. In bathrooms, storm troopers bearing bright gooseneck lamps would have homed in on my foreskinlessness, pointing with black-gloved fingers at the undeniable proof. But this being now I could pass. The approaching neo-Nazis might know chapter and verse of every Elder of Zion conspiracy, but it was all abstraction, stuff pulled off the Internet from right-wing sites in America. *Seinfeld* was on the TV, but how many real Jews had these would-be *Übermenschen* really seen, in the flesh? There were never very many Jews in Thuringia to begin with, and the original Nazis had managed to reduce that number from an estimated 4,500 to 450. In the GDR, if Jews appeared in the history books at all, it was as "victims," a "victim" being the lowest of concentration camp inmates, below "resistance fighters" and passive "mere survivors." It was a pejorative thing, to be called "a victim." Neo-Nazis often addressed their targets as "you victim" before stomping them.

Years ago a good friend of mine was on his deathbed. A grand, knock-around Heeb of the beatnik variety, once Muhammad Ali's press agent, friend of Norman Mailer and Bugsy Siegel, he would die within the hour. He asked me to place my ear close to his mouth because, after a life of raconteur patter, he couldn't talk above a whisper. He said he had two last things to say. The first was to ask me if I'd brought a joint because if he was going to die, he might as well go out higher than a kite. The second was a regret.

"I regret I never killed a Nazi," my friend said.

I knew what he meant, of course. When we were kids, it was another schoolyard Holocaust topic along with the lampshades: if you saw the baby in the carriage and you knew it would grow up to be Hitler, would you strangle it or not? It was a strange image, nine-year-olds from Queens with their hands around the neck of a baby, but we all swore our unwavering willingness to do it. But these Nazis? These latter-day street punk malcontents on Lisztstrasse? These anti-antifas? Would it have been worth it to strangle them in their cribs?

We passed each other without so much as a nod, ships in the night. They didn't know me, I didn't know them. They were probably too busy dreaming of pummeling Indian merchants and throwing a rock through the window of a kebab shop to care about this big-nose Jew. It was another one of those universalist/particularist problems. If Nazis weren't trying to kill you and turn you into a lampshade, this had to be progress, right?

TWELVE

I was in Mannheim, fifty miles south of Frankfurt, talking to Daniel Strauss, whose father, Heinz, or "Pappo," was a Buchenwald prisoner from the summer of 1944 until the end of the war. "He was there, and before that in Auschwitz, when he was a teenager," Daniel said of his father, now in his eighties and quite frail. "But he never talked about it. Except at night, when we heard him screaming from the nightmares.

"As a child, it scared me when he yelled," recalled Daniel, a balding, friendly man in his fifties. A scholar and activist, the younger Strauss runs the *Verband Deutscher Sinti und Roma Baden-Württemberg*, an organization dedicated to preserving the culture and history of the Sinti and Roma, people commonly, and pejoratively, known as Gypsies.

" 'What, Pappo?' I'd ask him. 'What do you see?' But he would never tell me. He said it was better if I didn't know."

Author of such articles as "Between Romanticisation and Racism, 600 Years of Sinti and Roma in Germany," Daniel, a Sinti, says no group besides the Jews were as systematically terrorized during the Third Reich as the so-called Gypsies. The 1935 Nuremberg Laws expressly forbid Sinti and Roma people from marrying or having sexual relations with Germans. In 1936 the Nazis instituted a campaign that sought to make Berlin "Gypsy-free" for the Olympic Games. In 1938, with the opening of the Reich Central Office for the Fight Against the Gypsy Menace, concentration camp internment escalated, with many imprisoned in the so-called *Zigeunerlager* ("Gypsy camp") at Auschwitz, where they became favorite subjects for Josef Mengele's race-based experiments. It is estimated that somewhere between 250,000 and half a million Sinti and Roma died in the camps. In the Romany language the period is called *Porrajmos,* or "the Great Devouring."

According to Daniel, Pappo's transfer to Buchenwald from Auschwitz in the spring of 1944 almost certainly saved his life. Only days after his departure, the remaining prisoners at the *Zigeunerlager,* nearly three thousand people, were gassed in a single night. But it wasn't until 1995, when Daniel went with his father to observe the fiftieth anniversary of Buchenwald's liberation, that Pappo decided to talk about his experiences during the war.

"I'll tell you once and don't ask me again," Pappo said. Seizing what he knew to be a singular personal moment, Daniel decided to make a video recording of Pappo telling his story. Beginning with a long segment of the old man playing the piano, his camp tattoo visible throughout, Daniel's video is a touching treatise on the nature of cultural survival. If you're in Mannheim someday, perhaps you might be lucky enough to see it.

Eventually Pappo told Daniel about his nightmares. "There were a lot of them," Daniel said. "People being shot in the back of the neck, hung, so many terrible things happened there." But one image appeared more than others.

"It was a woman. The Kommandant's wife . . . Frau Koch," Daniel said. She regularly invaded Pappo's dreams, more often than not coming out of nowhere on her horse, riding crop in hand. The lampshade also haunted Pappo. "Ilse Koch and her lampshades."

This was curious, since it seemed unlikely that Pappo had ever seen Ilse Koch, on horseback or not. If he arrived at Buchenwald in

April 1944, that was three years after Karl Koch's transfer to Lublin and a year after Konrad Morgen's investigation at the camp, during which time Ilse Koch continued to live in the so-called Villa Koch but was rarely seen in public by the prisoners. Her horseback riding days were long over.

Yet one hesitated to assign these dreams wholly to Pappo's imagination. At the Buchenwald reunion a number of other prisoners, some Sinti and some not, spoke of similar nightmares. "Ilse Koch and the lampshade, several of them mentioned this," Daniel said. Albert Rosenberg, who had been at the camp only after its demise, had said a similar thing in far-off El Paso, Texas. Ilse Koch was in his nightmares, too. "A beast of a woman," he called her.

When I asked Daniel if I might talk to Pappo, he was not encouraging. The elder Strauss had been in the hospital. He was very weak. Daniel feared it might be too stressful for him to talk about the camp days. Moreover, as far as Pappo was concerned, the Nazis had never gone away. Until quite recently, following the family tradition, he had continued to go around Germany operating his swing carousel, a staple attraction at Sinti traveling carnivals. The carousel appears, quite poignantly, in the final scenes of Daniel's video. Pappo sits with Daniel's young son in a seat of the swing, going round and round, an inviolate symmetry of cultural endurance. But there were always problems from the neo-Nazis, mostly skinheads, who would attack the Sinti carnivals. On a number of occasions Pappo had been beaten up and his carousel vandalized. Eventually, Daniel said, he and the rest of Pappo's kids convinced him to give up traveling because it was too dangerous.

Still, Daniel said he'd ask his father if he minded talking about Buchenwald and the lampshade. If such a thing really existed, it would be "important" to talk about. "It is something you don't ever want to show anyone but you want everyone to see," Daniel said. Sometime later, however, I heard that Pappo, after several nights of bad dreams, had passed away.

"He died with that woman in his head," Daniel said.

• • •

Perhaps Diane Saltzman from the U.S. Holocaust Memorial Museum had been half right after all. The lampshade might not be a myth, as she claimed, but it certainly was *mythic*. It had a life of its own quite apart from any conventional notion of physical reality. This went double for its spiritual creator, its most-cited progenitor, Ilse Koch. Routinely included in Internet polls as one of the ten most evil women ever, along with Countess Elizabeth Báthory, the Hungarian serial killer; Irma Grese, the vicious Nazi prison guard at Ravensbrück; and Isabella I of Spain, enabler of both Columbus and the inquisitor Torquemada, *die Kommandeuse* had entered what the French social philosopher Maurice Halbwachs, a colleague of Henri Bergson's and Émil Durkheim's, who died of dysentery at Buchenwald in March 1945, called "the collective memory," which "need not be exact" but nonetheless "carries a prestige reality does not possess."

Jorge Semprún, another Buchenwald prisoner who almost certainly never laid eyes on Ilse Koch, calls up her image in his novel *The Long Voyage,* published in 1963, more than thirty years before *Literature or Life.* Following long descriptions of the brutal train ride to Buchenwald, Gerard, Semprún's narrator, finds himself in a small-town café ten years after liberation with Sigrid, a young, "beautiful" German woman with "short hair and green eyes."

Gerard has questions, things he needs to know from Sigrid. Just who is she, what were her parents doing ten and twenty years ago? Perhaps she is the daughter of "Dr. Haas," a "Gestapo character." She puts out her cigarette and asks, "Why are you treating me like this?" Her father was not "Dr. Haas," he was not in the Waffen-SS, not any Totenkopf. Gerard keeps on, saying well, of course Sigrid's father could not have been a Nazi "because there were never any Nazis."

She shrugs this off, says he's drunk, inquires why he is "sad." It is the dim openness of the question, the alluring naiveté of her green-eyed face, that makes Gerard wonder: could it possibly be that Sigrid truly doesn't know about the hangings on Sunday afternoons in the Ettersberg woods, "beside the electrified barbed wire, the village beneath its quiet smoke, the winding road and the green, fertile Thuringian plain"?

Then they are in each other's arms, entwined in what Gerard calls "the burning tension . . . between the weight of this past and the refusal to remember this past." Her face is "smooth," "polished," and "eternally fresh," as if "washed by centuries of slow, Nordic rains." Her body is "perfectly suited for the appetite of juvenile perfection which vibrates within each of us." It is a face and body, Semprún writes, that has been "reproduced tens, perhaps thousands of times in the women's magazines" as if only "to make us forget the body and face of Ilse Koch, that straight, stocky body planted solidly on her straight, sturdy legs, that harsh, sharp, incontestably German face."

Years after liberation, Gerard is still held captive by the image of Ilse Koch, with her "iron gray eyes" fixed on the naked torso of her human prey, her gaze "already cutting out that white, sickly skin along the dotted lines of the tattoo which had caught her attention . . . picturing those bluish lines, flowers or sailing ships, or snakes . . . on parchment-like skin." It is the picture of Ilse Koch, "reclining on a couch" surrounded by adoring Waffen-SS officers, all of them bathed in the post-human light of her lampshades, that must be banished, Gerard says, if he will ever fully return to the living.

It is not unlike the drama Semprún will write about thirty years later in *Literature or Life,* the story of how Albert Rosenberg, a.k.a. "Rosenfeld," saved him from limbo. The hope here is that Sigrid (and who knows how many Sigrids before and after) with the softness of her unmarked skin will somehow rescue Gerard/Semprún from *das radikal Böse* of Ilse Koch's echoing laughter as she surveys her lampshade collection, "gathered like shells at the seashore on a weekend," restoring the narrator to a world where love and untainted sex are possible.

Many people of the post–World War II generations got their first look at Ilse Koch, or at least her facsimile, in one of the now vanished movie theaters on New York's Forty-second Street and in similar "grind houses" throughout the United States. Few films outsleazed *Ilsa, She Wolf of the SS.* Shot on the set of the cheery prisoner-of-war camp television comedy *Hogan's Heroes* and starring the spectacularly endowed 37D-22-35 Dyanne Thorne, *Ilsa, She Wolf of the SS* takes a number of liberties with the Ilse Koch story.

Far too immoderate a presence to be a mere Kommandant's spouse, Thorne's Ilsa functions as a Nazi Dr. Moreau, serving as both the *Kommandoführerin* and head doctor of Medical Camp No. 9. With this expanded portfolio, Ilsa eschews such ho-hum Third Reich medical practices as mass sterilization in favor of pet projects like a series of experiments bent on proving that women can tolerate more pain than men. While the apparent goal of breeding a race of Ilsa-like dominatrix Amazons to serve in the front ranks of the Reich's push for world domination remains unfulfilled, the tests do allow for a few extended, sapphically oriented S&M scenes. By night, Ilsa, an all-purpose *Hexe* when it comes to the unholy mixing of sex and death, orders male prisoners to her swastika-bedecked boudoir. Those who do not satisfy her are killed or merely castrated, depending on how close they bring her to orgasm.

Since Chaplin first pranced with his globe in *The Great Dictator,* mockery of Nazi leaders has been a staple of American popular culture. Why simply have a sleepy village attacked by zombies when you can dress the undead in SS uniforms and make them Nazi zombies? Few Reich figures, however, have provided as much cartoon mileage as Ilse Koch. Although offering few of the "fascinating fascist" contradictions inherent in a dashing character like Leni Riefenstahl, the plump Dresden secretary still supplies much fertile study territory to those seeking to explore the male fantasies that suffuse both the rise and fall of the Reich. Scholars like Alexandra Przyrembel, in her aptly titled essay "Transfixed by an Image: Ilse Koch, the 'Kommandeuse of Buchenwald,' " say Koch got a raw deal because she was one of the few recognizable females in the Nazi Party. The point appears irrefutable. Is it any surprise that in 1951, with so many

high-ranking Nazis already restored to positions of economic and political power, Ilse Koch was again sentenced to life imprisonment in
a German court where she was described as a "diabolical female," a
"red-headed cocotte," and a "robot of cruelty"? When the defendant
broke down in her cell, sobbing, "I am guilty! I am a sinner!" *Time*
magazine tastefully described the scene by saying "the fat-faced Bitch
of Buchenwald . . . no longer the doll-eyed ruminant, collapsed in a
hysterical heap." Who, after all, could be a better scapegoat than Ilse
Koch? Shortly after her conviction, *Neues Deutschland,* the Party-
approved East Zone newspaper, wished good riddance to the "symbol
of that period of the deepest disgrace and humiliation of all decent
Germans." But the transfixing image of Ilse Koch, like the lampshade, did not disappear. The cartoon was too compellingly drawn to
fade away.

Dyanne Thorne in *Ilsa, She Wolf of the SS*

Reached at her Las Vegas home, Dyanne Thorne, now in her seventies and "busier than ever," says she knew "very little" of Ilse Koch

when she agreed to take the *Ilsa* part. "I knew she was something of a despicable psychopath, a totally terrible person. I knew something about the lampshades. We read about that in the newspapers when we were little. That scared me, the idea I was going to be *her*.

"But I didn't choose Ilsa, she chose me," said Thorne, whose credits include *Sin in the Suburbs*, *Blood Sabbath*, *The Swinging Barmaids*, and *Hellhole*. "I studied at the Actors Studio with Lee Strasberg. We all wanted to play Shakespeare, to be Blanche DuBois in *Streetcar Named Desire*. But *Ilsa, She Wolf of the SS* was what I was offered. That is the way the business works. Say what you want, but it was a starring role and I wasn't going to turn my nose up at that. I've taken some flak over the character. A few people stopped talking to me. There were stares in the supermarket. But I never saw Ilsa the way others did. I always thought of her as a female James Bond, an exotic woman of action. It is the responsibility of the actor to see a character from different sides, to be aware of the saving grace in them."

Remembering afternoons inside the sticky-floored Selwyn Theatre on Forty-second Street when I sat between snorers and outpatients watching Ilsa dribble through a golden shower scene with a snivelingly kinky SS general, I wondered what Dyanne Thorne, who seemed like a very nice person, found to be Ilsa's saving grace.

Thorne laughed. "Well, she is a very strong-minded individual. A strong woman character. That's what you get when you take out the politics, isn't it? A woman who's *in charge*. Someone who scares the hell out of the men. Don't look at her the wrong way or she'll pull your skin off—*that's power*. That's Medea. Catherine the Great. I never imagined that Ilsa was something anyone would want to emulate. She isn't what you might call a role model. That's one reason I insisted Ilsa die at the end. She has to get what is coming to her.

"Still, Ilsa has been good to me. I get so many fan letters! I can't even answer them all. Fans send me such lovely artwork, pictures of me as Ilsa. What imaginations they have! I'm always flying to one film convention or another. We just got back from the Cleveland Cinema

Wasteland convention. Everyone was so nice to us. They treat me like a homecoming queen. Maybe *that* is Ilsa's saving grace: I don't know if it's nostalgia or what, but she makes people happy. Strange as it sounds, Ilsa is a beloved character."

Since her last film appearance in 1987, playing James Belushi's deeply cleavaged transsexual father in *Real Men*, Thorne has earned a Ph.D. in comparative religion, become an ordained nondenominational minister, and along with her husband, musician Howard Maurer, currently runs A Scenic Wedding, a Las Vegas–based wedding planning business. Billing themselves as "an alternative to chapels," the Maurers stage what are called "fantasy weddings."

"We've done them in canyons, on the shores of Lake Mead, with hot-air balloons. What I tell our clients is the only limit is your imagination," said Thorne, describing a recent wedding she and her husband presided over in a nearby forest, on horseback. To listen to her talk about it, the wedding, with unicorn-like trappings, had a distinctly Renaissance faire feeling to it.

"On horseback, like Ilsa," I threw in.

"We do a lot of weddings on horseback, deep in the forest; it is very popular. Everyone has a ball," Thorne said, pointing out that, as an accomplished horsewoman, she handled all the riding and stunts in the *Ilsa* movie herself.

Hearing this, it was difficult not to recall "the fantasy wedding" of the real Ilse Koch, to Karl Koch at midnight in the woods behind Sachsenhausen, with the steel helmet, the rings bearing runic symbols, the bread and salt, the white-gloved SS men.

"When you marry people, do they know you were Ilsa?"

"A lot of them do," Dyanne Thorne answered. "It's a kick, I suppose, getting married by Ilsa . . . but no one has ever asked me to *dress up* as Ilsa to marry them."

"Would you? If they did ask?"

Dyanne Thorne thought a moment. "Well, we're in business to give people the wedding they want. If Ilsa is their dream wedding, I guess I'd have to think about it."

• • •

I had an address for Uwe Köhler, Ilse Koch's son, in Bavaria, east of
Regensburg.

Born in Landsberg Prison in October 1947 following his mother's conviction, Köhler was Ilse Koch's fourth child. Her first three
children—a son, Artwin, and two daughters, Gisela and Gudrun—
were born at Buchenwald, each successive year from 1938 to 1940. It
is assumed that Karl Koch was the father of these children—a cradle
embossed with back-to-back *K*s, donated by a local family, is in Wolfgang Röll's special collection at Buchenwald—however there were
many rumors concerning Karl Koch's purported homosexuality, and
Ilse almost certainly had a number of lovers. Prominent among these
alleged paramours were the deputy camp commander, Hermann
Florstedt, and the camp doctor, Waldemar Hoven.

The brutal, gawk-necked Florstedt was Karl Koch's chief lieu-
tenant/henchman at both Sachsenhausen and Buchenwald before
replacing his disgraced boss as head of Majdanek, where he would
preside over a murderous regime that set the stage for the horrific
"Operation Harvest Festival," a mass killing spree that peaked on
November 3, 1943, when eighteen thousand Jews were reported to
have been shot. Hoven was another sort of Nazi. Darkly handsome in
a tragically Teutonic, Gregory Peck mode, the ascot-wearing Hoven
traveled in the United States, where he sought a career as a Hollywood romantic actor. Failing this, he returned to Germany, joined the
SS, and despite scant medical training became a camp physician. He
was later convicted at Nuremberg for dispensing lethal injections to
prisoners. Koch and Florstedt were shot by the Nazis as a result of the
Konrad Morgen investigation; Hoven was hanged by the Allies. This
makes Ilse Koch quite possibly the only woman ever to have sex with
men put to death by opposite sides in a world war.

Nonetheless, in the story of Ilse Koch, the conception and birth of
Uwe Köhler remains a singular event.

Prosecutors at the Dachau war crimes trial were dumbfounded

when the forty-one-year-old former Kommandeuse announced in open court that she was pregnant. This seemed impossible, even for the supposedly insatiable Bitch of Buchenwald. As the only woman among the thirty-one defendants at Dachau, she had been locked up in an isolated, heavily guarded cell. The disclosure set off a tabloid firestorm. The court officers believed the father might be Josef Kirschbaum, one of the military interrogators, a Jew. Could Ilse Koch be so man-hungry that she would welcome the company of a *Volk-defiling* Hebrew? Joshua M. Greene in his book about the trial, *Justice at Dachau,* writes that Koch's mystery lover was likely a prison kitchen worker who "dug a hole to her barracks," tunneling his way into the arms of the Kommandeuse.

The paternity question was never settled. Koch refused to talk about it. It was as if the birth were a magic thing, the uncoiling of the malign spirit that, in keeping with the vows sworn by Ilse and Karl during their midnight wedding, dwelled in the womb of SS women.

This was some onerous existential baggage with which to begin life's journey, I thought as I drove south through Bavaria to the town where I'd been told Uwe Köhler lived. Taken from his mother almost immediately after his birth, raised in a succession of foster homes, Köhler (Ilse Koch's maiden name) was unaware of his parentage until shortly after his nineteenth birthday, when he saw a newspaper article headlined, "No Pardon for Ilse Koch." Recognizing the name from his birth certificate, Köhler did some checking and in 1966 made contact with Ilse, then entering her sixteenth year of incarceration.

It was with "a creepy feeling" that he first approached the looming old Aichach prison one dank morning shortly before Christmas, Köhler told *New York Times* reporter David Binder in 1970. He wasn't sure what kind of reception he would get from this person who supposedly turned men into lampshades and also happened to be his mother. As it turned out, Köhler told Binder, it was "a joyous reunion" and he began to visit Koch every month, which was all the law allowed. Insisting on her blamelessness, Koch sent her son several poems she'd written in jail. One poem, entitled "Innocence," goes: "Still they keep me bound / counter to all justice / when guilt cannot be found . . ." One day, she writes, her fate will be "reversed," with honor paid to those who were "cursed," Hell's torments at an end, right "installed again."

"I always avoided talking with her about the war," Köhler told the *Times*. "She said she was the victim of libels, lies and perjury but I didn't discuss it with her further because it was painful for her . . . I can't really imagine what it was like. I am not even convinced she is guiltless. I feel she just slithered into the concentration camp world like any others without being able to do anything about it." Köhler continued to see his mother until one day in September 1967, when he arrived at the prison for his monthly visit to find that she had hanged herself in her cell the day before.

When he spoke with the *Times*, Köhler was twenty-three years old, "making a good living in the insurance business," and attempting to rehabilitate his mother's name, the prospects of which he called "practically hopeless." After that, Köhler disappeared from public view.

Given this past, perhaps turning up on Köhler's doorstep unannounced was a cruel thing to do. My only excuse was that I'd tried to call the number provided without success and my letter had gone unanswered. It is a reporter's sickness, this barging in. The truth was I didn't have any list of probing questions for Uwe Köhler. I had no right to put him on the spot. If his mother had turned men into lampshades, it was certainly no fault of his. Still, I felt a need to see him, to speak with him, if for only a moment. So much about the lampshade was fleeting, impossible to pin down. But here there was a connection, a direct line, in the blood. To stand next to Uwe Köhler might be as close as I'd ever get to Ilse Koch and whatever happened in the Buchenwald pathology lab.

I knocked. No one answered. I was thinking of leaving a note when a youngish, dark-haired man called to me from the road. He lived in the house, he said, and didn't recognize Uwe Köhler's name. Perhaps someone named Köhler had lived there many years ago, or resided in another house in the town. It was difficult to tell if the man was telling the truth or not. I couldn't imagine that I was the first lampshade hunter to arrive in town looking for Uwe Köhler. Either way, it was stupid to stand out here in the rain, the man said. He managed the tavern across the road, and I should come in and have a beer.

The bar was rustic in a cozy, deeply unsettling Bavarian way. It was a lucky thing I'd come by, said the man, now standing beside his cheerful blond wife, with whom he ran the tavern. A good friend of theirs was stopping in and he was bringing his accordion; this was a real treat, they said, especially since, as they were sure I would notice, he looked "exactly like our Austrian cousin, you know, Hitler."

A few minutes later, Mishi, a large, white-faced man wearing a denim mechanic's jumpsuit, came through the door carrying a mother-of-pearl-inlaid accordion. I had to admit, despite his huge size and lack of mustache, he did look a little like Hitler.

We drank and chatted, aided by the bartender, acting as translator. Mishi was very put out by the ingress of immigrants into Bavaria. It wasn't that he minded so much that "Munich is full of Arabs," Mishi said. What bothered him was "these people do not know to act in a proper German way." Mishi felt entitled to say this, being an immigrant himself. His family came to Bavaria from Kosovo in 1890, so he was not a native German and had never forgotten that fact. To become a "real German" was a long process. It wasn't as easy as making out a tax return. It was a matter of blood and soul, he said, picking up his accordion.

Settling in a chair, Mishi flashed a smile and shouted, "Since four forty-five we are shooting back." This apparently was his customary opener, the way another musician might say, "Hit it," or count off, "1, 2, 3, 4." Later it was explained to me that this was what Hitler said the morning the Reich attacked Poland to begin World War II: after a specious report of Polish gunfire, the Führer went on the radio to inform the *Volk* that as of 4:45 a.m., the German army was returning fire.

With that intro, Mishi launched into "Rivers of Babylon," a spiritual adapted from Psalm 137: "By the rivers of Babylon, where we sat down, there we wept when we remembered Zion." Mishi sang it beautifully, too, his pure tenor lifting over the squeezebox licks. Perhaps it was the odd confluence of tune and setting—the sad song of homesick Jews sung in a Bavarian bar by a man who was happy to look like Hitler—but by the time he got to the part about "so let the words of our mouth and the meditation of our heart be acceptable in thy sight," I was a bit choked up. When he finished, I clapped and told him how much I enjoyed his performance, especially since "Rivers of Babylon" had been one of my favorite songs ever since I first heard it in the Jamaican film *The Harder They Come*. Adapted from the biblical original by the Rastafarian band the Melodians, the song celebrates an otherworldly kind of logic, Rastas being under the impression they are a tribe of Africans stranded in a tropical Babylon where they do not belong. The idea of former slaves, forcibly exiled from their home, inventing such a seemingly outlandish yet sanity-saving cosmology has always touched me.

"Who?" Mishi asked.

"The Melodians. From Jamaica."

Mishi shook his head. "This is not from Jamaica. It is from Boney M."

Boney M. I had forgotten about Boney M., the disco band put together by German entrepreneur Frank Farian, who later was the mastermind behind the black duo Milli Vanilli, the only group ever to have their Grammy Award revoked for not really singing on their records. Like Milli Vanilli, Boney M. had a visual crossover racial appeal, but their voices were electronically altered to mask any undue evidence of ethnicity. In 1978 they had had what is called a "Eurodance hit" with a cheesy version of "Rivers of Babylon" that played in every hotel bar from Scottsdale, Arizona, to Mogadishu.

Mishi was done playing. On my way out he wished me luck finding "your friend Uwe."

Authenticity was a hell of a thing, I thought, driving across the Hitlerscape near Berchtesgaden. Were things ever as they were supposed to be?

Sixty-five years ago, as a member of the 133rd Engineers Corps attached to George Patton's Third Army, my father came through here. His unit built numerous bridges in advance of the front lines, and by the time they came to Berchtesgaden, it was June 1945. The war was over. My father had a picture taken of himself sitting on Hitler's balcony with the Alps behind him and sent it to my mother. My parents are both long dead, but the picture is my all-time favorite: a two-inch-square Brownie print with crinkle-cut edges showing Dad, in his uniform, puffing on his pipe, the same pipe I often saw him smoke after dinner in Flushing, Queens. It is a sunny day; the light glints off his wedding ring. You can't miss it. On the back of the photo, my father wrote, in his familiar angular handwriting, "On Hitler's balcony, me too, the ring is shiny, huh?"

I may have never taken the time to notice it while growing up, but my parents had a brilliant, thrilling romance. They were married only days before my father shipped out in 1944 to return to the Old Country from whence his own mother had fled the Cossacks and a whole galaxy of anti-Semites. Now he returned to help vanquish the greatest of Jew-killers. My parents' fate, and my own, was tied up with beating the Germans, crushing them to rubble. To sit on Hitler's balcony, smacking the ashes of his civil servant's pipe onto the grounds where the Führer once took tea with Eva Braun, that was the payoff, a most perfect spike of the football. I look at the reflection from my father's ring and know that, even before I was born, at least some of its glow was intended for me, his way of sharing that moment of love and triumph with the unborn son who soon would be cracking up his Plymouth station wagon on the West Side Highway.

For my night in Obersalzberg, I checked in close to the Eagle's Nest at the Hochlenzer hotel. It was an older place, perched on the side of a hill, at forty-five euros probably the cheapest around. I could see why. While perfectly well maintained, the hotel had an eerie timelessness about it, as if nothing had changed since 1938, the year the watercolor landscapes hanging above my bed were painted. In the lobby, one photo stood out among many. Its frame bolted to the wall with heavy screws (other prints had been stolen), the picture, labeled *"A. Hitler an Hochlenzer,"* showed a smiling Führer looking jaunty in a double-breasted suit and fedora as he shook hands with a number of people on the patio of the hotel.

One person in the photo, a man in a corduroy jacket and leder-hosen, looked familiar. He was blond and tall like the man standing beside me in the dining room of the Hochlenzer right now. "This hotel has been in the family for many, many years," the man said, slapping down a plate of cold cuts before me, unhappy that my late arrival had required him to reopen the kitchen.

As I ate the lonely slices of *Jagdwurst* in the empty knotty-pine dining room, the light suspended above the table caught my eye. The lampshade, perhaps a foot high and sixteen inches across and made of a thick brown paper, was of little interest. The trim, however, the pink and gold embroidery stitching, rang a bell. It wasn't identical to the pattern on the New Orleans lampshade, but it was close. Very close. Not that this was a great surprise. If the accoutrements of a human skin lampshade couldn't be found here, in these mountains, where would they be? I was in the zone.

David Jacobson on Hitler's balcony, 1945

• • •

I had one more address. It was for David Duke, Louisiana's most famous fascist. If you happen to be in possession of a lampshade possibly made in a German concentration camp that turned up in a
flooded building in New Orleans after the storm of the century and
you want to find someone who best personifies the psychic connection between those two points, David Duke is your man.

Over the past several years, outside of occasional sightings in the
deli department of the Mandeville Winn-Dixie, Duke had all but disappeared from the shores of Lake Pontchartrain. Now I was told he
was residing, deliberately under the radar, a mere hour's drive from
the Eagle's Nest. This was a switch, a Nazi hiding in plain sight amid
the *dampfnudeln* bakeries and T-shirt shops of an Alpine tourist town
rather than down a Buenos Aires back alley or deep within the Brazilian jungle.

Back to the days of Napoleon, who sold half a continent to finance
a doomed attempt to conquer the world, the snake oil–drenched world
of Louisiana political theater has had its outsized players, megaloma-
niacs of every stripe. There was Henry C. Warmoth, a Reconstruction Republican who was elected governor in 1868 at age twenty-six
by a grand total of two votes and then proceeded to run the state debt
from $6 million to nearly $100 million in a few short years. More recent times have included segregationist kingpins like Judge Leander
Perez Sr., unchallenged ruler of the Plaquemines and St. Bernard
swamplands, who in 1960 unleashed a call to action against the inte-
gration of New Orleans schools: "Don't wait for your daughter to be
raped by these Congolese. Don't wait until the burr heads are forced
into your schools. Do something about it now." Then, of course, there
was the Long trinity: Russell Billiu Long, who served thirty-nine years
in the U.S. Senate, and his uncle Earl Kemp Long, the three-time
governor and self-proclaimed "last of the red-hot poppas," who was
quoted by his occasional Boswell, A. J. Liebling, as saying he wasn't
against nobody "for reasons of race, creed, or any ism he might believe

in except nuttism, skingameism or communism." And sitting at the
top of it all, Earl's brother, the Kingfish—Huey Pierce Long, who, it
is often conjectured, dreamed of overthrowing Franklin Roosevelt's
U.S. government and making himself a latter-day Napoleon of a self-
styled share-the-wealth, Libertarian, downhome National Socialist
state, albeit with much better food, music, and manners.

David Duke, loner son of a largely absent Shell Oil executive father
and an alcoholic mother, entered this ripe tapestry as a full-blown
race fascist in 1967 when, at age seventeen, having carried a copy
of *Mein Kampf* to classes at John F. Kennedy High School in New
Orleans's Lakeview section, he first appeared in public wearing a Ku
Klux Klan hood. By his early twenties, Duke, the self-anointed Grand
Wizard of his own Knights of the Ku Klux Klan (the KKKK), was
hosting LSU campus birthday parties for Adolf Hitler while wearing
a knockoff Hugo Boss SS uniform.

Duke soon smoothed these rough edges and positioned himself as
a kinder, gentler, Ayn Rand–reading racialist for the post–civil rights
era. Rather than one more troglodyte blocking the school door like
George Wallace, here was a soft-spoken young man tricked out as a
network anchor type (rumors of early-career plastic surgery earned
Duke the nickname "the nose job Nazi"), a dreamboat of a National Socialist to appeal to doublewide-dwelling *Frauenschaft*. After a bizarre
interlude during which he wrote a sex manual for women, *Finders-
Keepers,* under the pen name Dorothy Vanderbilt, Duke ran for public
office in the late 1980s, with surprising success. In 1989, campaign-
ing as a Republican in a Metairie district adjacent to New Orleans,
he was elected to the Louisiana state legislature. A year later, in a
U.S. Senate primary, Duke received a shocking 44 percent of the vote,
just missing a runoff with the stalwart seventeen-year incumbent,
J. Bennett Johnston.

This set up one of the most phantasmagorical elections in state
history, the 1991 gubernatorial "race from Hell" pitting Duke, who
had astonishingly vanquished the sitting governor, Buddy Roemer, in
the primary, against the coolest cucumber of all Louisiana pols, the

wily, unashamedly graft-ridden three-time chief executive Edwin Edwards. Edwards's presence in the race was something of a surprise. By the late eighties, after he was implicated in a far-reaching series of scandals involving such disparate individuals as Carlos Marcello, the New Orleans mob boss often mentioned as a possible plotter in the John Kennedy assassination, and Tongsun Park, a South Korean rice magnate accused of bribing a wide range of U.S. officials, Edwards's political career appeared finished. According to the *Shreveport Journal,* the only way the former governor could get elected again would be "to run against Adolf Hitler." In David Duke, he had the next best thing.

Matched with a canny cracker-barrelist like Edwards, Duke, never your *Triumph of the Will* spellbinder, came off like a cue card–reading ideologue, more *Volk* than folk. The election was basically over when the famous slogan "Vote for the Crook—It's Important" began to appear on bumpers throughout the state. Zingers from Edwards, a noted philanderer—stuff like "The only thing David Duke and I have in common is we're both wizards under the sheets"—only ran up the score. Edwards, unsurprisingly, went on to preside over an administration racked with impropriety and would eventually be jailed for racketeering. Still, Duke received 671,000 votes, including 55 percent of whites, leading the undeterred candidate to declare, "I carried my constituency."

Duke's electoral career peaked with the Edwards defeat. By the 1996 Senate primary he was under 12 percent and sinking fast. His regular-Christian-guy pose was blown with the 1998 publication of his seven-hundred-page autobiography, *My Awakening: A Path to Racial Understanding,* in which Duke contends, among many other things, that more than 25 percent of all African Americans have "an IQ of under 75" and that the Jewish-controlled media is covering up the existence of the "Aryan gene." Under investigation for fraud and tax evasion, he pled guilty in December 2002 to embezzling several hundred thousand dollars in donations from supporters and gambling it away in Gulf Coast casinos. He was sentenced to fifteen months in the federal lockup in Big Spring, Texas, a minimum-security prison that didn't even have an Aryan Brotherhood, which was probably just as well from Duke's point of view. After his release in 2005, having alienated most of his better-heeled followers, Duke relocated to eastern Europe, where, he said, he felt "more in tune with the demographic."

The address I had for Duke turned out to be a small apartment house a few blocks from the picturesque but largely deserted (the ski season was winding down) main drag. The eight buzzers all had German names next to them and random bell pushing produced no result. Nearby an older man was playing Frisbee with a blond-haired boy about nine. "Are you looking for the American?" the old man asked. "He is there." With that the old man unlocked the building's door, walked up the wooden staircase, and knocked on a door.

A moment later there was Duke, coming down the staircase in a lime-green satin bathrobe, tan puffy bedroom slippers, and a bathing cap on his head. The skin on his face was red and curling; it seemed as if I'd caught him in the middle of a chemical peel.

"David Duke," I said.

"No," he said. "My name is *Ernest* Duke." Ernest is Duke's middle name and he sometimes signed articles as "Ernest Duke." It was not clear if Duke preferred to be addressed as Ernest or whether he was pretending to be a wholly other person.

After a pause, Duke abandoned this tack and asked me who I was and how I'd found him. I said I was a reporter, I'd been given his address by some people in Vienna, and since I was in the neighborhood, I thought I'd drop in. I was writing a story on Katrina and its aftermath, and since he'd once been a hair's breadth from occupying the Louisiana statehouse, I thought it might be interesting to hear what he had to say about the storm, from the leadership point of view. All of which was completely true, more or less.

I handed him my *New York* magazine card, which Duke looked over. "New York, huh?" he said. Then, he focused on my name in what appeared to be three distinct, escalating takes: Jew . . . *Jew* . . . *JEW.*

"Who gave you my address?" Duke asked again, sharper than be-fore.

"I don't have an ax to grind. I just want to hear views," I offered.

"Okay," Duke said, putting my card in the pocket of his bathrobe. "I'll talk to you. Go down to the café at the corner. Wait there. Let me get dressed. Be a few minutes."

The café was closed for the season, so I sat down at a metal pic-nic table outside and surveyed the scenery, which was copious, with mountain peaks in three directions. Small packs of bicyclists rode the sloping curve in the road, tapered spandex butts in the air. Austria. For years I couldn't think of the place without recalling the line attrib-uted to Arnold Schwarzenegger during his bodybuilding days: "The Germans are nothing without an Austrian to lead them."

It was taking Duke a while to come down. I figured he was on the Internet trying to find out who I really was. The wait gave me a chance to mull over the time I'd attended a seminar for middle and high school teachers back in New Orleans on how to present Holocaust and civil rights curricula to students from backgrounds not in tune with the current thinking on these topics. The seminar leader, the estimable Plater Robinson, had invited some members of the small New Orleans Holocaust survivor community, including Anne Levy, then in her seventies but still in the Garden District an-tique business and very spry. Separated from her family as a young girl, and having grown up as a street urchin in the Warsaw Ghetto, Levy was very upset when David Duke began running for office. "It was like they'd come after me again," she said when we talked.

Levy described coming face-to-face with Duke. It was during Duke's term in the legislature; Levy was in Baton Rouge to see an exhibit about the Holocaust. "I was looking at some photos," she re-called. "Then I see, right beside me, David Duke. The way he was standing there, his hands clasped behind his back, it was exactly the way I remembered the Germans standing in the Ghetto, when they made us line up and looked us over. Sometimes they'd pull people out of line. You never saw them again.

" 'What are you doing here?' I yelled at Duke. He didn't respond. It was like I wasn't there at all. I said it again, 'What are you doing here? Why do you want to look at pictures of something you say never happened?'

"Finally he looks at me and says, 'I didn't say it never happened. I said it was *exaggerated*.' I guess I was yelling at him, because some cameramen started coming over. Duke started walking away, faster and faster. He didn't want to have his picture taken with me. But I wouldn't let him go. I started running after him. The closer I got, the faster he went. Here I am, this five-foot-tall Jewish grandma and David Duke is running away from me. They got shots of it; it was in all the papers."

Duke was walking toward the café now. He'd changed into tight-fitting blue jeans neatly cuffed to show off a high-end pair of hiking boots. A partly zipped buckskin jacket covered a striped Ralph Lauren shirt. His blond hair, haphazardly dyed, sat on top of his head like a half-fallen soufflé. Now nearly sixty, Duke, his teeth whiter than buffed Chiclets, seemed intent on presenting the aspect of a man twenty years younger.

Duke said he didn't know how much time he had. Even though his position in "the cause" had shifted over the years to "more of an elder statesman, an adviser, a historian and philosopher, rather than the young Turk I used to be," he was still very busy. He wrote columns for his website, DavidDuke.com, and did a radio show three times a week with Don Black, who runs the "white rights" Stormfront site. There was also the matter of putting the finishing touches on his new book, *Jewish Supremacism: My Awakening to the Jewish Question,* which he'd begun as part of the Ph.D. he got in history from the Interregional Academy of Personnel Management in the Ukraine.

Beyond that, there was a chance of a great sunset and Duke wanted to photograph it. "I've always been an amateur shutterbug," he said, but since moving to the Alps he'd become "inspired as never before." He was currently displaying his pictures, many of them Obersalzberg landscapes, at DavidDuke.com, where framed 20 × 28–inch prints were available for sale, each one personally autographed in "a special gold ink."

Duke took a deep gulp of Alpine air, which he said was "the world's finest." There was simply something about "being around the mountains" that brought out the best in him. "Up here you feel free . . . You wouldn't have anything like Katrina up here, that's for sure."

Katrina was a "cataclysm of race and neglect," Duke said. "I watched those images and was heartsick to see what has happened to our country. It was like Uganda in New Orleans. As if a lovely city had been thrown back to the Stone Age. It was a massive failure of government on every level, but it was also an even more massive failure of people. Face it, black people were out of control in those streets. I have a lot of good friends on the NOPD. The stories they've told me you won't believe. The public will never know the half of it because it is suppressed. The scene in the Convention Center and the Superdome was way, way worse than anyone knows. There were dozens of rapes. People were just defecating right there in their seats. Right where they sat!

"You ask me what I would have done if I was governor during the storm? What could you do, short of letting the police and military have their way with the criminals, but is that what you really want, all those people shot down in the streets? You can't give people like Nagin and Bush a free pass, but New Orleans was so far gone before Katrina that the disaster was inevitable. It might be a dead city now but it has been dying for years. Look at the basic structures, look at the schools. Everyone says the public schools in New Orleans are bad for black kids, but they're hell for white kids. I went to a good segregated public school in New Orleans. I got a good education. Now a white kid would be lucky to make it through a day.

"People talk about a post-racial society. You might as well call it a post-human society, because race is the natural order of things. It dictates behavior. Tell me, do you think if you had twenty thousand

Anglo-Saxons in the Superdome, you would have had people acting like that? Twenty thousand Germans, twenty thousand Danish or Swedish people? You think any of that would have happened?"

There was every chance the entire American enterprise was going to go the way of New Orleans, Duke said. The white Europeans who had founded the country, built it into a great nation, were getting the short end of the stick.

He related the situation to his own criminal conviction. "They had nothing on me. The whole thing was going to be dropped. But then I made an appearance on Al-Jazeera talking about how the Iraq War was about nothing but Zionist domination of American foreign policy. It wasn't a war about oil. It was a war about what Israel wants. A war dictated by Israel. Dictated by Israel to the American president. That's what I said to an audience of ten million. I guess some Zionist in the State Department must have heard it and asked around, 'What do we have on Duke?' Then, the next thing I know, I'm arrested, facing something like twenty years in jail with the threat of an all-black jury hanging over my head. So I took the plea. I didn't want to, but I did. That's what happens to people who speak out against the real power structure."

Duke had been talking for going on two hours. He'd missed his date to photograph the sunset, but no matter. The sun would go down tomorrow, too. He had a lot more to say, an anxious, even desperate need to explain himself to this Jew who dutifully wrote down most everything he said in a skinny reporter's notebook. It was "good to talk to a Jewish man who likes to listen," Duke said.

Which was true. There was a strange comfort in hearing Duke spin out these moth-eaten theories, these conjectures about how my people (not me, of course, but my people) were the true power behind Bush and every other asshole currently wrecking the world. After encountering the anti-antifa in Weimar, those inscrutable black-clad figures harboring who knew what newer and more opaque kind of "Ossie" fascism in their hearts, here, at least, was the Nazi I knew.

I wouldn't say I felt sorry for him, but Duke did have a seriously hangdog aspect. It seemed a sad Dick Shawn act, shacking up in this college party resort in such close proximity to the Berchtesgaden mother lode. Was he so friendless in his secret Aryan Valhalla that he didn't even mind opening up to a big-nosed Jew?

Duke became expansive. Did I know, for instance, that white people had settled the New World before the so-called Native Americans?

"It is called the 'Solutrean hypothesis,'" Duke explained: "A professor at the Smithsonian Institute came up with it based on the arrowheads they've found. There is also a lot of genetic evidence, an overlapping between the DNA of European groups and skeletons found in America. All these years we've had to listen to how horrible the white race is. How much terrible stuff we've done. They say the white man wiped out the Indians. Well, here's proof that it was actually the other way around."

I asked him if he ever misses Louisiana.

"Well, I go back there a lot. I have no restraining order against me preventing it. And I do love it. I loved growing up there," Duke said. "When we were kids, we'd string hooks with worms, dig for hearts of palm. We'd go out on little boats for days at a time. Swim with the gators. We all swam with the gators. Then you'd wake up early to see the sun rise over the water. I guess you can say I'm torn because as much as I love the bayou, I love the mountains, too. When I'm here I feel more religious than I ever have in the church. There's so much *strength* in the landscape. But when it comes down to it, I'll always be a Louisiana boy at heart."

We'd bonded now, Duke and me. He gave me his personal number and told me to call whenever I "get a hankering." There was only one thing left to discuss, the lampshade.

"Can't talk about that," Duke replied, his mood suddenly cold. "Nothing about the Holocaust."

In the mongrelized USA, Duke could say whatever he wanted, but here in the cradle of National Socialist romance and idealism, there was no First Amendment. No license to say the first moronic thing that came into your head. It had only been a couple of years since the Austrian government had sentenced David Irving to three years in jail for maintaining there were no gas chambers at Auschwitz. If you were going to "talk politics," as Duke called it, you'd better watch your mouth.

A flock of geese flew overhead. Duke looked up. "You can see eagles here, owl eagles," he said, noting he'd like to do more photography of Alpine bird life. Then, leaning over, Duke lowered his voice. "Those lampshades are a myth. Everybody knows that."

PART 3

THIRTEEN

For twenty years, I thought the opening line of Bob Dylan's "Blind Willie McTell" was "Seen the arrow on the *dartboard,* saying this land is condemned." Then I found out that he's really saying, "Seen the arrow on the *doorpost* . . ." The song was already one of Dylan's most desolate, with that business about the "ghosts of slavery ships" and "power and greed and corruptible seed," and the change only added to the bleakness. Since the next line, one I had right from the start, was "all the way from New Orleans to Jerusalem," "Blind Willie McTell" became the mournful soundtrack to the few weeks before I boarded a plane to Ben Gurion Airport.

I saw the story of the lampshade breaking down into three parts: A) getting it, B) having it (the attempt to understand the history and the nature of the thing), and C) getting rid of it. I was up to C, or so I thought after speaking to renowned Holocaust scholar Yehuda Bauer. In contrast to other Holocaust professionals, Bauer, former director of the International Institute for Holocaust Research at the Yad Vashem Holocaust Martyrs, and Heroes, Remembrance Authority in Jerusalem, senior adviser to the International Forum on Genocide Prevention, and winner of the coveted Israel Prize, said he was more than willing to entertain the possibility that the lampshade might be real.

"Why shouldn't I believe the Germans made lampshades out of Jews?" said the then eighty-three-year-old Bauer when I reached him in his Jerusalem office. When it came to atrocities, "I wouldn't put anything past those people."

Dr. Bauer had arrived in Palestine in 1939 after his family fled Prague, and he fought in the 1948 War of Independence. He and I had been emailing each other for a few weeks, and after receiving a copy of the Bode lab DNA report, he pronounced himself "officially intrigued" by the Katrina lampshade. "These colorful details you describe, with these oddball characters, seem unbelievable, but it is not unusual that such things like this lampshade might appear in the wake of upheavals," the historian said. "In any disaster, and this New Orleans flood is certainly a disaster, the foundations and the framework of a time or place become shaken, causing strange things to wash up."

Bauer was "not surprised" at my difficulties in getting a major Holocaust institution to take the lampshade off my hands. Holocaust institutions did a wonderful job in the preserving of memory and raising consciousness regarding genocide in general, he said, "but they were still institutions, given to institutional thinking." This meant "fitting things into categories. I am not certain this lampshade of yours has a category."

I asked Bauer about the "ownership" of the lampshade. If it was made from a human being, as the science indicated, who did it belong to? Was it possible for anyone or any entity to claim title to something like the lampshade?

"Who does it belong to?" Bauer wrote back. "I am no expert on legal issues like that, but clearly it belongs to you, at the moment at least, and you are perfectly entitled to do with it whatever you think fit. However, if what we both fear—that it comes from a camp—can be proved beyond a shadow of a doubt, perhaps it can be said to belong to the Jewish people. And in that case it should be at Yad Vashem."

On the phone Bauer said he had an upcoming dinner date with his longtime colleague Avner Shalev, the former Israel Defense Forces brigadier general and current Yad Vashem chairman. "I will talk to him about it," Bauer said. If Mr. Shalev agreed, as Bauer felt he probably would, it might be possible for Yad Vashem to undertake some further testing on the lampshade. I could either ship the lampshade or, better yet, bring it myself. Jerusalem was quite nice in the fall, at least after the High Holy Days and the rest of the Jewish holidays, which Bauer, a noted atheist, called "endless."

If I could see my way to bringing the lampshade to Jerusalem, Dr. Bauer said, we could discuss it over a cup of coffee. "I know I would like to see it."

If Yad Vashem would accept the lampshade, that would be that. Who could claim that by handing the lampshade over to the ultimate Holocaust authority, headquartered smack-dab in the middle of the Holy Land, I had not fulfilled my solemn responsibilities? Yet as I packed my bags, cold feet set in.

There had been some changes regarding the lampshade, and my relationship to it. For one thing, it was no longer in the box with the Sugar Ray Robinson stamps. If I was going to travel sixty-five hundred miles with the shade as a piece of carry-on luggage, it would need a sturdier container. An antique and art shipper on the Brooklyn-Queens border said he could make a nice box with a foam-core interior. I brought the shade to his shop; he took one look at it and asked what animal it was. There were several new laws on the books pertaining to shipments of animal products; he was not interested in having anything to do with the skins that might have come from an endangered species. Not to worry, I told him, probably a tad too flippantly, this species was not endangered. Far from it.

"Not endangered—I was afraid of that," the box maker said, turning a bit pale. After a pause he said that even though his services usually included packing the item, he could not do so in this case. He would make the box, that's all. I would have to pack it myself and pay cash. A couple of days later the box was ready and I went to pick it up. It was snow white with a bloodred handle affixed to the top. Was this the only color he had, or was it commentary?

I never knew how people were going to react to the lampshade. I'd been talking with "Mr. Paul," a high-end lighting designer from India, who worked with Hugo Ramirez, the Argentine-born owner of a marvel-filled antique lighting store on East Fifty-ninth Street in Manhattan. Mr. Paul and Hugo Ramirez were fascinated by the human skin lampshade. They spent a good deal of time examining it, and had a few disagreements about its construction, notably whether the stitches that joined the skin panels together had been done by hand or machine. Ramirez felt a machine had been used. Mr. Paul, pointing to the varying spacing between the stitches in certain spots, insisted that the shade was hand-sewn. Their debate grew louder by the moment, causing uneasy looks among the browsers in Ramirez's store.

In the cause of further research, Mr. Paul suggested we drive out to East New York in Brooklyn to talk to Eppie G., who learned to make lampshades from animal skins in her mountain village in Ecuador. A tiny, dark-haired woman in her fifties with a no-nonsense, market-lady demeanor, Eppie looked over the lampshade, noting the "greasy" feel of the panels. She wanted to know which animal it was made from. When I broke the news to her, she screamed and ran out of the house, leaving the front door wide open to the winter air.

It was several minutes before she returned. Now totally calm and businesslike, she said, in Spanish, "I would cut the pieces from the back and the belly, because you cannot use one piece. You tan it . . . in the sun, then you cut. With a big knife." She went through the whole process with a craftswoman's precision, as if it were just another job she'd done a dozen times.

If there was one thing everyone agreed on, it was that I was insane to keep the shade at my house. How could I stand to be around the thing? After a while, if someone asked where the shade was, I'd lie and say it was in a storage unit or a safe-deposit box. It was simply too hard to explain that after a while I wanted the lampshade around me. That being away from it didn't feel right.

Doña Argentina, the Dominican medium in Union City, New Jersey, said the spirit of the lampshade "trusted" me, that "he" placed "his fate" in my hands. But how could you take this sort of talk seriously? Soon after receiving the lampshade from Skip Henderson, I'd stopped in at Priestess Miriam's spiritualist parlor on Rampart Street in New Orleans. Miriam had a local rep for being able to contact the dead, so I thought I'd try her on the lampshade. The priestess's storefront is right below the apartment where, in a frightening case, Zackery Bowen, an Iraq War veteran, murdered and dismembered his girlfriend with whom he'd ridden out Katrina. Bowen had kept the body parts in the apartment for days on end. I asked Priestess Miriam about that and she said, somewhat huffily, "That's upstairs. I pay rent down here."

In the months since seeing Doña Argentina, I'd grown closer and closer to the "spirit" of the lampshade. Like hurricanes, the shade had acquired a name. "Ziggy," I called it, a nice German-Jewish name, American for Sigmund, as in Freud. Feeling nervous the night before leaving for Jerusalem, I put Ziggy on my bed and lit one of the candles Doña Argentina had given me. On cue, the flame lurched from a flicker to several inches high.

Watching the glow of the candle flit across the diaphanous surface of the skin shade was to allow the consideration of any number of intellectual and emotional propositions. To paraphrase the Russian "harlequin," Kurtz's disciple in *Heart of Darkness,* the lampshade had "enlarged my mind." In his presence I was invited to ponder the most basic of Zoroastrian dualities, the distinction between light and dark, which made sense since what was a lampshade (lamp/shade) but a device designed to simultaneously shed and constrain illumination—an interplay of obfuscation and radiance that yielded, for lack of a better term, meaning. Goethe the polymath had tackled similar issues in his major scientific work, *A Theory of Colors.* Discussing his findings with his faithful secretary and biographer Johann Eckermann as they strolled the Ettersberg forest, the master said, "We see that darkness itself is part of light. It sounds absurd when I express it: but so it is. Colors, which are shadow and the result of shade, are light itself."

From the beginning, the lampshade had been talking to me, making itself known in small and often oblique ways. It was a conversation I'd gotten used to, grown protective about. There was no way to banish the possible horror scenarios of how the lampshade came to be, the indelible images of the unlucky prisoner plucked from the Buchenwald *Appellplatz* by a former Dresden secretary on a white horse, the misery of being lain prone on the tiled tabletop in the pathology lab, the shearing blades ripping away skin in sheets, the weeping cobbler working deep into the camp night to add a bit of style to the frame as a loving, if perverse, tribute to a doomed friend who was now to be given as part of a birthday gift to a Nazi Kommandant. If this was the story of the lampshade, so be it. Yet eventually, inevitably, the revulsion, the fear, even vengeful anger faded away before a vast wave of sympathy. The thing had been a person. With the candlelight shooting higher, it was still a person. A human being who had asked me to look out for him and deserved no less.

So, with respect and as gently as I could, I placed the lampshade into its new, stark-white home with its bloodred handle. The customs people and the cops might order me to peel back the Velcro that held the box's lid closed. They might demand to look inside. If so, what would they see? An old, torn lampshade. They were looking for bombs, C-4, pistols, box cutters, not souls.

A few days after landing in the Holy City, I was sipping a cup of tea at the Three Arches Restaurant inside the Jerusalem YMCA on King David Street, engaged in a conversation with Yehuda Bauer regarding particularism and universalism as it pertained to the lampshade found in New Orleans. Attired in a jaunty royal blue windbreaker with racing stripes down the arms and describing himself as "quite lively for a semiretired eighty-three-year-old with a foot and a half in the grave," Bauer listened patiently as I made my case about how the Bode lab's DNA test, which identified the shade as being of human origin but did not specify the kind of human, might place the object in "a no-man's-land of murder," belonging to no one and no group. "To me that makes it a potentially universalist object," I said to the famous scholar.

Bauer's own position on the issues of universalism and particularism are well known among Holocaust scholars. Speaking in front of the German Bundestag in 1998, he had asked, "How is it possible to compare the tragedy of a Jew, or a Russian peasant, or a Tutsi, or a Cambodian Khmer? It is, surely, impossible to say one mass murder is better or worse than another, that the suffering of one person is greater or less than that of another. Such a statement would be repulsive."

Yet in the Holocaust, Bauer continued, "for the first time in the whole of history, people descended from a particular kind of grandparent—in this case Jewish—were condemned to death just for being born. This, the mere fact of their having been born, was by itself their deadly crime that had to be avenged by execution. This has never happened before, anywhere."

At the Jerusalem YMCA, Bauer received my lampshade claims with the patience of a bemused elder, as if they were part of an overblown but not uninteresting grad student paper. He was willing to entertain the possibility that the lampshade might qualify as "an icon of genocide." Likewise, the "tantalizingly inconclusive" DNA report was "intellectually provocative." But as for what any of these notions proved, if anything, Bauer would not venture a guess.

Not that he had any doubt that the lampshade was real, Bauer said. When I took the shade out of its white box, he hesitated before approaching it. "A sobering sight," he said. But if the science of the shade was a matter for the lab workers, what it meant—the position it might take in the Holocaust narrative or the wider discussion of human affairs—was a trickier business. "I think you should not worry

too much about arguments about things like universalism and particularism. These discussions are for academics, people like me," Bauer
said, dipping a piece of pita bread into a plate of hummus.

"You are a writer, you tell stories. The meaning comes from the
telling, and the retelling." Not to make any comparisons, Bauer said,
but this is what he often thought when he encountered Holocaust
survivors: "Tell your story. Don't stop telling it." For Bauer, oral history was mutually beneficial to the teller and the listener. In the past
decades, he'd heard so many stories. "Thousands of terrible stories,
rattling around in my brain." Some of these narratives were more revealing than others, but all of them, even the lies, had value. One day,
however, the last survivor will die. Then, even though he and many
other historians had written down the stories, finding the truth of
things will become more difficult because the voices, "the sound of
them, the voice of the teller, will never be heard again."

This was why he liked hearing about the lampshade from New
Orleans, Bauer said, and why I should keep telling the story. "This
Dominici, for instance, he is quite a fellow," he remarked, leaning
back in his chair. Bauer couldn't hear enough about the former cemetery bandit. "The role of the thief is always interesting, the ambi-
guities of so-called good and evil in situations of extremis," he said,
captivated by the account of how Dominici had talked himself into
the psych ward at the OPP by insisting on immunity from prosecution owing to his status as the locator of "the Nazi lampshade."

"*What a character!*" the scholar exclaimed.

On the Dominici front, there had been some recent news. Since I
visited him at the OPP, he'd been convicted on a number of charges
and sent to the state pen in DeQuincy, in the swamplands near the
Texas border. In a letter I received from him, Dominici maintained
a steadfastly upbeat account of his life and times, reporting he was
keeping his "nose clean and mouth shut," promising to be "back-at-
ya" in no time. DeQuincy was no picnic, but being locked up was
"a blessing in disguise" since it gave him plenty of time to work on
his autobiography, which he planned to call *Or Else Is Here—Drugs,*

Money, Graveyard Robbery! A Drug Addict's Insane Ideas to Keep from Being DopeSick!

"*Or Else Is Here?*" Bauer repeated, trying to grasp the gist of Dominici's title. Then, looking up with a wide grin, Bauer, who purports to be "a world-class collector of Jewish jokes good, bad, and indifferent," said, "Oh. Now I get it. *Or Else Is Here.* You either do this, or else. You didn't do it, so now *Or Else Is Here!* A marvelous concept, I think. *A very Jewish concept.*" In a way, he said, Dominici's title also described the history of the State of Israel. "Or else is *always* here."

When I met Bauer at the Y, the Israeli invasion of Hamas-ruled Gaza was still weeks away but clearly in the wind. Hamas had been firing rockets into Israeli territory with increasing frequency. Reaction by the IDF was inevitable. "The Army will go in there because it will be seen as necessary and they will do it with great popular support," Bauer said. Despite his long involvement with the now marginalized left-wing Israeli "peace" parties like Mapam and Meretz, Bauer could see no other way of looking at the realpolitik of the situation. He had no doubt about what he called the "genocidal mind-set toward the Jewish people" on the part of Hamas and other radical Islamic groups. "What do you say to people who claim to prefer you were dead?" he asked. This threat worked both ways, added Bauer. In 2003 he had caused something of a stir when he said that in the armed conflict between the Israelis and Palestinians, "if one side becomes stronger, there is a chance of genocide." Asked by shocked observers if he was really suggesting that the State of Israel might be capable of committing genocide against the Palestinians, Bauer, professor of the Holocaust, said, "Yes."

Five years later, the Israeli situation was no better. Relations with the Palestinians had reached a numbing antipathy on both sides; the rise of Muslim fundamentalism with its eliminationist rhetoric had only grown louder and more dangerous. Ahmadinejad was hosting meetings in Tehran to deny the Holocaust. Throughout western Europe, hostility toward Israel, especially on the left, was often translated to mean anti-Semitism in many quarters. Inside Israel itself, the liberal, secular society envisioned by many of the *yishuv,* the early Zionist settlers, kibbutzim idealists who'd fought to establish a nation, was under siege. Many intellectuals had left the country. To live in Jerusalem now was "to be squeezed by various fundamentalists on all sides," Bauer said, including the ever-growing community of the ultra-Orthodox, or Haredi, members of the various Hasidic sects, each with their own rebbes, who would throw stones at your car if they saw you driving on the Sabbath.

One of Bauer's most penetrating essays, "Theology, or God the Surgeon," critiques Haredi attitudes toward the Holocaust, describing what he calls "the convoluted arguments" used by the ultra-Orthodox to explain how an all-powerful, all-merciful Lord could allow his chosen people to endure such a travail. Sweeping away the "elementary" notion advanced by some rebbes that humans are simply "too puny" to understand the methodology of the Deity, Bauer focuses on the often-voiced Haredi view that the Holocaust was God's punishment upon the Jews for falling from the strict path of the Torah. As an illustration of this thinking, Bauer cites an "invented" parable employed by the late Lubavitcher rebbe Menachem Mendel Schneerson. Schneerson, still thought to be the *moshiach,* or messiah, by many followers despite his death in 1994, characterized the Holocaust as an operation by God, "the specialist surgeon" who cuts off a "hopelessly poisoned" limb in order to "save the life of the patient," i.e., "the Jewish people." Bauer is disgusted by what he calls this *mipnei khata'einu* "because of our sins" explanation for the death of almost fifty million people in World War II, only 10 percent of them Jews. To conjure a God so obsessed with the fate of the Jews is, Bauer argues, to remove the Holocaust from the realm of human history, thereby "absolving" the Third Reich of its crimes and assigning Adolf Hitler, whom Schneerson refers to as "a mad goy," the role of divinely appointed agent of mass murder.

It was in the context of talking about the Haredi influence in current Israeli society that Bauer broke the news to me that even with additional testing there was no chance Yad Vashem would take the

lampshade into its collection or store it on its premises. "They are prohibited by law from doing so," he explained, owing to an agreement
with the religious community that holds that human remains must be
buried according to the rituals that prepare the body for its final rest.

This brought me up short. I was aware of the Jewish law regarding human remains. It went back at least to the Pentateuch, with
who knew how much halachic amendment since. Back in New York
people were telling me not to worry about customs, the real danger
were the ultra-Orthodox, who, as one friend told me, "will hit you over
the head and bury the lampshade, and they won't be sending it to any
lab to see if it is real or not first." But I had no idea this attitude would
apply to a museum and learning center like Yad Vashem.

Noting my dismay, Bauer, while allowing that he might have mentioned this earlier, asked me what was wrong. Looking at me with a
stern impatience that seemed distinctly rabbinical, he wondered if
I'd really been listening when he was talking about the value of telling the lampshade story. Why had I bothered to go to Jerusalem in
the first place? Was this all I hoped to get out of this journey, an opportunity to have people from a museum lock this "symbolic object"
into a closet? Would that be a proper end to my inquiry regarding the
lampshade, the best end of the story I was telling?

"Do you want some advice?" he asked.

"When you see Avner Shalev," Bauer said, referring to my upcoming meeting with the head of Yad Vashem and the museum curators,
"don't bring up that business about seeing the spiritualist lady with
the cigars and the rum in New Jersey. And don't call the lampshade
by a name. Things like that are all right for me. For me this is all part
of the story. Mr. Shalev is an Army guy. He is very smart, but very
practical. He will want to hear what you say, but certain things will
make him wonder how serious you are. So be careful how you tell the
story, you'll get more out of him, believe me."

• • •

Yehuda Bauer was right about Avner Shalev. Director of Yad Vashem since 1993, Shalev retained the brusque but not unfriendly aspect of a military man, a bearing no doubt honed while taking part in the negotiation of the peace treaty with the Egyptians following the 1973 Yom Kippur war. Now seventy years old, a blocky man in a blue suit, he sat at a conference table along with Yehudit Shendar, the museum's senior art curator, and Haviva Peled-Carmeli, the senior artifacts curator. It was quite a high-level turnout to hear the story of a humble lampshade scavenged from a wrecked house in the aftermath of a New Orleans hurricane.

I gave them the whole spiel, from Skip Henderson's purchase of the lampshade all the way through. We discussed the DNA report. Questions were asked and answered. The lampshade sat on the conference table, a mute, stoic sentinel. "It is larger than I imagined," Peled-Carmeli finally said. Shalev was surprised at the design of the frame, which he called "somewhat artful." No one wanted to touch the thing. When I put it back into the box, everyone appeared to breathe easier.

The meeting was largely transactional. I got to tell the story of the lampshade to a highly prestigious, respectful audience. They got to listen and explain why they couldn't have anything to do with it. Yehudit Shendar said that while the lampshade was an interesting object, for Yad Vashem the most important thing was to follow good museum policy, which was based on solid research. "What matters is the provenance and dating," she explained. "Where did it come from and when? Everything here has to be Holocaust-related and one hundred percent proven."

Avner Shalev assumed the mediator position. While reiterating that there was no way Yad Vashem could accept the lampshade "legally or morally," he wondered if there was some way the museum might be able to aid me in my inquiry. More testing could be done, said Peled-Carmeli, perhaps some carbon 14 dating. She gave me a small folder of materials she'd put together, some Nuremberg transcripts and a picture of the Buchenwald Table.

A few minutes later the meeting was over. We exchanged cards, Peled-Carmeli saying she would call a few people to see about some testing. Avner Shalev thanked me for my "curiosity and persistence," wishing me good luck "in getting to the bottom of this lampshade story."

If Yad Vashem was not eager to get involved with the lampshade, Avi Domb, chief of DIFS, the Israeli police Division of Identification and Forensic Science, thought he might be able to help. I was given Domb's contacts by Joseph Almog, former head of DIFS and current director of the forensic chemistry department at the Casali Institute at Jerusalem's Hebrew University. I'd run into Almog, the inventor of a spray that turns red when coming in contact with urea nitrate, a compound often used in the construction of homemade bombs ("That way we catch them red-handed," he said), a few months earlier at the Marriott Hotel in New Orleans, where the International Association of Forensic Sciences was holding its convention. By chance, we were seated next to each other at a talk given by Clyde Snow, the forensic anthropologist who, among many other high-profile cases, identified the bones of Nazi doctor Josef Mengele.

I told Almog about the lampshade, said I was planning to come to Jerusalem, and asked him whom I should look up. "That's easy," Almog said. "Avi Domb. Avi sits in my old chair. He deals with strange things every day."

Domb came over to my hotel off Jabotinsky Street the morning of my meeting at Yad Vashem. A copy of *Haaretz* under his arm, Domb, fifty-five but tall and lean like a retired power forward, exuded that formidable action-hero model of Judaism not generally known back in the Queens of the 1950s. To us, Israelis, those unstooped sabras straight out of the Negev, seemed another species altogether with their sexy, hair-on-their-legs kibbutz girls and blazing Uzis. If Avi Domb did not present himself as a Promised Land hard-ass, you knew he could.

Sitting on the edge of the bed in my hotel room, Domb examined the lampshade with a wary confidence, then turned his attention to the Bode DNA report. He'd heard of the lab and knew they had done "good work" in the aftermath of 9/11. Still, it was possible to miss things. Perhaps "this lampshade has more to tell us about itself. Let's see if we can make it talk," he said.

"Give me a few days," Domb said. I wasn't in a rush to leave Jerusalem, was I?

No, I told Avi Domb: no rush.

The truth was, Jerusalem was giving me the heebie-jeebies. It had been going on for weeks, long before my arrival. The sensation began as a low-timbre but unmistakable uneasiness, a dull buzz, and slowly swelled to a borderline anxiety fit. It made no sense. After all, I'd been to Jerusalem before. I'd walked those ancient, narrow streets, been to the Western Wall, counted the Stations of the Cross, visited the Dome of the Rock. I knew the history, the six thousand years of possession and loss, during which the Holy City had been ruled, conquered, or occupied by Jebusites, Israelite kings, Arabs, Babylonians, Hittites, Persians, Philistines, Seleucids, Romans, Byzantines, Mamluks, Crusaders, Ottomans, and Brits, to say nothing of Alexander the Great and the Frankish Crusaders. The place was a power spot, all right; whatever was here, people wanted more of it. They never got enough. The array of belief, sublimation, and desire was all crammed together in a few thousand square yards.

The last time I was in the Holy City, in 1999, on the eve of the new millennium, local officials expected a large outbreak of the so-called Jerusalem syndrome, defined by doctors from the Kfar Shaul Mental Health Center in a paper published by the *British Journal of Psychiatry* as "a psychotic decompensation . . . related to religious excitement induced by proximity to the holy places of Jerusalem." From 1980 to 1993 more than twelve hundred people had been referred to Kfar Shaul for what were described as "severe, Jerusalem-generated mental problems." The symptoms fell into three basic types, the report explained: 1) Jerusalem syndrome superimposed on previous psychotic illness; 2) Jerusalem syndrome superimposed on and complicated by idiosyncratic ideations—such as when already religious people undergo sudden and radical conversions to other creeds; and 3) Jerusalem syndrome in a discrete form, uncomplicated by previous psychopathology. Considered to be "perhaps the most fascinating" by the report writers, this final category described people who "fall victim to a psychotic episode" while in Jerusalem, including "the need to scream, shout, or sing out loud psalms, verses from the Bible, or deliver a sermon in a holy place."

Given this data, it made sense that in late 1999, with incessant chatter of Y2K, there would be a serious outbreak of the syndrome. However, despite the increased number of people converging on the Holy City at the eve of the new millennium, the Kfar Shaul Center reported no appreciable rise in the number of Jerusalem syndrome cases. As one doctor told me then, "The calendar, which is made by men, says one thing, but Jerusalem keeps a time of its own."

With the comparatively quiet state of Palestinian-Israeli relations in 1999, it was no problem for the visitor to enter the Dome of the Rock on the Temple Mount, the spot from which Muhammad is said to have risen to heaven, or even walk among the faithful inside the massive Al-Aqsa Mosque. Crowds were everywhere, but after midnight, with the metal shutters of the candy and T-shirt merchants drawn, you could hear the sound of your footsteps on the ancient stones. Above, the stars were still there, fixed in the sky just as they were when King David viewed them nearly three millennia before.

A decade later, however, following Ariel Sharon's famously provocative visit to the Temple Mount in 2000 that helped spark the Second Intifada, 9/11, worldwide terror attacks, wars between Western and Muslim nations, Hamas in Gaza, the collapse of the "peace process"—the list goes on—Jerusalem seemed a far more forbidding place. In the Old City, pairs of IDF soldiers, rifles at the ready, patrolled the Beit Habad Road inside the Damascus Gate. The Islamic sites were off-limits; the Al-Aqsa, built in 705 CE, was no longer considered by many in the city a religious building but regarded as the headquarters of the Martyrs Brigade.

The Jerusalem syndrome was now pandemic. On Friday night, at the Western Wall, the young men davened, *paises* flying, black hats a blur. A Lubavitcher man had his cell phone pressed to the wall; over the phone speaker you could hear several voices, as many as a small congregation, praying. The people on the other side of the line could have been anywhere, as far off as Australia or Paraguay: like the Jesuits, the Chabad, the Lubavitch outreach project, was all over the globe now. But via satellite phone, their voices, the force of their devotion, coalesced in this spot.

The modern city was no more serene. All over were half-finished construction projects, stalled in the economic turndown. Buses were shrink-wrapped with the dour countenance of Arcadi Gaydamak, the self-made Russian oligarch who was running for mayor of Jerusalem. Best known for his alleged role in a gun-smuggling scandal in Angola, Gaydamak was spending millions. He barely spoke Hebrew, hence his campaign slogan, "He doesn't talk, he acts." When the buses covered with his ubiquitous ads sideswiped cars, as they often did, enraged drivers screamed they'd been "Gaydamaked." Even the weather was out of whack. One morning it snowed, not all that much, but it was only October.

"Chaotic times produce chaos," said Farid Abu Gosh, as we drove past the last checkpoint out of the city. Chairperson of the Trust of Programs for Early Childhood, Family and Community Education, Farid, a neatly attired man of sixty with an urbane, friendly manner who has been involved in "the social aid business" for going on three decades, had offered to give me "a short tour" of the West Bank.

I met Farid at the American Colony Hotel, the still elegant outpost in eastern Jerusalem. He had a "sentimental attachment" to the place, Farid said. "I used to come here when I was young, hopeful, and had some hair on my head . . . I could not afford it then and I cannot afford it now, but it brings back memories." The Trust works almost exclusively with West Bank Palestinians attempting to deal with rampant problems such as abuse of women and violence in schools, but Farid has always identified himself as "an Israeli Arab," an accurate description of his status as an Israeli citizen of Arab descent. He was born in 1949 near Abu Ghosh, the only Arabic-speaking town in the so-called Jerusalem Corridor, the disputed stretch between the coast and the Holy City, to remain neutral during the 1948 war. It is for that reason, most say, Abu Ghosh, where King David is said to have once abandoned the Ark of the Covenant, was not attacked by Jewish forces during the Israeli independence war and still exists today while surrounding Arab towns have long disappeared.

"Neutrality in the cause of survival is not to be underestimated," Farid said of his namesake hometown with the weary ease of a character in a Sidney Greenstreet film. "But it can be difficult to maintain, harder every day."

Fox News likely wouldn't refer to Farid's West Bank tour commentary as "fair and balanced," but the sights spoke for themselves. There were so many places like this, favelas in Rio, the slums of Mumbai, Central City in New Orleans—ramshackle pits of misery so close to yet so far from centers of great wealth. The West Bank, or at least the parts Farid chose to show me—the battered, unmaintained dirt roads, the abandoned buildings in Ramallah, the piles of garbage picked through by children and old men—was a derelict society, living on the margin. The new Jewish "settler" communities that continued to be built with their freshly paved blacktops and gated access only made the contrast more extreme.

Looming above it all was the wall, what is euphemistically known as the "West Bank Separation Security Barrier." Projected to stretch more than four hundred miles when finished, twenty feet high in some spots, with Sing Sing–style watchtowers, the wall was shockingly awful, a far more formidable and depressing presence than one might imagine from reading the *New York Times*. Plotted along the jagged, gerrymandered Green Line, one minute the wall was in front of you, the next it was behind. It surrounded you. If graffiti is defiance, there was plenty of that. Somewhere near East Jerusalem, "CTRL + ALT + DELETE" was scrawled in ten-foot-high letters, as if cosmic reboot were the only solution.

Farid and I drove through this ravaged zone talking of the lampshade. The lampshade story was "incredible," he said, yet here, on the edge of Ramallah, it made perfect sense to him.

"You know, I have visited Yad Vashem. Some years ago, as an Israeli Arab, a secular man, a nonpolitical man. I thought it the right thing to do." Farid described how he went through the exhibits, seeing "the terrible, terrible things the Germans did to the Jews." One thing that stuck with him was "how, in the end, after you have been through all that misery, you come out onto a patio where there is a fine view of the countryside. It was as if to say, we have suffered, the Jewish people have suffered the worst crimes, yet here is the reward, what God has promised us: the State of Israel, a land of milk and honey. What I want to know is, where is the Palestinian reward for *this* suffering? Where is our view of the Promised Land? This wall?

"People are always asking me how the Jews can act in such a way after what the Germans did to them. How can they do this to us? I understand what they are saying, but what gives anyone the idea that being brutalized teaches people not to brutalize others? It is too bad, but this is not human nature."

Farid said he often saw graffiti in which swastikas were painted inside Stars of David. "This is a tragedy. It is wrong to equate these two circumstances. But this is a violent place; the parents are disaffected. The children grow up angry, confused. When I hear them say the Jews are Nazis, I say calm down, I have been in this country my whole life, dealing with Israelis since birth. I have many good friends. The goal is to stay rational, do your job, provide some help. It can be a trying experience.

"But when you bring up this lampshade—making a lampshade out of a human being—this is an act of gratuitous cruelty. It is outside the general program. It is terror. Sheer terrorism. It makes me think of the stories one hears from Lebanon, the reports that the IDF places bombs inside of toys, which explode when the children pick them up. This is a similar thing."

I had heard these same stories, how bombs were secreted by Israeli forces inside soccer balls and dolls, but I thought that they had been proven to be false, a bit of heavy-handed propaganda.

"I didn't say this was positively true," Farid replied. "How would I know? I am not there. I am only saying that this is what many people believe. It is difficult to stand in the way of that. You know how these rumors start and become more powerful than the truth."

The ride back to Jerusalem was quick. It is barely a half-hour drive from Ramallah back to Jerusalem, and with Farid's blue *teudat zehut* ID card, getting through the checkpoints was a breeze. If his ID were green and his car had a Palestinian license plate, the same trip could have taken hours, if we'd have gotten through at all. "Another benefit of neutrality," Farid said.

• • •

Back at the hotel I fell asleep in my clothes before the sun went down and woke up at three in the morning, sweaty and jangled. The situation called out for Xanax but the six-foot walk to the bathroom seemed way too strenuous. I stayed in bed, scanning the room. I could see the lampshade sitting on the desk beside the television cabinet: Ziggy, in his snow white box, the crimson handle grayish in the gloom.

At Yad Vashem they wanted "provenance and dating," but this was a dodge; there was no way I would ever be able to trace the lampshade back to a specific concentration camp at a specific time. I had asked Yehuda Bauer if the murders of Ed Gein could be connected to the Holocaust, if the Wisconsin fiend got the idea to make human skin lampshades from reading articles about Ilse Koch. The professor said it would be "a persuasive argument." Not that this sort of cultural studies analysis was likely to pass museum muster. It was fine to adhere to strict standards of provenance and dating, but museums made mistakes all the time; the Museum of Natural History in New York had the wrong head on the *Apatosaurus* skeleton for fifty years. Besides, why should the lampshade be subject to more stringent proofing than some of the most famous pilgrimage spots in Jerusalem?

It was a city of fakes, full of the unreliable, the unprovable.

One afternoon I went up to the Chamber of the Holocaust, a small museum on Mount Zion at the southern edge of the Old City, where I'd been told they had a lampshade on display. Among the first assemblages of Shoah-related objects in Jerusalem, the "Chamber" lived up to its name. A dank series of cavelike rooms below an Orthodox yeshiva, the place had a musty, subterranean feel, as if the Golem were crouching in the next passageway.

"You want what?" came the voice from behind me. It was Aharon S., a pasty-faced man wearing the sort of wide-brimmed fedora usually associated with the Lubavitch Hasidim. Formerly of Brooklyn, Aharon, who could have been any age under fifty, identified himself as "the only watchman and curator" currently employed by the

Chamber of the Holocaust. I asked him if he had a lampshade in his collection.

"We don't have the lampshade. We have the soap."

"You have soap?"

"Soap from Jews. Soap and ashes. From the Holocaust. It is in there." He put down the old-style heavy black telephone receiver he'd been screaming into and pointed to the dark hallway leading to the exhibit halls. "I cannot accompany you to the soap. You will have to go alone. I can't go into that room. I am a *Kohen*."

This meant that, as a Jew whose patrilineal line could be reputedly traced back to Moses's brother Aaron, Aharon was a member of Judaism's priestly caste, descended from those who were thought to have conducted services in the Temple. The *Kohanim* are subject to a vast number of rules and practices aimed at preserving ritual purity, including a prohibition of proximity to the dead. They must not touch the deceased or enter any space in which a dead body or part of a dead body may be found.

I wandered through the mazelike rooms of the museum. The place felt like a cluttered basement, a scary place down creaky steps filled with piles of regrettable things better kept from the light of day. Devoid of the professional curatorial hand, the exhibits had an uneven, homemade quality. A series of famous photos from the camps and the Warsaw Ghetto, cut from magazines and haphazardly taped to poster board, sat beside remarkable items such as a jacket made from Torah parchment, supposedly fitted by Jewish tailors on the orders of a Nazi officer. A number of grotto-like rooms contained marble tablets commemorating the names and places of shuls and congregations destroyed by the Nazis. There were hundreds of these irregularly sized plaques with names of vanished, forgotten communities like Abgustov, Adalin, Adan, Bacav, Backa-Palanka, Bacsalmas, Cakovec, Chamatiz, Chanuzev. It went on and on, a succession that numbed the mind with loss and sorrow. Here, in the claustrophobic chambers, with the unswept floors, broken pipes, and mildew, you returned to a sort of Jewishness that must have haunted Kafka, with all the poverty, superstition, fear, and unwelcoming strangeness typically edited out of museums set in buildings designed by I. M. Pei.

Finally I came around to the soap and the ashes. Bearing the inscription "From Jews whose dying words proclaimed their faith in the Almighty," the soap, surrounded by a dozen or so striped porcelain urns affixed with a red star, was piled up inside a long-unwashed glass cabinet about a foot high. Dark gray, the stuff looked petrified. It could have been chunks of anything. I took a picture and went outside, where Aharon sat talking with a few old men.

"The soap," I said. "Did they ever have that tested?"

Aharon squinted. "Tested? What for?" he asked.

"To see if it is real."

"Of course it is real. The rebbe says it is real."

"The rebbe is a scientist? You know, they say soap made from Jews is a myth. That there's no such thing."

"Who says that?"

"At Yad Vashem they say that. I was just there."

"Yad Vashem! Don't talk to me about Yad Vashem!" He got up and summoned me to follow him. He led me out the gate and into the vestibule of the yeshiva around the corner.

"I can't talk in front of those people," Aharon said hurriedly. He had some things he wanted to tell me but first needed to know whom he was dealing with. Examining my card, he placed his fingertips against his forehead, marshaling his thoughts.

"You are Jewish, so I will tell you. You cannot listen to what Yad Vashem says. It is full of Germans."

I wasn't aware of the German influence at Yad Vashem.

"Who do you think gives out all the big grants for Holocaust research? Germans. The Germans decide what will come out and what won't. Not everything. But a lot. *A lot.* That's why they say what they say about the soap and other things. I have done a lot of research on this. I could send it to you. You could write an article. An exposé."

Aharon scribbled his email address on the brochure for the

Chamber of the Holocaust, placed it in my hand, and ran back inside. Without him, he said, no one was available to watch the museum.

Almost directly across the narrow Mount Zion Street, a busload of English tourists was queued up in front of the Tomb of David. A staple on sightseeing tours, the tomb, formerly used as both a Byzantine church and a French monastery, is an old building even by Jerusalem standards. It was in the twelfth century CE, during the Crusades, that the place was first declared to be David's tomb, in other words, about two thousand years after the erstwhile shepherd boy supposedly killed Goliath. However, there is no proof as to the veracity of this claim. No scientific documentation has been attempted on the contents of the coffin, nor is there any definitive evidence that any body, let alone David's, was ever buried here. But that does not stop the crowds from filing into the building, pausing to deposit a few shekels into the venerable *tzedakah* donation box, and snapping copious photos of the blue-velvet-draped sarcophagus.

This was the syndrome throughout the Holy City, where the dialectic between science and belief, truth and faith, went blooey. The sacred, supposedly absolute, eternal, unchanging I Am was instead a movable, protean thing. It was in the eye of the beholder, expanding like air to fill the space. What, for instance, are the chances that the so-called Stone of the Anointing inside the Church of the Holy Sepulchre is really the same rock where Jesus' body was prepared for burial? The church itself was severely damaged in a fire in 614 and again in 966; the present stone only appeared in its current spot in 1808. Yet people still come, they still lean over the rock, shed their tears upon it. How much of that belief has to be directed before a regular rock, a dumb piece of geology, is transformed into a holy slab, floating through outer space like the monolith that ennobled the tribe of apes in *2001: A Space Odyssey*?

I looked at the lampshade, sitting in its box on the desk in my darkened Jerusalem hotel room. Since the thing had arrived at my door in Brooklyn, I'd been attempting to find out who and what it was. And now that I was in a place where a rock can be said to become divine simply because enough people wish it to be so, I could feel the questions I'd been asking about the lampshade turned back on myself. Was this part of the Jerusalem syndrome, to imagine that a human skin lampshade was capable of administering the third degree to its supposed keeper? Who knew, but certain questions of identity suddenly felt unusually pressing.

Farid Abu Gosh, the Arab Israeli, said there was no getting around it: when there's a wall, inevitably, no matter the color of your identity card, you will be asked which side you are on. Years ago the late Jack Newfield, a treasured friend and mentor who in his reportorial calling lived by the Old Testament credo "An eye and an ear for an eye," said, "Don't back down, speak your mind, but when the topic of Israel comes up, play dumb, because whatever you say, *it just won't be worth it.*"

This remains good advice in Greenwich Village. Except here I was, in *Eretz Yisrael,* and a surprising thing had happened. I'd gone to the West Bank, found conditions there to be more miserable than I had imagined—more miserable, in fact, than many of my sweet liberal, Palestinian-supporting buddies back in New York had presented them to be—and I returned to Jerusalem with a newfound sympathy for the Israelis.

This didn't mean I wanted to move into a settlement financed by some Bokharan oligarch, vote for Benjamin Netanyahu, or become an acolyte of Rabbi Ovadia Yosef, spiritual leader of the ultra-Orthodox Shas Party, who said Hurricane Katrina was "God's retribution" for a lack of Torah study in the area and because black people "have no God." But I did attend a pleasant *Shabbos* lunch at the home of Robby Berman in the nice proto-yuppie neighborhood off Emek Refaim Street.

I had met Berman in New York at a lecture he was giving on behalf of the Halachic Organ Donor Society (HODS). A Harvard Kennedy School graduate who prefers to ride a bike and doesn't mind sleeping on floors, Berman, HODS founder and president, is engaged in a campaign to encourage religious Jews to donate vital organs despite the widespread teaching that Jewish law forbids the practice. He also seeks to alter religious thinking on the moment of death. Many Orthodox rabbis maintain that the body can only be said to be dead when the heart stops beating. Berman counters by saying this is often too late to save other organs, arguing instead that "brain stem death"—the moment when the body stops functioning of its own accord—should be accepted as the end of life. Another issue that came up all the time, he said, was who should get these donated organs. "People say they'll donate, but it has to go to a Jew." These were thorny problems, Berman said, but what it came down to was "when is a Jew dead, and who should control his body when that occurs."

These questions seemed intriguing, so when Berman called me to say he was inviting me to *Shabbos* lunch and that several interesting people would be there, it was easy to say yes. It was a good thing, too, being at Robby Berman's house for *Shabbos* and spending several hours talking to Uriel Simon, the seventy-eight-year-old professor emeritus of biblical studies at Bar-Ilan University and longtime peace advocate, about whether God's obsessive call to Saul to kill all the Amalekites and "to blot out the memory of Amalek from under heaven" constituted true genocide or not. It seemed a perfectly normal conversation to be having on a Saturday afternoon, pretty much the conversation I would be having at *Shabbos* lunch if I were a liberal-minded Israeli, hard-pressed to keep morally and politically sane in present-day Jerusalem.

Yeah, I said to myself later on, in my hotel bed, when people are building walls, barriers that must be adhered to regardless of what you might think of their legitimacy and legality, choices eventually must be made. Perhaps it was cowardice, or sheer convenience, but you go where you're wanted. It wasn't that I couldn't imagine a Palestinian inviting me to lunch, even *Shabbos* lunch. It just didn't seem like it was going to happen, not here, not now.

But was that really enough? "What do you think, Zig?" I addressed the lampshade. "That enough to make you draw the line, between us and them?"

It was such a drag the way particularism had all the logic on its side. This was just the way things worked. But I didn't like it. To accept a wall was to accept the iron gate shutting behind you at Buchenwald: *Jedem Das Seine,* to each his own. But you didn't have to give in, did you? No, you didn't. You could keep yourself open, a citizen of the universe.

"Isn't that right, Ziggy?"

I don't know how long this went on, but I must have fallen asleep eventually because the sunlight was streaming through the curtains when the phone rang and woke me up. It was Avi Domb. His forensic people hadn't been able to find out anything new about the lampshade. "I'm sorry about this," Domb said. "I honestly thought we could make some progress. But apparently we can't beat what you already have. Your lab is good. My person said, 'If this was our case, we might have had to send it someplace like that ourselves.' So it looks like the lampshade will have to remain a mystery a while longer."

He apologized again, wished me a good trip home, and hung up.

A couple of nights later, having purchased a number of "Guns and Moses" and "Uzi Does It" T-shirts in the Old City market, I was at the airport with the lampshade. It was the usual Israeli security question-and-answer period. A sweet-looking woman in her twenties asked me where I was from, if I was bar mitzvahed, and at what temple. Then she handed me off to another group of officers who did their visual scans of the luggage and asked if I was in the antique business. I told them no.

"You always travel with lampshades?" one officer asked, with a smile that told me lying was useless.

"Just this one."

FOURTEEN

The idea that the lampshade should be buried in New Orleans took hold in the days before the third anniversary of Katrina's landfall.

After months of delay, the city was rushing to finish a memorial to the hurricane victims at the north end of Canal Street, in the section of the old Charity Hospital Cemetery formerly used as the municipal potter's field. It was here, at the last stop of the streetcar marked "Cemeteries," that the last eighty-two unidentified or unclaimed storm victims would find their final rest.

The journey "home," as they say, had not been easy or quick for these mostly anonymous souls. In early 2006, five months after the storm, the dead were stored inside refrigerator trucks at the large federal morgue near St. Gabriel in Iberville Parish, seventy miles west of New Orleans. The feds were pushing to bury these bodies in a four-acre field out in the Cajun countryside, but Mayor C. Ray Nagin protested. "I told them we cannot be burying New Orleanians outside of New Orleans," Nagin said. Turned over to the city, the unclaimed corpses were moved to a downtown warehouse where they would remain for the better part of the next two years. Eventually, after much discussion and alleged foot-dragging, enough public and private money was raised to build the Canal Street memorial, which consisted of six black granite mausoleums arranged about a central circle built to represent the eye of a hurricane.

The burial ceremony, timed to coincide with the Katrina anniversary, would be split into two sections. On the first day the vast majority of the bodies, seventy-five of them, would be interred. According to the planners, primarily a consortium of largely black-owned funeral homes in conjunction with Frank Minyard's coroner's office, this was to be a "semi-private" occasion. Local press were not invited. The next day was scheduled as the public section of the program. The remaining seven bodies would be laid to rest amid solemn municipal fanfare under the banner of the "One New Orleans," a city hall initiative largely deemed to be a government-funded promotional vehicle for Mayor Nagin, who was scheduled make the keynote speech.

Aimed at providing what the mayor called "some closure to this challenging chapter in the history of our great city," the memorial was subject to last-minute uncertainty. This being the season, another storm, Gustav, was making its way into the Gulf of Mexico. As Nagin made clear, the new tempest had the potential to make Katrina seem like a mere capful of wind. Calling Gustav quite possibly "the storm of the century, the mother of all storms," Nagin announced that he would be ordering a mandatory evacuation along with a dawn-to-dusk curfew. With reminders of the Katrina disaster still present throughout the city, few residents, even those prone to drunken bravado, were talking of riding out this new storm.

"Katrina and Gustav, together again in unholy matrimony," Skip Henderson cried out as he went about triaging his dwindling number of prized possessions in preparation for fleeing the beloved city yet again. "Why don't they just call them Adolf and Eva? Nazi hurricanes!"

As Gustav's deadly vortex churned northward through the Gulf, August 28, 2008, dawned clear and hot in New Orleans. It was barely seven a.m. and the temperature was already past eighty. On upper Canal Street, lined up as far as the eye could see, sat long, black hearses, idling in the early morning sun, air conditioners humming. The few drivers standing outside their vehicles, attired in their black funeral suits and peaked caps, dabbed away sweat with oversized white handkerchiefs. An edge was in the air, with everyone anxious to send these last victims of Katrina to a better place before the next fresh batch of Hell hit. Yet there was a holdup. The landscapers hired to prepare the memorial weren't quite finished. They'd worked through the night, under floodlights, but there was still plenty of sod to lay.

That was post-Katrina New Orleans for you, said Stephanie Rhodes-Navarre, as we sat talking in her charming apartment on upper Esplanade Avenue. "Poor souls out in the wilderness for three years, and these fools are putting down grass."

Sharp as a tack and stylish with a blond rinse on her short-cropped Afro, Ms. Rhodes-Navarre, along with her three sisters, Sandra Rhodes-Duncan, Joan Rhodes, and Kathleen Rhodes-Astorga, own the Rhodes Funeral Home. Founded by Duplain W. Rhodes, in 1884, operated by their father, Duplain W. Rhodes Jr., for five decades, the Rhodes Home remains among New Orleans's most iconic family businesses, thanks in no small part to the status of the funeral home in the African-American community. In places like New Orleans, death was as segregated as everything else, making undertaking a singular pathway to social and monetary success for an ambitious black businessman.

"The fact is," Stephanie said, "black people just don't do death like white people. A white person dies, and at least as far as the funeral part is concerned, it is a two-day thing. Black people need more than that. They have to have a week, even more. In New Orleans it is more complicated. There are all kinds of special family requests. Some might need a jazz funeral. This isn't just for show. They *need* these things and it is our job to give it to them. That's why we have to have a closer relationship with our clientele. People know us and we know them, for generations. We're not just someone you get out of the phone book at the last minute and we show up at the door with a shovel."

This was why, Stephanie said, the Rhodeses and the other famous funeral families, the Charbonnets, the Labats, the Glapions—a large portion of the "aristocracy" of Creole New Orleans—banded together with other black undertakers around the state to "make sure this Katrina burial happened, and it happened *the right way* . . . because this has been a nightmare, from even *before* the storm came ashore."

Three years on, the episode continued to haunt and infuriate her. "We had twelve funerals booked for those days, which meant there were several bodies already in house, aboveground. But once Katrina came, we couldn't get them buried. Everyone—the grave diggers, the cemetery people—were getting out. Then came the floods. What were we supposed to do then? But when people leave their loved one to you, that is a bond that must be taken seriously. When everyone was running for their lives, we were trying to save the dead."

This meant, Stephanie said, keeping the bodies out of the water and transporting the ones who couldn't be buried in New Orleans to the Rhodes Facility in Baton Rouge. "We stayed in the funeral home for twenty-one straight days, my family and our staff. Every day we dressed in our normal business clothes because you've got to provide confidence, make people understand that no matter what happens, you are going to remain professional, that we are going on.

"What I'm talking about here is not just business but continuity between life and death. You can't separate those two things. If you ask me, that was one of the main things that went wrong during Katrina: making everyone leave, keeping them out of town for weeks. It was that displacement that cut the cord a lot of people had with New Orleans. There's lots of people who now live in Atlanta. Ask them where's their home and they'll say New Orleans, but they're in Atlanta. That's the real disaster, because things like Katrina had happened before, maybe not as bad, but we never left, and we survived. We would have survived this, too."

It was during this period that the Rhodes family and others in the New Orleans undertaker community met with state and federal officials in Baton Rouge to talk about what to do with the Katrina dead, several of whom were still locked in attics or floating in the flood-waters.

"We sat down with people from Governor Blanco's office, and Louis Cataldie, the state medical examiner," Stephanie said. "It was like talking to the wall. I thought it would be obvious: we're from New Orleans, we *know* New Orleans, we've been dealing with New Orleans dead for a hundred years. Once we tried to explain what could be done and how much it would cost, they threw up their hands and said, 'Oh, so this is about money.' I was shocked that they would think that. As if we were trying to make a buck off the misery of people we grew up with. The next thing I know they've hired Kenyon, from Houston, it's a done deal. What a mess. In Iraq they might have had Halliburton, but here in New Orleans we had Kenyon."

Stephanie Rhodes-Navarre was alluding to charges of cronyism involving Kenyon International's then parent company, Service Corporation International (SCI), the Texas-based "end-of-life" concern, which under its various "Dignity" brands owns more than half of all funeral homes and cemeteries in America. This success has no doubt been aided by the political connections of Robert Waltrip, the long-time (four decades and counting) CEO of SCI. A venerable member of the Bush family inner circle of financial backers, Waltrip has contributed mightily to the presidential library of George H. W. Bush as well as the gubernatorial and presidential campaigns of George W. Bush. Despite this access to power, many claimed SCI's performance during Katrina left much to be desired.

In the fractious two months of Kenyon's employment by the State of Louisiana, the company recovered a total of 535 bodies, for which it charged $6 million, or over $11,000 per body. Expensed items such as $14,000 for beef jerky raised eyebrows. According to many relief workers, Kenyon's $800-a-day "search and recovery specialists," while expert in such incidents as plane crashes, were unfamiliar with New Orleans; mistakes in noting where bodies were found made identification more difficult. There was also the question of why the state would do business with SCI to begin with, or if it was even aware of Kenyon's parent company's legal troubles. In December 2003, the firm agreed to a payment of $100 million to settle a case involving mishandling of the dead at two Jewish cemeteries they owned in Florida. According to the suit, SCI employees routinely buried people in the wrong place, broke open vaults, and in some instances removed bones from gravesites and tossed them into maintenance yards.

On August 28, 2008, with the Rhodes family running things, the burial of Katrina's last victims came off without a hitch. One by one the hearses pulled up to the arched wrought-iron gateway of Charity Hospital Cemetery and dispatched their cargo. The metal caskets, each topped with a single red rose, were wheeled up the bank of mausoleums. Behind the pallbearers marched a six-piece brass band led by local legend Lionel Batiste, a sticklike man of indeterminate age wearing a sash saying "Jolly Bunch" and twirling a cane. When the coffin was positioned in one of the drawers of the mausoleum—a modified version of the "oven vault" tomb often accorded poor people in New Orleans—the band began to play the spiritual "Just a Closer Walk with Thee." Once the coffin was pushed into its space, a board was affixed to the open end of the mausoleum, the seams caulked with plastic sealant pumped from industrial-sized tubes. The board was then covered with a granite slab, which was screwed into place.

When the last of the bodies were pushed into the mausoleum, Stephanie Rhodes-Navarre's sister Joan, who'd been up since four in the morning, took a deep breath. "It went good," she pronounced, looking exhausted. "Everyone got their flower, everyone got their music."

As people were packing up, I chatted with the trumpeter from the band, whose standard brass band cap was emblazoned with the word TREME above the visor. Asked how many times he'd played "Just a Closer Walk with Thee" in his life, he said, "Damn, I just done it a hundred times today. Altogether, might be a million." Did he ever get tired of it? He shook his head.

"Why should I get tired of it? If you're playing funerals, sending people home, what *would* you play but 'Just a Closer Walk with Thee'? That's the gig, man."

Funeral band for Katrina's unclaimed dead, August 28, 2008

Now that Washington and Jerusalem had rejected the shade, there was a case to be made that it belonged in New Orleans, along with the rest of the unclaimed. This topic had come up earlier in the day, when I ran into Frank Minyard, the parish coroner, who was serving as the president of the Katrina Memorial effort. Scheduled to speak and play his trumpet the next day at the public ceremony, Minyard had come over "to pay my respects." Attired in an electric blue shirt and baggy nautical pants, the coroner had a wraithlike aspect to him as he beckoned me toward a lone gravestone just inside the cemetery's iron gate.

"I have often wondered, for fifty years I wondered," Minyard said in his slow drawl, "whatever happened to those cadavers we used to dissect back in school. You know, a cadaver is very important to a young medical student. Sometimes you'd take a piece home. A hand, or even a whole arm, so you could look at the insertion of the tendons, things like that. You didn't want anyone to see you on the streetcar with it, but you cared about your cadavers. You became attached to them, even gave them names. And now, I see, here they are."

Minyard pointed to a monument erected by the Bureau of Anatomical Services honoring those "who have donated their bodies to science."

The coroner took a moment before asking, "So did you ever find out more information about that lampshade?"

I briefly filled Minyard in on all that had happened since we'd last talked, and I told him that with so many other options off the table, I was thinking of burying the lampshade in accordance with Jewish religious law.

"Burying it here in New Orleans?" Minyard said, rolling the idea around in his head. "Well," he said, "this is the end of the river. Biggest river system on earth, things carried along with the current from as far off as Montana. A lot does get buried here."

Then Minyard spoke of the coming storm, Gustav, remarking that the weather reminded him of the days immediately before Katrina. He asked me if I was getting out of town. I said I had a flight back to New York, but if the airport closed, I'd drive to Houston and fly from there. Minyard said that sounded all right. "Just make sure you go."

It was something to think about as I walked across Canal Street to the old Jewish cemetery, called the Dispersed of Judah, a phrase that appears often in the literature of exile, most prophetically, according to many Christian Zionists, in Isaiah 11:12, where God, after speaking metaphorically of an anointed "branch" that will grow from the roots of the tree of Jesse, informs the prophet of his plan to "assemble the outcasts of Israel," to "gather together the dispersed of Judah from the four corners of the earth."

Opened in 1846, the cemetery differs from the other, better-known New Orleans Cities of the Dead in that the bodies are buried in the dirt rather than in aboveground crypts and mausoleums. Like using biodegradable, nail-free pine boxes as coffins, this Jewish practice, devised in a desert land many thousands of miles from the soggy swamps of the Mississippi Delta, is based on the notion that the body, like dust, should eventually return to the earth from whence it came.

Even with Gustav still two hundred miles out into the Gulf, the gravestones at the Dispersed of Judah, mute witnesses to so many storms, had a forlorn aspect. A few flowers might have spruced things up, but not many people place flowers on the graves of people who died in 1867. Certain names came up again and again on the lichen-stained headstones. Present were several members of the D'Meza family, who like Judah Touro were descendants of the first waves of Spanish and Portuguese Sephardim expelled from Europe during the Inquisition. There was the large monument for Abraham D'Meza, dutifully noted as the "president of this congregation," and his wife Zipporah, dead within two months of each other in 5632, or 1872. A far smaller stone marked the grave of Estelle D'Meza, aged ten months, who succumbed during the influenza outbreak of 1878, or 5640. Also well represented was the Marks family, once of the London Jewish community. Monuments noted the graves of Joseph Hart Marks, David Hart Marks, Theodore Marks, Edwin Marks, Marion Marks, and Washington Marks, all of whom enlisted on the Confederate side during the Civil War. Washington Marks, a colonel and later a Democratic party politician, so distinguished himself at the Battle of Vicksburg that a statue was erected in his honor.

So this was where these Jews, these particular dispersed of Judah, their families hounded across the globe, residents of the Louisiana once governed by *le Code Noir,* which decreed practicing Hebrews be banished, had found their final rest. If Jews turned up in the most incongruous places in the world, so did their dead. Yet, after Buchenwald, Auschwitz, and the rest, it is a blessing to see the graves of a thousand Jews who weren't dead from violence between 1933 and 1945. Confederate or not, these Jews, like my dead relatives in Elmont, New York, had gotten through an entire lifetime without being murdered by a Nazi.

Yes, I thought, if I were a human skin lampshade who might or might not have been constructed by a doomed Jewish shoemaker at the behest of a mad red-haired woman on a horse, and then found sixty years later by a dope fiend in an abandoned house after the worst storm in United States history, there could be worse places to return to the earth than inside the gates of the Dispersed of Judah. Being right across the streetcar tracks from the monument to Katrina's unclaimed, the spot made a good deal of sense.

Shiya Ribowsky, the forensic cantor and my adviser on Jewish clerical matters, told me that if I truly wanted to bury the lampshade, I might as well find an Orthodox rabbi "just to be on the safe side." Who knew what the Reformists and the like believed in a place like New Orleans? They were probably holding crawfish boils as some kind of Lenten ecumenical outreach program. If the Orthodox rabbi had any Halachic issues, Shiya said, I should inquire about the possibility of burying the lampshade along with *shaymos*—sacred ritual objects like tallis prayer shawls and tefillin phylacteries that, being inscribed with the name of G-d, were to be interred with the same respect as the human body.

"Ask them if they can put it in with the *shaymos,* mention the building fund, and you should be fine," counseled Shiya, offering to fly down to New Orleans to sing the mourner's Kaddish at the burial ceremony.

The Orthodox rabbi selection in New Orleans is not extensive, but the choice of Rabbi Uri Topolosky, the energetic thirtysomething installed as the spiritual leader of the Beth Israel temple in 2007, was obvious from the start. For one thing, Beth Israel was the congregation most affected by Hurricane Katrina. Founded in 1904, it was once the largest Orthodox temple in the South, observing the High Holy Days in a lavish Byzantine Revival synagogue on Carondelet Street. The congregation moved to the "safe" Lakeview section in the 1960s, where temple membership had declined to a hundred families by the time the storm surge from Lake Pontchartrain left ten feet of water in their Canal Boulevard shul. Fearing for the fate of its seven Torahs, the temple contacted representatives of ZAKA, the Jerusalem-based emergency response unit (the name in Hebrew stands for "Disaster Victim Identification"). In Israel, ZAKA volunteers have become a familiar sight in the aftermath of terror attacks and other disasters, collecting body parts and spilled blood of Jews to ensure they receive a proper religious burial. (In Jerusalem I'd called them to see what they had to say about the lampshade and was told, "If it is Jewish, it should be buried. If it is not Jewish, it can also be buried, but we're not involved.") The group, which also rescues sacred materials, arrived in New Orleans via National Guard helicopter to retrieve Beth Israel's holy scrolls, which they whisked away in motorized inflatable boats. Its temple ruined, Beth Israel, minus nearly half its congregation, had no choice but to accept temporary quarters at the Gates of Prayer, a Reform temple in Metairie, the district David Duke had once represented in the state legislature. It was then, their rabbi opting to remain in Tennessee, that Beth Israel hired Uri Topolosky, who had been an assistant rabbi in the Riverdale section of the Bronx.

I first saw Rabbi Uri in a picture on the Internet. *Kippah* on his thick mat of black hair, his young son in his arms, a huge smile on his face, Topolosky was talking with a full-headdressed Mardi Gras Indian. They seemed a good match, since the Mardi Gras Indians—black people dressed as Indians who famously sing and shout on Fat Tuesday—were, like Topolosky's congregation, a dwindling bunch. With 30 percent of the Jewish population gone following the storm, Beth Israel was participating in an appeal to get Jews to move to New Orleans. Thirty thousand dollars in interest-free loans and half-price tuition at Hebrew school were among the financial incentives offered newcomers. Meanwhile, the Mardi Gras Indians, key to the town's carnival tradition, were suffering demographic problems of their own. Between hip-hop and the crime situation, fewer and fewer young people wanted to spend the twenty weekends or so it took to sew the ornate parade costumes that when finished weigh as much as seventy-five pounds. Many Indians had died recently. Just months before Katrina, Allison "Tootie" Montana, the eighty-three-year-old leader of the Yellow Pocahontas "tribe," the Big Chief of all Big Chiefs, appeared at the New Orleans City Council to decry what he called the NOPD campaign to "wipe out" the Indians, just as the real Native Americans of the area—the Chitimacha, the Acolapissa, and the Atakapa—had been wiped out. Chief Tootie barely got the sentence "This has got to stop!" out of his mouth when he suddenly clutched his chest and died of a heart attack on the spot. The Rhodes family handled the funeral, one of their biggest ever. As a musician himself who likes to call attention to the similarities between the raucousness of Mardi Gras and Purim, Rabbi Uri said he was "terribly saddened" to hear of Chief Tootie's passing.

From his "Okay, let's tee it up" invitation to his tiny congregation to begin the somewhat laid-back but still stirringly pious Friday-night services, where a Walmart-style screen separates the bare minyan of older men from the ladies, there was a lot to like about Rabbi Uri and what he called "modern Orthodoxy in the context of New Orleans lagniappe." Rejecting the Shas Party idea that God had unleashed Katrina on New Orleans because of its paucity of Torah readers, Rabbi Uri said, "If Katrina is a divine disaster, then there is nothing to be done about it because we, as people, cannot know why God does what he does. Only a maniac would claim to know the mind of the Creator. But this was really a human disaster. The levees failed; they failed for several reasons, human reasons, which is why we are in control of how to respond."

This sounded like someone who might consider presiding over the burial of the human skin lampshade. When I went to visit Rabbi Uri in his Metairie office, after a momentary shock he said, "I don't see why I couldn't do it. It is a probable body remnant. I'll look over the texts to see if there is anything preventing it." The *shaymos* idea was a potentially good one, Rabbi Uri said, "but I don't know about a second line. I'll check into the Halacha on brass bands to see if it is appropriate. I kind of doubt it, but you never know."

Standing amid the graves of the Dispersed of Judah Cemetery, that more or less settled it, at least for a moment, I thought. Intellectually and practically, the lampshade could pass back into the earth in this place. I'd been halfway around the world with it. I'd done my part.

That was the working plan: to bury the lampshade in a Jewish cemetery, have Rabbi Uri and Shiya Ribowsky do the service, invite those who wanted to be there, and create the sort of "closure," however artificial, that Mayor Nagin and every other politician liked to prattle on about when it became obvious that events were out of control and they had no clue what to do next. Skip Henderson, as part owner of the shade, was okay with the idea as long as the thing wasn't buried in his backyard for his dog to dig up. "I can't have Tina coming over in the middle of the night panting with it between her teeth like 'Look what I found.'" A New Orleans funeral wasn't a perfect end, but it was an end, and if the lampshade was more of a story than anything else, as Yehuda Bauer suggested, it had to stop sometime.

But there were snags, loose ends that couldn't be ignored, which Dr. Volkhard Knigge, director of the Buchenwald Memorial, pointed out to me when I went to see him on a cold winter day in early 2009. Born in 1954 in Westphalia, son of a Lutheran priest, Dr. Knigge described his childhood surroundings as "a kind of deadening boredom, full of oppressive piousness." The atmosphere changed during the 1968 demonstrations, when all of Europe "seemed to come back to life." Seeing young people in the streets, saying what was not supposed to be said, convinced Knigge that "there were other kinds of angels in the world, another kind of heaven." He went off to the university, where he studied Lacanian psychology, began to travel, married an Israeli artist, worked with Lutz Niethammer on an extensive German oral history project, and became the director of the Buchenwald Memorial in 1994. Owing to his longtime involvement with the camp, along with his customary attire of a black hat, long black coat, black shirt, and black jeans, Knigge has a reputation as something of a melancholy fellow. At least this was the impression I'd gotten from Hans Ottomeyer, the general director of the Deutsches Historisches Museum in Berlin.

I'd spoken to Professor Ottomeyer, a robust, red-faced man with a grand helping of metallic gray hair, on the recommendation of a friend who had met him at a gala in Berlin. According to my confidant, when the conversation turned to the matter of Third Reich–era artifacts and their proper representation in the museum context, Ottomeyer mentioned that he'd heard a rumor that a human skin lampshade had been found in America. Thinking this had to be the New Orleans shade (and marveling at the remarkable spread of such memes), my friend replied that Professor Knigge at Buchenwald had expressed interest in the object. "Well," said Ottomeyer, "we can do whatever Knigge can do. I wouldn't mind looking at that myself." By the time I arrived in his sumptuous office on Unter den Linden with a grand view of Kaiser Wilhelm's Berliner Dom, however, Professor Ottomeyer seemed to have changed his mind about the German Historical Museum's involvement with the lampshade.

"There is an undue concentration on the darkness of the German history," Ottomeyer said. "This is not to say there is not darkness. But there is light as well, as I'm sure you know. This is what we try to do here at the museum, present a balance. So it is best that you take this lampshade to Professor Knigge. He deals with this sort of object, and to tell the truth, I don't know how he does it. Every day in that gloom, surrounded by those terrible things. I have a lot of respect and sympathy for him."

Listening to this as he sat in his office in the former SS barracks at Buchenwald, Knigge sighed. "Well, he does have Hitler's desk in his museum, but it is a very nice, very well made desk, I can assure you of that," he said. Knigge did, however, agree with Ottomeyer's assessment that Buchenwald was the proper place for the lampshade, at least at this moment, better than the German Historical Museum, better than a hole in the ground in New Orleans.

"It is too early to bury this lampshade," Professor Knigge said during our first meeting. "It is not ready for the earth." He ran his hand over the graying fuzz on his head and looked out the window. It had begun sleeting. Rain, sleet, snow—this was how it was in the Ettersberg in February, especially at the end of the Blood Road.

"How can I explain?" Knigge said, cursing his English. "You say the lampshade is a story, and I would agree, but what kind of story do you want to tell? When I first came here, there was nothing that could be depended upon to be the truth. When the GDR decided they wanted to memorialize the camp, the first thing they did was tear the place down and reconstruct it in the image of what the state wanted it to be. This wasn't Auschwitz, not a death camp, so it was important to make Buchenwald more horrible, more bloody, because the GDR wanted to tell the story of the antifascist heroes, what in German is called *Heldengeschichten*.

"But now the GDR is gone, the Cold War is gone, and so are these stories. What are we left with? We have what the survivors tell us, and we have the objects. For us it is daily life to be confronted by objects which we know to be part of the concentration camp but in most ways remain silent. Did the Nazis shrink heads at Buchenwald? We have evidence that they did. Did Ilse Koch conspire to make lampshades out of human beings? We cannot be sure. We keep trying to find out because by confronting these atrocities, we hope that it will change the minds of people and, in a way, perhaps make the world a better place. So now we are in a different situation because you have this lampshade that is made of human skin. This mythic object that is suddenly real. And because it exists, there are new questions to ask. We may never get an answer, but we continue to ask. That is why it is too early to bury this lampshade. It is still asking questions."

Knigge acknowledged that the lampshade held for him a personal "fascination." Myth or reality, reality and myth, the lampshade was inextricably tied to the history of Buchenwald. For many people, it was all they knew of the camp. There was no tossing it out of the narrative here. If I wanted, he suggested, I could ship the lampshade from Brooklyn to the Ettersberg. Some further scientific investigation could be arranged. Funds for this purpose were in the memorial budget.

This was the best offer I'd heard. So, yes, I told Volkhard Knigge, strange as it sounded, perhaps it was a good idea for the lampshade to come to Buchenwald. But I couldn't ship it. I couldn't take that chance. I'd have to bring it myself.

Some of Knigge's unanswered questions came up as soon as I left the Ettersberg and traveled two hundred kilometers east to Dresden. The very next day was the sixty-fourth anniversary of the February 13, 1945, firebombing during which Allied aircraft destroyed the previously untouched city, considered by many to be the most beautiful in Europe, the baroque "Florence on the Elbe."

Like most Americans, most everything I knew about Dresden came from Kurt Vonnegut's book *Slaughterhouse-Five,* the odd tale of Billy Pilgrim, the optometrist of Ilium, New York, who, after being captured by the Nazis in the Battle of the Bulge, is sent to work in a Dresden slaughterhouse. Surviving the attack by hiding in a meat locker, Billy emerges to a ruined world, the shock of which causes him to be "unstuck in time," a mystic state that enables him to travel to various periods of his life and eventually leads to communication with the extraterrestrial Tralfamadorians, a race of mostly all-knowing two-foot-tall aliens Vonnegut describes as looking like upside-down toilet plungers. It is from the Tralfamadorians that the eternally traumatized Billy learns that time, which includes life and death, is basically subjective, part of an unbroken continuum, any segment of which can be revisited over and over again.

I always liked *Slaughterhouse-Five,* a perfect book for the smart fourteen-year-old, for the way it breaks through the usual jingoist stuff about which side you were on and in its own fabulist way attacks the human condition of killing other humans, even Germans. Few books rail against the finality of death with such passionate invention.

The fact that it is based on Vonnegut's own experience as a witness to the Dresden firebombing (Billy Pilgrim is the author, up to a point) only deepens the reader's appreciation for the work.

Yet to be present in Dresden on the anniversary of the bombing, with the church bells ringing at 9:45 p.m., the moment the RAF wing commanders in their Lancasters and Mosquitoes began the attack, is to be confronted by unsettling events that Vonnegut couldn't have foreseen when his book was published in 1969.

On the Ammonstrasse, the Nazis were marching. In fact, these members of Germany's more visible ultraright wing have been marching in Dresden on the anniversary of the bombing since reunification. For them, the Allied firebombing of the city during which untold thousands of civilians were incinerated in their wood-frame houses— Vonnegut, using figures cited by the then not-so-controversial David Irving, placed the death toll at 130,000; most historians now estimate the dead at 20,000 to 40,000—was nothing less than *Massenmord*, mass murder, a *Bombenholocaust* on a par with anything that happened to the Jews.

Dresden, capital of Saxony, hometown of Ilse Koch, has always been a right-wing stronghold. The NSDAP was dominant here and the present-day hard-right NPD, the *Nationaldemokratische Partei Deutschlands*, also does well, outpolling the old-line left-of-center Social Democrats (SPD) in local parliament races. This local sentiment, along with the ongoing controversy over the attack, which many regard as an unnecessary act of revenge on the part of the Allies (during the GDR it was presented as an instance of Anglo-American imperialism), has turned the bombing anniversary into a rallying point for the nationalist movement in present-day Germany. With each passing year the demonstration has grown. The night I arrived there were several thousand in the streets, taking part in a silent torchlight procession. It was part of the largest such gathering in Germany since the end of World War II.

Deep into my second year on the lampshade beat, I had a more nuanced critique on the German right wing than during my early visit to

Weimar, when I couldn't tell the difference between an antifa and an anti-antifa. The people walking down the Ammonstrasse in silence with their candles and signs in Reich typeface about how the *Heimat* (homeland) was reduced to *schutt und asche* (dirt and ash) by the *verbrecher* (criminal) Allies were the *Kameradschaften,* the "Society of Comrades." These were the mostly young, often violent "autonomous" nationalists who took their inspiration not from the "führer model" of Hitlerism but rather from the brothers Strasser, Otto and Gregor, the intellectualized, ultranationalist racialists who broke from the NSDAP in the early 1930s to follow their own doomed, anticapitalist path to German hegemony.

Not content to fall in line with the dreary old farts of the top-down NPD and their tired Reich-nostalgic rhetoric, the *Kameradschaften* were anarchist, antiglobalist, kaffiyeh-wearing neo-Nazis, mostly East German youth who understood the duplicitous ways of the overlords and believed the true threat to the purity of the *Volk* lay not with the Jews in the classic "bacillus" sense of their mere existence but rather with the ever-encroaching modern world—that bastardized, one-size-fits-all-consumerist, Internet-addicted culture with no moral or physical barriers, where everything was for sale, including blood and honor. The new enemy was not the Jew himself but rather the identity-free, self-perpetuating quicksand of existence that at its core was Jewish, whether individual Jews like myself, paying off their credit cards at 30 percent like any oppressed Gentile, knew it or not.

Yet what was one to do as the young flag-wavers passed by, Wagner music blaring from the DJ speakers? Point out that many military historians think the Dresden attack was actually the correct decision, given the city's industrial capacity, which included vast factories of slave workers manufacturing bombsights for the Luftwaffe? Was it the time to split hairs over where "legitimate" wartime destruction ends and criminality, even genocide begins? The fact remained that people had been killed here, burned to nothingness, leaving no trace by which scientists could run the DNA to see if they were members of the Nazi Party or not. As Yehuda Bauer had told me, in such matters "dead was dead."

Right-wing march, Dresden, February 13, 2009

It was all so familiar, I thought, as the *Kameradschaften* walked by, heads bowed in the appearance of solemn prayer. Dead might be dead, but playing dead also looked the same the world over. The way these Nazis, in their black hoodies and skull masks, skeletons painted on their chests, came out of the torchlight murk, they would have fit right in on a hazy Mardi Gras morning at the corner of Clouet and Dauphine streets marching alongside the Bywater Bone Boys. That was the essence of Mardi Gras: behind the mask, when you're just a bag of bones, you could be anyone.

But who exactly were these *Kameradschaften* passing in silence on the Ammonstrasse? There were statistics on neo-Nazi violence: how many Turks and Africans they had attacked over the years, in how many murders they had taken part. A day later a bus carrying trade unionists, in Dresden to protest the right-wing march, was stopped by nationalists; several of the union people were badly beaten. The left-wing blogs said, "Nazis attack bus." Still, lots of people get called Nazis—terrorists, totalitarians, idiot gay-baiters, gangsters. When crystal meth freaks in Idaho are drawing Hitler mustaches on Barack Obama, who is to say who is a Nazi and who isn't? But this obfuscation is unfortunate, because there are real Nazis out there, and it is good to know who they are, what they're capable of.

Could they, for instance, make a lampshade from a human being?

Professor Knigge suggested that the lampshade was not finished asking questions, and here was one: given the chance, would these teenage torchlight marchers, in some distant racially pure future they claimed to long for, find it within themselves to capture large numbers of human beings whom they'd labeled the enemy, murder these people, strip the skin from their backs, tan that skin in the sun, order prisoners skilled in leatherwork to fashion the skin into a lampshade, attach the shade to a fixture wired for electricity, bring the finished project home to the house where their beloved children played, put the lamp on a bedside table, and pass a pleasant evening reading by the lamp's light, and then flip off the switch to get a sound night's sleep?

Did these *Kameradschaften,* these skeletal mourners, these anti-globalists in their Pali scarves, have the stomach for that?

How does one know when one is confronted by true evil? The Talmud says there are 7,405,926 demons, or *mazikin,* in the world. Seems as good a number as any; I'm not going to dispute it. I am also grateful that Hashem, in his infinite mercy, is said to block from us the sight of these ubiquitous demons, for as Abba Benjamin, sage of the Babylonian captivity, says, if their multitudes could be seen, no creature could endure knowledge of their presence. Seeing too many demons could drive you crazy, and if Jerusalem has its own syndrome, for someone like me, Germany does, too. It is an ingress of paranoia, a shadow that follows each smiling beer maid and train conductor, a miserable, unshakable slime trail of the past. And standing on that Dresden street watching *Kameradschaften* "dead" walk by, I could feel myself becoming "unstuck in time" just as Billy Pilgrim had before me. Likely this sensation was cued by one of the banners being held by the marchers, which translated from the German read "worse than Hiroshima." It was, as I recognized, a paraphrase of a line in *Slaughterhouse-Five,* where the narrator, named "Kurt Vonnegut," says that "not many Americans knew how much worse it had been than Hiroshima."

Worse than *Hiroshima* . . . The word itself is enough to cue the newsreel inside the brain, the series of slow dissolves set to musical portent: Einstein, Oppenheimer, Fermi. Paul Tibbets and the B-29 named after his mother, Enola Gay, the kiss she gives will never fade away. And then the wide-open sky, the blinding light brighter than a thousand suns, a pan across the shattered landscape, the woman crawling through the wreckage, her arm upraised to the sky, beseeching heaven, as if that would help.

"Worse than Hiroshima." What could be worse than Hiroshima? Who was qualified to make such a declaration? Not "Kurt Vonnegut," not these masked neo-Nazis, not me. The world was full of victims and perpetrators. Every so often the victims and perpetrators would change places, as if in some vicious, unending square dance. So it goes, as Vonnegut would say. The duality was present in the lampshade. On one hand there was Ziggy, the victim, the poor schmuck who got turned into a lampshade, and there were the awful people who'd done it to him. Sometimes it was one thing, sometimes the other. Only the Nazi stayed the same. Him and Hashem, immortal, immutable opposites, who deserved each other.

The rumor on the Ammonstrasse was that the antifa had arrived to take on the *Kameradschaften,* but the Dresden cops, in full riot gear, had the leftists bottled up inside the train station. In Dresden the cops were like that, people said, bent on attacking the leftists, protecting the Nazis. That was too bad, I thought, because I wouldn't have minded some action, a little duke-out between the true believers. As it was, I almost got to throw a punch myself, and take one, too, no doubt. What set me off was another of those Nazi banners being held by four or five skeletons. It read "10.5 Million Germans

Ask Why?". The statistic was the reputed number of German citizens, soldiers included, who met their death during World War II.

Reading that, I might as well have been back in the old Queens schoolyard, with the sons of sanitation workers shaking their fists, claiming that if I didn't shut up they were going to turn me "into a lampshade." In this case it wasn't the threat that ticked me off. It was the plaintiveness, the earnest, weak whine of the appeal, exactly the sort of sheep-to-the-slaughter attitude the *Übermenschen* Germans attributed to the lowly Jews, that alleged pathetic helplessness that only triggered more *Blutrausch,* the frenzy of killing that once begun could not be stopped.

"10.5 Million Germans Ask Why?"

"Why? You want to know *why? I'll fucking tell you why!*" The voice was mine but it might as well have come from the lampshade itself.

A few months later, into the fall, I again found myself riding the number 6 bus up the Blood Road, to Buchenwald. On my lap, having once more flown across the ocean in an overhead rack, was the lampshade. If you want, you could call it a homecoming of sorts.

Volkhard Knigge was waiting in front of the old SS barracks. In his customary all black, he looked like a taller Johnny Cash as he stood under a large umbrella in the sharply falling freezing rain. Since our last meeting, Knigge had become what he called "a little famous," owing to the worldwide coverage of President Barack Obama's visit to Buchenwald in July 2009. Knigge could be seen on websites everywhere chatting with Obama, as well as German chancellor Angela Merkel, Elie Wiesel, and Wiesel's fellow survivor Bertrand Herz, as they walked across the *Appellplatz.*

Obama's Buchenwald stopover was foreshadowed by a misstatement he had made during his generally impeccably modulated presidential campaign. During a speech to a veterans' group, Obama said his great-uncle Charles Payne, a member of the Eighty-ninth Infantry Division of George Patton's army, had assisted in the liberation of Auschwitz. This was incorrect. Actually, Payne had taken part in the liberation of the Buchenwald satellite camp at Ohrdruf, where General Eisenhower first saw sights that "beggar description." Obama's error recalled the flap over the 1992 documentary *Liberators,* which portrayed the segregated, African-American 761st Tank Battalion as the first U.S. Army unit to reach Buchenwald in April 1945.

Nominated for an Academy Award and seen by almost four million people on NET public television, *Liberators* was given a special screening at the renowned Apollo Theater on 125th Street in Harlem on December 17, 1992, in the wake of the Crown Heights riots. Sparked when an ambulance accompanying the motorcade of the Lubavitcher rebbe Schneerson ran over and killed a young Guyanese boy, an incident that led to the murder of a yeshiva student by a group of black youths, the riots threatened to destroy whatever remained of the old liberal black-Jewish voting coalition in New York. The screening of *Liberators* was supposed to help begin the healing process. David Dinkins, New York's first and only African-American mayor, then running for reelection against a fully locked-and-loaded Rudolph Giuliani, addressed an audience that included Jesse Jackson, District Attorney Robert Morgenthau, Congressman Charles Rangel, and Elie Wiesel, as well as many rabbis and church pastors. *Liberators* should be seen as "a step along the road to mutual understanding and respect," Dinkins said. "When we see those brave African-American soldiers freeing Jewish prisoners from the concentration camps, let us remember all that binds us together."

Unfortunately, as NET officials would later admit, the film's version of the liberation of Buchenwald was "seriously flawed." The 761st may have landed on Omaha Beach, punched a hole through the Siegfried Line, and risked their lives for their less-than-loving country many times during the push through Europe, but they had nothing to do with Buchenwald's liberation. They weren't even in the area at the time.

"I think it is somewhat like the GDR, another of those Buchenwald stories that are difficult to resist telling—black people from

America, suffering from discrimination, oppression, coming here to save the Jews. It is an instance of something we perhaps wish was true but is not," Knigge remarked. As for the visit of Barack Obama to Buchenwald, during which the president spoke of the "need to reflect on the human capacity for evil and our shared obligation to defy it," Knigge remained thrilled, albeit in his sober way.

"He is very impressive," he said. "We spoke for almost two hours. He is very interested in making a museum about slavery in Washington and was asking about that."

The Buchenwald Memorial offices were undergoing renovation, so we entered the old SS building through the basement. It was dank and cold and Knigge pointed out the boilers where forced laborers once shoveled coal around the clock. We went up the staircase, the same stairs used by officers of the Death's Head order, strode past rooms once inhabited by vicious camp overseers like Martin Sommer, who, according to the Nazi judge Konrad Morgen, kept a secret compartment for his torture instruments and slept with dead bodies under his bed. Kommandants Koch and Pister, and likely Ilse Koch herself, used these hallways.

A few more doorways and we were in the room where Herr Röll had first shown me the contents of his cabinet. It being late Friday afternoon, Knigge's staff—Röll, Harry Stein, Sabine Stein, and the rest—were already gone for the day. Dr. Knigge placed the lampshade on a table where Herr Röll would be certain to see it and wrote a note. "Herr Röll, this is the lampshade made from human skin. Please handle it with the utmost care."

The plan, as Knigge outlined, was to take the lampshade to the offices of the Landeskriminalamt Thüringen, which he described as the Thuringian office of "the German FBI." They had a copy of the Bode lab DNA report and had agreed to give the lampshade a forensic workup, including testing the frame, the tassels, and the threads used to attach the panels. If no meaningful results were obtained, Knigge said, there was a possibility of sending the lampshade to a genetic testing lab in Leipzig.

The professor wrote out a receipt, acknowledging that I had dropped off the lampshade at Buchenwald for "further examination" and that it would be returned to me "upon request." I insisted on this last phrase. Bringing the lampshade to Buchenwald, to the scene of the alleged crime, was bothering me. To leave it here any longer than necessary would have been an unforgivable betrayal. I couldn't let that happen, not on my watch.

Knigge and I drove down to Weimar, had a bite to eat. The rain had turned to snow. "This is the perfect weather for this place, every day more of the same," Knigge said.

It took until the new year before I got Knigge's email with the results of the German forensic testing, which were the same as I had gotten from Avi Domb in Jerusalem. The German FBI had tried but could not find anything more than what was already in the Bode report. They did, however, ascertain that the Mardi Gras–colored tassels were a later addition to the shade, but that was no news.

"Now we come to the end," Knigge's email said. "The police research confirmed what we already know. To get further technically isn't possible. Sorry about that . . . So there will be no last certitude about the object for now. That's how history works. Here it's snowing heavily which fits the issue at hand. Have a happy New Year anyhow, yours, VK."

Six weeks later, Fat Tuesday came again, the fifth time since Katrina. We Bone Boys were out there, at Clouet and Dauphine, nice bunch of white homeowners in the tentatively stirring Bywater real estate market, augmented by a few of the post-Katrina social justice types, some St. Claude Avenue guerrilla art gallery owners, and a couple of stray gutter punks, ready to wake up the town for "da holiday," as Big Chief Bo Dollis and the Wild Magnolias sing in "Meet Da Boys on Da Battlefront." When we started marching, in the antediluvian days of 2005, there were twelve Bone Boys, "no dues, no officers, no meetings, not bound by circumstances." Now there were more than a hundred Bones, every one playing some version of dead. With a picture in the *Times-Picayune*, us Bones were a coming krewe, a staple of conversation in the hipster downtown bars and coffee shops. In the manner of New Orleans, where everyone thinks they own the town and its legacy, there were grumbles that things were getting too big, too full of Johnny-come-latelies. Being unbound by circumstance was cool, but like the old-line krewes uptown, you couldn't be parading with just anyone, you know.

If the storm had laid a brutal kind of poetry on New Orleans, created a one-of-a-kind landscape of desolation in the country's most romanticized city, a new vibe was in the air. According to the papal calendar, Mardi Gras fell on February 16 this particular year, and only a few days before, the city had been turned upside down in a single weekend. On Saturday, February 6, with Ray Nagin prevented from running again by term limits—and his own 20 percent approval rating—Mitch Landrieu had been elected the new mayor. Brother of Louisiana U.S. senator Mary Landrieu, Mitch was the son of Moon, the last previous white New Orleans mayor. After thirty-two years of black clubhouse leadership and nepotism dominated by the Morials, Dutch and Marc, along with Nagin—a period of population loss, financial decline, rampant (but hardly unprecedented) corruption, and off-the-charts murder—it was considered time to make the only political change that the majority of people recognize down here and to let the whites back in at the trough. Not everyone was happy about this (Landrieu received barely 28 percent of the eligible vote), as the hosts on WBOK, a black talk station, made clear. Hour after hour the airwaves were rife with fulmination against the so-called Shadow Government, the white, uptown ruling class that had been calling the shots for centuries and would continue to do so. It was important for blacks to control the mayor's office and the patronage it offered, people said, as a counterbalance. No one doubted the soundness of this analysis, but cooler heads agreed that, given a chance to do something truly heroic both during the storm and beyond—to at least *pretend to,* like Giuliani did in 9/11—Ray Nagin had blown it, big-time. Besides, as one WBOK caller said, "White people are like the weather. You can't get away from them. You just got to figure how to work around them, like we been doing here for the past four hundred years."

But this chatter was mere background noise compared to what happened the next day, Sunday, February 7, when after four decades of mostly miserable football, the New Orleans Saints won the Super Bowl. By the final gun, grown men were crying in the street, people were drinking and partying so hard that it was a wonder they could manage to get out for Mardi Gras only a week later to drink and party some more. The town was still pretty much a disaster area. The Army Corps of Engineers was probably screwing up the levees worse than ever. Buildings two blocks north of St. Claude Avenue had three walls or fewer, the murders kept coming every day. But, *who dat!* The Saints won the Super Bowl! It was a gift only the most churlish could refuse.

This was the mood as the Bone Boys stepped off to wake up the town for Mardi Gras 2010, rattling our dead man shovels on the uneven pavement behind us. It was time to remind the predeceased that their days were numbered, to assault the vain fetish of living flesh with this year's slogan, "Tomorrow, your face!" Skulls painted on mirrors were held aloft in case anyone missed the point. The route had been expanded to include the streets closer to the Industrial Canal: Mazant, Alvar, Pauline, Lesseps, Bartholomew, all the way over to Poland. This was where, according to Dave Dominici's instructions, I had spent several days knocking on doors to see if anyone knew anything about a lampshade made of human skin. That was in 2007. Back then half the houses were boarded up, wrecked. In 2010 some ruins remained, places with the once-ubiquitous Gas Off signs, but much of the neighborhood had "come back." Houses were painted in those marvelous wack-job parish colors, offset by magenta shutters. Businesses like the Jesus Is Lord Plumbing Company had popped up.

It was the coldest New Orleans winter in three decades, so everyone was extra-fortified by Jack Daniel's behind the skull mask. Stumbling through the neighborhood, I had the thought that perhaps the lampshade wasn't man-made after all but rather an organic bit of hybrid plant/animal matter that germinated in places where terrible, willfully forgotten things had occurred—like, say, maintaining one of the world's largest slave markets for a hundred years. Maybe the shade had grown in the same way that nooses had appeared like strange fruit one day on the branches of a tree in front of a high school in Jena, Louisiana, which shares a name with Jena, Thuringia, where Nazi Hans F. K. Gunther once headed the Department of Race Sciences (work that was honored by a Goethe arts and sciences medal in 1940) at the same university where Volkhard Knigge teaches the psychology of history today. A noose, after all, isn't all that different from a lampshade, being one more innocent-seeming household object, a neutral piece of rope, until coiled into a certain shape and knotted. In my tipsy botanical conception, these malicious blooms were widely occurring, their habitat just about anywhere, but they weren't necessarily perennial. At some point the curse could come off the land from which they sprang and they might wither and die, at least this was the hope.

The Bone Boys were making a joyful racket by the time we turned on Royal Street and, following the vanished tracks of the streetcar named Desire, came to the corner of Piety, where Skip Henderson had bought the lampshade from Dave Dominici. The year before, the house had had the look of one more abandoned structure. Now Dominici's daughter had moved in, along with her boyfriend and their two children, Dave's grandchildren; they'd fixed the house up, brought it back to life.

I talked to Dominici a couple of days later when he called up his ever-loving, endlessly patient seventy-eight-year-old mother, Patsy, at her house near the Metairie/Kenner border. It was the only way to talk to Dave, said Patsy. Dave would have loved to contact me directly, but he was still locked up, this time near Shreveport, and prisoners are not allowed to call cell phones. "Wouldn't you know it," Patsy said, "just about everyone David knows has a cell phone. So he rings me, like, ten times a day, with the charges reversed, of course."

What a great stroke of luck it was, getting to talk to me, Dominici said, now "totally clean" but sounding the same as ever, not counting the occasional clunk of AA phraseology. He'd just put the finishing touches on his autobiography, *Or Else Is Here,* and I'd be doing him a great favor if I would "grab the bull by the horns" and "get the ball rolling" by calling up the *Oprah* show because he was certain the talk show host was going to have her socks knocked off by the book and make it a major selection of her literary club. After his release, which he said would be any day now, pending a few hearings, he planned to buy a new suit so he'd look good for his TV appearances.

It wasn't the money that he wanted, just the opportunity to show how sorry he was for his "previous screwups," and to prove it, he was going to take only 50 percent of the profits from *Or Else Is Here,* leaving the rest to the fund to save New Orleans's cemeteries and to "the members of my family that I have let down." He was a new man, he said, I'd see that soon enough. Until then, Dominici said he wanted to thank me for taking the lampshade "to the next level" and continuing the work he started by "bringing this thing to light." He got in one last "Back at ya" before the electronic voice said, "Five seconds," and terminated the call.

The morning after Mardi Gras, I always go with Skip Henderson to 7:30 mass at St. Louis Cathedral on Jackson Square, which was first constructed in 1718 and remains the oldest continually operating church in America. First we drive over to Bourbon Street to see the trash. This is the only time of the year Skip intentionally goes to Bourbon Street. The city used to make a big deal out of weighing the trash picked up in the French Quarter the morning after Mardi Gras; the more garbage, the better the party. Everyone was always trying to throw stuff away to beat the record. When Ray Nagin, the technocrat, was elected, trash weighing and the bets taken on the final poundage were considered déclassé, so the practice was abandoned. But you could still eyeball it, estimate the drift-size of the detritus, assign a degree of wretchedness to the pooled bodily fluids. This year's

Mardi Gras had outtrashed any other since the storm. Did this mean Katrina was finally over? I asked Skip.

Skip Henderson, Bywater Bone Boy

"Katrina will never be over. Not until the last person moves back. Not until the last *X* is off the last house," he answered, melodramatically. After all, Skip knew that for every one resident who'd returned since the storm, two had stayed in Houston or Atlanta. As for the *X*'s, the so-called Katrina tattoos painted by the National Guard during their body search, several residents, certainly those in Bywater, were keeping them as souvenirs. Many of the new people regarded the tattoos as badges of honor, hard-to-come-by authenticity in an ersatz era. At the end of Montegut Street a sculptor had enshrined his building's *X* in bronze. You wanted one on your house, just in case the angel of death came this way again. The marks had become part of the city, like the storm itself, one more personality-building scar.

What Skip really wanted to know was what I was going to do with the lampshade; it was still half his, he had a right to know.

"If you're not going to bury it, then what?" Skip half pleaded. "What?"

We were in the cathedral now, the mass under way, the priest quoting Genesis 3:19: "For dust thou art, and unto dust shalt thou return." It was as Skip always said: there could be no Fat Tuesday without Ash Wednesday, the gorging of carnival being incomplete without the spare reminder of life's fleetingness. The bead-decked yahoos drinking themselves into oblivion on Tuesday who didn't show up to mass on Wednesday, whatever religion they were, were clueless as to the real meaning of Mardi Gras.

The lines to receive the ashes were long, probably twice as long as in the past couple of years, another sign that the town, the Big Easy once more, was back and open for business. It was going to take Skip at least twenty minutes to receive the sacrament. This gave me plenty of time to think things over, which was a good thing because I like to be in churches, especially ones as handsome as St. Louis Cathedral. It is good to be surrounded by the sacred mumbo jumbo, especially when it isn't *your* sacred mumbo jumbo. Sitting in a temple, even a fancy momma like Emanu-El in Manhattan, was never so relaxing. In temple there were issues, questions of childhood, history, tradition, faith. In church none of that applied. Whatever was stirred up here was Skip Henderson's problem, not mine.

The lampshade had opened a special portal, all right, I thought, recalling a story told to me by Plater Robinson, who ran the Holocaust education seminars at Tulane. It was about Henry Galler, a New Orleans Holocaust survivor and longtime proprietor of Mr. Henry's tailor shop on Jackson Avenue. Henry and his wife, Eva, also a survivor, were forced to evacuate to Dallas during Katrina. They lost almost everything, including a piece of soap Henry said he'd gotten at the concentration camp. Soap supposedly made from Jews, kept all these years, dissolved in the flood.

The connections piled up. One morning I heard from Shiya

Ribowsky, who sounded excited. Most of the time, if you ask Shiya how well he sang at *Shabbos* services, he'll say he was awful, that he had a head cold or phlegm in his throat, something that kept him from being the greatest cantor west of Galicia, which, in his heart, he knew he was. This past *Shabbos,* however, Shiya said, "I was on. Smoking." After the service ended, a large black man "with these gigantic biceps" came up and shook his hand. "Really dig your music, man," he said.

"I didn't know who he was," Shiya said. "We have some black congregants, six or seven, but I'd never seen him before. Then he tells me he's Aaron Neville. He came over to the shul with a friend. I said, 'Well, thanks, dig your music, too.' "

I'd even talked to David Duke from time to time, most memorably on the morning after the 2008 election. He was driving to Memphis to address a long-planned convention of his "white rights" group, the European American Unity and Rights Organization (EURO), and I asked him what he thought of the presidential results. "It is an Obamanation! It is the nadir of the country. The end of America as we know it," Duke said before shouting, "My God, I think my front tire is coming off. I'm going to have to call you back."

After receiving the German FBI report on the lampshade, I called Volkhard Knigge to tell him I'd pretty much decided not to bury the lampshade. "This is the way it is with these kinds of objects; a historian is always lingering between the realm of hope and disappointment," Knigge said, with the curious cadence that sometimes made him sound like he was talking in an ethereal blank verse. "You are forced to accept the idea of limits. There are things you will never know. It can be frustrating to be confronted by these structures of silence and the fantasies they produce. This is why it is helpful to be organized in your approach, to establish frameworks for thought.

"With this lampshade you can say it had a first history, which is that identification with the Buchenwald camp and people like Ilse Koch. The lampshade on the Table with people passing by. Then there is the second history. The history with you. Your adventures and your thoughts. There is the strange and frightening idea that someone would make a lampshade out of a person and it has arrived in New Orleans after a storm. This interests you, so now the first history becomes infused by the passage of years and a new context. Then we would come to a third possible history, one we cannot guess. Who gives us the right to close the book for the future? The questions must be kept open. The best thing to do is treat it with respect, and we will see what happens next."

That was probably good advice, I thought. If the lampshade was a story, I was only writing one part of it. The thing would continue on, like the line of people waiting to have a bit of ash smeared onto their forehead. It would stay in the world, as it should. Someone would find it again.

ACKNOWLEDGMENTS

Writing this book has been a disturbing but rewarding experience. The goal was to look at a frightening object from as many angles as possible and try to make sense of it. But you have to start somewhere, and that would be with Skip Henderson. As noted, I've known Skip for some time, but our friendship was probably always pointed toward the moment he purchased the lampshade from Dave Dominici. It is something about Skip: He has the air of destiny about him. No one else I know could have found the lampshade and known, immediately, of its importance. His sensibility, however cockeyed, informs these pages.

This said, to write such a book—or rather to simply see it as a book that could be written—one needs early supporters, trusted fellow travelers who know you, know what you can do, what fears you must confront to do good work. I have been lucky in this regard to have friends like Michael Daly; my longtime running mate Jonny Buchsbaum; Lou DiBella, the world's greatest Harvard-educated boxing promoter; the nonpareil Steve Earle; and the fabulous Zarela Martínez (whose hospitality and margaritas were most welcome).

Encouragement is nice, but one cannot proceed without a more tangible kind of faith offered in the form of business acumen and a checkbook. I consider myself very fortunate to be a client of my agent, Flip Brophy, of Sterling Lord Literistic. Flip knows a good idea from a bad one and doesn't mind telling you so. Flip deserves credit for demanding we take this idea first to David Rosenthal, then the grand poo-bah at Simon & Schuster. I knew David would understand what I was hoping to accomplish. We have, after all, done business before, coming up together through the old magazine jungles of the 1970s. He was very smart then, even smarter now, but still very *hamish*, certainly for a poo-bah.

This book would not exist without the participation of the major "characters" I write about, people like Farid Abu Gosh, Andy Antippas, Doña Argentina, Yehuda Bauer, Bob Bever, Denier Bud, Avi Domb, Dave Dominici, Dr. John, David Duke, Skip Henderson, the brilliant and thoughtful Ken Kipperman, Volkhard Knigge, Frank Minyard, Cyril Neville, Stephanie Rhodes-Navarre, Wolfgang Röll, Albert Rosenberg, Aharon Seiden, Avner Shalev, Harry Stein, Daniel Strauss, Dyanne Thorne, and Rabbi Uri Topolosky. All these people contributed to this book in ways I could not have imagined before I spoke to them. In this cast, I'd like to single out Shiya Ribowsky, the forensic cantor, who sent the samples of the shade to the Bode lab and advised me on a number of seemingly indecipherable issues. A rabbi of the best sort, a mensch of epic proportions, Shiya will someday be offered the job of running the world but will be too smart to take it.

This would have been a different book without the efforts of Anetta Kahane, founder and chairperson of the Berlin-based Amadeu Antonio Foundation. An indomitable neo-Nazi fighter, Anetta's scholarship, hell-bent attitude, and voluminous Rolodex opened many corridors of investigation that would have been shuttered to a non-German-speaking American reporter. She is a wonder. I must also thank Andrés Nader and Heike Radvan, also of the Amadeu Antonio Foundation, for their assistance. Others who must be mentioned are Joseph Almog, Alvin Babineaux, Michael Berenbaum, Robby Berman, Micha Brumlik, Melvin Bukit, the Bywater Bone Boys, Dan Christian, Rabbi Edward Cohn, Joe Coleman, the mysterious D, Dani Dominici, Patsy Dominici, Lawrence Douglas, Gaynielle Dupree, Steve Fishman, Terry Fredericks, the late Jamie Gillis, Sallie Ann Glassman, Gitty Grunwald, Rio Hackford, Taylor Hackford, Joe Hargrave, Deborah Harris, Baruch Herzfeld, Werner Herzog, Lance Hill, the late Khalil Islam, the late, much-missed Bob Izdepski, Susan Izdepski, Cathy Kahn, Ben Kiernan, Paula Kipperman, Yaakov

Kleiman, Antonin Kratochvil, Anne Levy, Wynton Marsalis, Guy Martin, Steve Mass, Michael Melnitzky, Dr. Charles Melone, Terry Melton, Case Miller, Priestess Miriam, Captain Frederick Morton, the Mütter Museum, Aaron Neville, Art Neville, Charles Neville, Levi Okunov, Mr. Paul of Bon-Bon Lighting, Lawrence Powell, Hugo Ramirez, Walter Reich, Plater Robinson, Thane Rosenbaum, Diane Saltzman, Dr. Raynard Sanders, Barry Scheck, Isaac Schoenfeld, the late Budd Schulberg, Tom Segev, Bob Shaller, Uriel Simon, Larry "Ratso" Sloman, Christy Smith, Clyde Snow, Sabine Stein, Steve the Biker, Michael Taussig, Scott Thode, Ed Ward, Allison Wells, Denis Woychuk, Peter Zeitlinger, and Sylvia Zeitlinger. Extra shout-out to Roi Melech for being in the right place at the right time: keep shaking and baking, baby. Special thanks to James Hamilton, my longtime colleague and treasured friend who took the lampshade photo on the book cover.

Since living is important when writing a book, I must offer fond gratitude to Adam Moss, my boss at *New York* magazine, for allowing me to write this and not firing me. My good friend John Homans, who edits my magazine stuff at *New York,* read an early draft of this book and, as always, had a few, but decisive, comments. Editors are really the writer's friend, except when they're not. Ruth Fecych at Simon & Schuster is a friend indeed. She fine-toothed through this pile of pages with rapier zeal and much-appreciated good cheer. I don't know how she turned out to be right about so many things, but she was. Adam Parker helped with some nifty fact checking. Beyond all that is the family, my ever-lovin' wife, Nancy Cardozo, and *der kinder,* Rae, Rosalie Sue, and Billy Jacobson. They're older now, in college and through it, and have gotten used to snarly ol' Dad typing away. They humor me; they weren't crazy about having the lampshade in the old homestead for two years, but were good sports. Love to them, always.

In the end, though, there is the lampshade itself: anonymous soul, surviving memory of terror, mute redeemer.

NOTES

Part One

7 The story of selling one's soul to the devil for temporal reward has long been among the most reliable narratives in world culture, but for Goethe and his German readers it was essentially a local story, with its roots quite close to the Ettersberg forest. An early mention of "Faust" turns up in a letter sent from one Trithemius, abbot of Würzberg and noted occultist, to Johann Virdun, an astrologer in Heidelberg. Dated August 20, 1507, the letter warns against a "Magister Georgius Sabellicus, Faustus junior," who has been passing himself off as the "prince of necromancers." Six years later, in 1513, there is a mention of a "Georgius Faustus," who is now described as "cheiromancer," or palm reader, supposedly operating in Erfurt, fifteen miles from Weimar. This was followed, in 1587, by the first of the "Faust books," under the all-inclusive title *History of Dr. Johann Faust, the notorious Magician and Necromancer, how he sold himself for a stipulated Time to the Devil, What strange Things he saw, performed and practised during this Time, until at last he received his well-merited Reward*. A popular hit, it was widely read in Weimar, as was the later Christopher Marlowe adaption of the legend. Goethe's version signified something of a homecoming for the Faust story.

23 Clarksdale, known as "The Golden Buckle of the Cotton Belt," was the key commercial center of the Mississippi Delta, the most fertile (along with the Nile Valley) cotton growing area in the world. The concentration of cotton plantations and the later sharecropping system in the Delta did much to create the dynamic that produced African-American blues music. For an excellent overview of the social and economic conditions of the Delta at the time, see Nicholas Lemann's *The Promised Land: The Great Black Migration and How It Changed America* (Vintage, 1992). Muddy Waters's sharecropper shack once stood on the Stovall Plantation near Clarksdale until it was purchased and hauled away by the House of Blues on a flatbed truck. Many sign-waving local music fans chased after the truck screaming, "Don't take Muddy's house away."

26 The monument Skip Henderson helped erect at Mount Zion Church was never intended to mark Johnson's actual burial spot. The other "gravesites" are at the Little Zion Missionary Baptist Church in Greenwood, Mississippi, and near the Payne Chapel Memorial Baptist Church in Quito, Mississippi. Robinsonville, a small town near the Tennessee border where Johnson lived for some years, is now home to several legalized gambling casinos with lounges mostly featuring second-string country artists, an irony the soul-selling Johnson might have appreciated.

28 NASA's version of the Ed White spacewalk incident includes no mention of any feelings of intoxication on the astronaut's part. It does, however, quote the astronaut as saying his extravehicular activity (EVA), which lasted twenty-three minutes, was "the most comfortable part of the mission," and that having it end was the "saddest moment of my life."

29 The most interesting work on New Orleans's ever-changing geography has been done by Richard Campanella. A New Orleans resident, his books include *Bienville's Dilemma, Time and Place in New Orleans,* and *Geographies of New Orleans: Urban Fabrics Before the Storm.*

42 Buchenwald doctor Erich Wagner, whose thesis on tattooing was supposedly read by Ilse Koch (the thesis itself appears on the Buchenwald Table, at the base of the lampshade), was brought to the United States as a prisoner of war. Escaping custody, Wagner returned to Europe, where he practiced medicine under an assumed name until he was recaptured. He committed suicide in prison in March 1959. Wagner's work in the identification of "criminal types" seems to lean heavily on the ideas of Cesare Lombroso, the nineteenth-century Italian psychiatrist and surgeon who is generally considered to be the father of modern criminology. Born into a well-to-do Sephardic family in Verona, Lombroso believed that "born criminals" could be recognized through eugenic-based characteristics of "biological determinism" such as handle-shaped ears, hawklike noses, and insensitivity to pain. It was Lombroso's belief that individuals displaying these signs of "atavistic stigmata" were more likely to have tattoos. Studies of the connection between tattooing and criminal activity of groups like the yakuza, Russian crime societies, and Latin American gangs are now standard police work. While gang tats can be quite elaborate, the old-style jailhouse tattoo remains an entire genre of self-branding. Most prison tats are quite primitive, owing to the meager resources at hand, with colors restricted to blue or black. Most are still done "freehand," by a needle dipped in ink, but homemade tat machines, usually powered by a small motor and a 9-volt battery, are also common. For a wide array of what's available to the long-term jailbird, check http://www.eviltattoo.com/pr.

69 For DNA report from Bode lab, see Appendix.

76 Accounts of Dave Dominici's career as the New Orleans cemetery bandit can be found in many *Times-Picayune* articles, from his arrest in February

1998 until the trial in March 2000. Short of Dominici's own accounts, probably the most interesting and idiosyncratic rendering of the story is in *Lost Souls in the Cities of the Dead* (1st Books Library, 2001), "a fictional police mystery novel" self-published by New Orleans Police Department detectives Lawrence Green and Frederick Morton, the arresting officers in the case. As Morton, who is now an NOPD captain in charge of the evidence and property room, told me, the book was started by his late partner, who saw it as "a chance to get a lot of things off his chest about the job and his relationship with his father." When Green abandoned the project, Morton took over and wrote the second half, which contains the cemetery bust. "I really jazzed it up," said Morton, an outgoing individual who promotes mixed martial arts cards on the side and maintains an abiding interest in New Orleans prosecutor Jim Garrison's investigation into the Kennedy assassination. According to Morton, the cops "kind of felt sorry for Dominici," who is called "D'Angelo" in *Lost Souls in the Cities of the Dead*. "He really got the short end of the stick in all that with the art dealers," Morton said. "But what can you expect? Dominici is a total potatohead."

Part Two

103 Ideas expressed here owe a debt to Professor Lawrence Douglas's article "The Shrunken Head of Buchenwald: Icons of Atrocity at Nuremberg." Douglas's discussion of the psychological motivation of the Nuremberg prosecutors is quite cogent. The article also includes the remarkable photo of Thomas Dodd holding a shrunken head in his hand, "like Hamlet contemplating the skull of Yorick."

104 Some of the items on the Buchenwald Table were tested to determine their validity, others were not. Three "tattooed skin hides" were sent to the Army Section of Pathology in New York. A report dated May 25, 1945, signed by Major Reuben Cares, describes "Piece A" as measuring "13X13 cm., is transparent and shows a woman's head in the center and a sailor with an anchor near the margin." "Piece B," a similar size, "is a tattoo of several anchors resting on an indefinite black mass. To the right of this mass is a man's head." "Piece C" is "truncated," with the upper portion showing "two nipples" sixteen centimeters apart. A "black dragon, with fire coming from the mouth, measures 28 cm." To the left of the dragon "is a man in a coat of mail, with a sword being apparently stuck in the dragon." According to the report, "all three specimens are tattooed human skin."

115 According to Israeli author Tom Segev, who was completing a book about Wiesenthal when I spoke to him in Jerusalem, the famous Nazi hunter later changed his mind on the soap issue. "He came to the conclusion it wasn't so," Segev said.

120 Buechner's books *Adolf Hitler and the Secrets of the Holy Lance* (Thunderbird Press, 1988) and *Hitler's Ashes—Seeds of a New Reich* (Thunderbird

Press, 1989) were written with the pseudonymous "Captain Wilhelm Bernhart." Buechner, a much-respected medical professor in New Orleans and a regular at many uptown society gatherings, claims "Bernhart," whom he presents as "a former U-boat captain," was privy to much of what went on between Hitler and Himmler regarding the Spear of Destiny. In Buechner's account, the spear was recovered from beneath the South Pole ice in 1979 and now is back in Europe, in the possession of a mysterious organization called the Knights of the Holy Lance. Buechner has also advanced the theory that the ashes of Hitler and Eva Braun were similarly buried and retrieved from Antarctica.

Buechner's work on the Dachau Massacre, which he claims to have witnessed, is far less fanciful. As recounted in his book *Dachau: The Hour of the Avenger* (Thunderbird Press, 1986), 520 German prisoners of war were murdered by American forces under the command of 1st Lt. Jack Bushyhead of the 3rd Battalion, 157th Infantry Regiment. Bushyhead, Buechner reports, was a "full-blooded Cherokee Indian" whose ancestors had been brutalized during the infamous "Trail of Tears," a race-based death march in which thousands of Native Americans were forced from their homeland to reservations in Oklahoma. In murdering these Germans, Bushyhead was motivated, Buechner conjectures, by a kinship with the Jewish people who, like the Cherokee, had been "harassed and driven from country to country for thousands of years." This idea is echoed in the recent Quentin Tarantino film *Inglourious Basterds*, in which Brad Pitt plays a Native American leading a platoon of Jews to take vengeance on the Nazis.

121 In his memoir, *The Course of My Life,* British prime minister Edward Heath writes of how as a young man he saw "tattooed human skins on lampshades" among the exhibits at Nuremberg, which is somewhat puzzling since no tattooed lampshades were introduced in evidence at the war crimes trials.

139 For the curious, Denier Bud's work can be found in many web locales. Since these addresses tend to change from time to time, the entry of "holocaust denial videos" or "denier videos" into Google is a fairly reliable pathway. Presently *Buchenwald: A Dumb Dumb Portrayal of Evil* can be found at http://www.holocaustdenialvideos.com/buchenwald. For *Nazi Shrunken Heads*, see http://www.holocaustdenialvideos.com/nazishrunkenheads.

149 David Cole was widely attacked by militant Jewish groups following his appearance on the *Phil Donahue Show*. In an article entitled "David Cole: Monstrous Traitor," the extremist Jewish Defense League, referring to Cole as a "low-life beast worse . . . than the Julius Streichers and Joseph Goebbels" and an "evil monster" who "does not deserve to live on this earth," offered "a monetary reward" to anyone supplying his correct address. In 1998, supposedly in response to JDL pressure, Cole recanted his "revisionist" position and has rarely been heard from since. It is "intimidation" like this, according to Denier Bud, that has sapped much of the energy from the "revisionist" movement. But there are unmistakable signs that the "movement," at least in its "scholarly" application, has been fading away since the Deborah Lipstadt–David Irving lawsuit case. In a January 9, 2009, article, Mark Weber, the longtime head of the Institute for Historical Review, publicly asked, "How Relevant Is Holocaust Revisionism?" Weber wrote: "Over the past ten years, sales of IHR books, discs, flyers and other items about Holocaust history have steadily declined, along with inquiries about Holocaust history and requests for interviews on this subject." This was countered by a more than equal rise in sales of items dealing with "Jewish-Zionist power, the role of Jews in society, and so forth." It was Weber's conclusion that "In the real world struggle against Jewish-Zionist power, Holocaust revisionism has proved to be as much a hindrance as a help." Asked if this signaled the end of formal Holocaust denial, Denier Bud said, "Well, maybe I'm going to be the last man standing."

157 The Desire Projects, 262 low-rise structures on outlying terrain on the way to New Orleans East, were built in 1949 as part of a major urban renewal effort. Known as "the dirty D," the area was crime-ridden even before the famous streetcar (which never reached the projects) stopped running in the middle 1950s. When the projects were torn down in 2003, the area was slated for a major housing upgrade, a plan that was derailed by Katrina. Some new housing has been built, but anyone exiting the I-10 at Louisa Street cannot fail to be struck by the abject desolation of the area. The fact that many of the unpaved streets have names like Abundance, Benefit, and Humanity only adds to the end-of-the-world squalor. The lamentable state of the old Desire area has often been mentioned as a cautionary note by activists who protested the demolition of New Orleans's other projects after Katrina.

160 On January 27, 2003, Jorge Semprún addressed the German Bundestag as the keynote speaker of a Day of Remembrance for the Victims of National Socialism, and once again called up his memories of Albert G. Rosenberg. Retired from his post as the Spanish minister of culture, Semprún recalled his days at Buchenwald, saying that even if it was his "good fortune to meet many individuals of exceptional humanity, intellectual acumen, possessed both of anger and moral courage," it was Rosenberg that he remembered most. He spoke of their talks about philosophy, their drive across "the landscape of Goethe, on the Ettersberg," and recollected the quiet authority Rosenberg displayed while speaking to the Germans from Weimar, telling them not to say they were innocent when they were not. Semprún explained he'd changed Rosenberg's name to Rosenfeld in his book *Literature or Life* because he did not know if the American was dead or alive, and to avoid the possibility that Rosenberg would feel "disturbed or injured" by his depiction. Mentioning that Rosenberg himself had lost twenty-eight family members in the Holocaust, Semprún said he knew the story of the American soldier was far from over. Perhaps someday, the then seventy-nine-year-old Semprún said, he would write about Albert

Rosenberg again. When I saw Rosenberg in El Paso in 2008, five years after Semprún's Bundestag speech, I asked him if he'd ever heard from the writer. No, Rosenberg said. But that was fine.

195 New Orleans's ethnic riots did not all involve members of the black community. The anti-Italian riots of 1891, during which eleven immigrants were murdered, rank as the largest mass lynching in American history. The incident was set off by the assassination of New Orleans police chief David Hennessy, who had arrested a number of reputed Mafia racketeers. Hennessy's reported dying words, allegedly whispered to an NOPD captain, "Dagoes did it," set off a chain of events that culminated in a mob storming the Orleans Parish Prison and dragging out all Italian prisoners. The lynchings were defended by New Orleans mayor Joseph Shakespeare, who said, "The Italians had taken the law into their own hands and we had no choice but to do the same."

195 On February 11, 2009, 117 years after Homer Plessy's arrest at the corner of Press and Royal Street, 113 years after the watershed *Plessy v. Ferguson* Supreme Court case, the City of New Orleans finally got around to putting up a plaque on the site. A heartwarming story it was, too, at least as depicted in the *Times-Picayune,* which told of how Keith Plessy, a fifty-two-year-old New Orleans bellhop and great-grandson of Homer Plessy's first cousin, collaborated with Phoebe Ferguson, great-great-granddaughter of John Howard Ferguson, the judge who ruled to uphold the city's "separate car" laws, to make sure the city finally commemorated the historic spot. Some people, Skip Henderson among them, were less than impressed. Skip had been trying to get the vacant lot where the railway station once stood turned into a "Civil Rights Park" for years with no success. "Looks kind of like a historical marker you drive by on the interstate," Skip said of the two-foot-square brown and yellow plaque. But still, it was better than nothing.

212 For a discussion of anti-Semitism in the German Democratic Republic and issues of right-wing activity in the current Germany, see the work of the Amadeu Antonio Foundation, http://www.amadeu-antonio-stiftung .de/start.

231 Long before her surrogates lit up the screens of American grind houses, the sexual legacy of Ilse Koch was a sub-rosa sensation in Israel. For a whole generation of horny Israeli teenage boys, vivid comic books depicting female SS officers abusing camp prisoners were just about the only pornography available. The books, called "stalags," followed similar plotlines to the Ilse film: sadistic, busty camp guards decked out in full bondage gear tortured prisoners until the underlings rose up to kill the vicious women, usually raping them along the way. Since Ilse Koch was the worldwide model for the evil Nazi sexual predator, it would be fair to say her image was at least the initial inspiration for these cheesy but undeniably compelling books. The fact that the Holocaust was rarely discussed in Israel prior to the Eichmann trial no doubt added to the subconscious appeal of the works. A film documenting the phenomena, *Stalags: Holocaust and Pornography in Israel,* played at the 2007 Jerusalem Film Festival, engendering much controversy.

Part Three

275 In the middle 1990s, Professor Karl Skorecki and his collaborators established the existence of the "Cohen Modal Haplotype," a DNA configuration thought to be distinctive to descendants of Aaron, brother of Moses, the first *Kohen Gadol* (high priest) of the twelve tribes of Israel. Since then many Jews, in both America and Israel, have undergone DNA testing to see if their particular arrangement of Y chromosomes qualifies them as *Kohanim,* or members of the priestly class. "Not everyone is *Kohanim,* but lots of people wish they were," said Rabbi Yaakov Kleiman when I talked to him in a café not far from his house in the Old City of Jerusalem. Author of a number of books on the topic, including *DNA and Tradition: The Genetic Link to the Ancient Hebrews,* Rabbi Kleiman, a *Kohen* himself (and a big Dr. John the Night Tripper fan), sees the discovery of the priestly gene as a powerful linkage between modern Jews and those of biblical times. "Jews have spent so much time and effort debating who is a Jew and who isn't. Now science is helping us, making some of the decisions for us. We're living in the golden age of Jewish population genetics," Rabbi Kleiman said. "I think that fifty years ago, if you had asked a Jew, especially a Jew in Israel, if it was possible to trace their origin straight back to Aaron, they would have looked at you like you were nuts. Now we can. Perhaps that explains a lot of recent history, because when suddenly things you think will always be hidden are suddenly revealed, that changes a lot."

288 Probably the best source for information about the New Orleans Jewish community is Catherine Kahn, coauthor of *The Jewish Community of New Orleans,* former president of the Southern Jewish Historical Society, and longtime archivist at Touro Infirmary. An exceedingly charming lady who has been known to greet a visitor with a hardy "Shalom, y'all," Cathy Kahn is Albert Rosenberg's cousin. When I was in El Paso visiting Rosenberg, he said, "Well, if you want to know anything about Jews in New Orleans, call my cousin Cathy. She has it all down." Offering to make an introduction, Rosenberg dialed his cousin's number. She wasn't home, so he left a message. "Hello, Cathy, this is Albert, calling from El Paso . . . Look, I'm talking to this nice young man who is doing some research on a parcel found in your neck of the woods. It is a lampshade made of human skin. Help him if you can, would you please? *Ciao.*" Hanging up, Rosenberg, a sardonic glint in his eye, said, "That ought to get her attention." The next time I was in New Orleans, I looked up Cathy and we had a nice chat. She asked me what I was writing about; I told her about the lampshade. "Oh, so that's what Albert was talking about," Cathy exclaimed. "I knew it was something strange."

302 Shortly before dropping the lampshade off at Buchenwald, I stopped in to visit Gert Schramm at his home in Eberswalde, thirty miles northeast of Berlin. Now in his early eighties, Schramm, son of a German woman and an African American, was the only black prisoner at Buchenwald. His father, Jack Brankson, an engineer from San Francisco, met his mother in Erfurt, where they fell in love and were married. When the Nazis came to power, Brankson was arrested and sent to Auschwitz, where presumably he was murdered. Young Gert was incarcerated in the children's barracks at Buchenwald. He managed to survive, was embraced by the East German regime, and made a good living running a cab company. Schramm was present in the camp on April 16, 1945, when the Buchenwald Table was shown to the people from Weimar. "Yes. I remember it well," Schramm said, pointing out that the white background seen in the Buchenwald Table photo was probably a sheet held up by prisoners so the photographer could get a better shot. He recalled the shrunken heads most vividly and "had no doubt whatsoever" that the Nazis skinned prisoners at the camp and made them into lampshades. In regard to the *Liberators* controversy, Schramm, who had an Obama sticker on his car, said he did see a number of black soldiers at the camp in the first days after liberation. "This was incredible to me. Outside of my father, who had already been missing for so long, I'd never seen a black person until the Americans came. I knew these people looked like me but I never thought of myself as black. I was a German and this was how I looked. This is what I saw in the mirror, myself, that was all. So I was amazed to see the black soldiers, but they were not *all* black. The story that blacks liberated the camp is not true." Schramm said being black in Germany has not been a problem for him. "I often think that this was a very good thing, because from what I have read and what people have told me, my life would have been much harder in America." Retired now, Schramm is writing his life story and makes a point of giving speeches to schoolchildren warning about the rising neo-Nazi movement. He still sits on the prisoners' advisory board at Buchenwald but as a son of the GDR retains reservations about the "Wessie," or western, influence at the former camp.

309 But the *bon temps* does not *rouler* for long in the Crescent City. Only two months after Skip Henderson received the sacrament of Ash Wednesday, he was back on the Bus, in emergency mode. On Tuesday, April 20, 2010, the 121st anniversary of Adolf Hitler's birth, the *Deepwater Horizon* rig blew up in the Gulf of Mexico, fifty miles off the Louisiana coast. Eleven people were killed and the resulting spill, the biggest in American history, threatens to wipe out the fishing industry on the Gulf Coast and befoul millions of acres of wetlands. Even as the *Treme* TV show reprised the nightmare life following Katrina on HBO, the fabled, wounded city suffered another blow. Again, the old, bad feeling of neglect from both the private and public sectors was ambient. One thing that was sure, the price of a po' boy made with real, unfrozen shrimp was going to go through the roof. From Skip Henderson's point of view, it meant more weeks of getting up at four thirty in the morning to drive the Bus down to Port Sulphur in Plaquemines Parish. The Plaquemines unemployment office was wrecked in the storm and never rebuilt, so Skip was enlisted to help out. "I *am* the Plaquemines Parish unemployment office," he wailed. What was worse was the return of the national media to the Louisiana coast. Skip called me the other day from Port Sulphur to complain about the way things were going, when a loud noise came across the line. Screaming over the din, Skip said, "They're landing a goddamn helicopter, right next to the Bus. There's no end to this."

Gert Schramm in Eberswalde with the lampshade

REFERENCES

Abzug, Robert H. *Inside the Vicious Heart: Americans and the Liberation of Nazi Concentration Camps*. New York: Oxford University Press, 1985.

Aly, Götz. *Hitler's Beneficiaries: Plunder, Racial War, and the Nazi Welfare State*. New York: Metropolitan Books, 2007.

"Anti-Semitism in Former East Germany." Amadeu Antonio Foundation exhibition, Berlin, 2007.

Armstrong, Louis. *Louis Armstrong, In His Own Words: Selected Writings*. New York: Oxford University Press, 2001.

Bankier, David, ed. *Secret Intelligence and the Holocaust: Collected Essays from the Colloquium at the City University of New York*. Jerusalem: Yad Vashem, 2006.

Bauer, Yehuda. *Rethinking the Holocaust*. New Haven, Conn.: Yale University Press, 2001.

Blassingame, John W. *The Slave Community: Plantation Life in the Antebellum South*. New York: Oxford University Press, 1972.

Breitman, Richard, Norman J. W. Goda, Timothy Naftali, and Robert Wolfe. *U.S. Intelligence and the Nazis*. Cambridge: Cambridge University Press, 2005.

Breytenbach, Breyten. "A Visit to Buchenwald." *MLN* 118, no. 5 (December 2003): 1274–97.

Brinkley, Douglas. *The Great Deluge: Hurricane Katrina, New Orleans, and the Mississippi Gulf Coast*. New York: William Morrow, 2006.

Brown, Dan. *The Da Vinci Code*. New York: Doubleday, 2003.

Browning, Christopher R. *Ordinary Men: Reserve Police Battalion 101 and the Final Solution in Poland*. New York: HarperPerennial, 1993.

Cheney, Annie. *Body Brokers: Inside America's Underground Trade in Human Remains*. New York: Broadway Books, 2006.

Codrescu, Andrei. *New Orleans, Mon Amour: Twenty Years of Writings from the City*. Chapel Hill, N.C.: Algonquin Books of Chapel Hill, 2006.

Cohn, Nik. *Triksta: Life and Death and New Orleans Rap*. New York: Vintage, 2007.

Cole, Tim. *Selling the Holocaust: From Auschwitz to Schindler: How History Is Bought, Packaged, and Sold*. New York: Routledge, 2000.

Coleman, Joe. *Internal Digging*. Berlin: KW Institute of Contemporary Art, 2007.

Conner, Steven. *The Book of Skin*. Ithaca, N.Y.: Cornell University Press, 2004.

Conrad, Joseph. *Heart of Darkness*. London: Penguin, 2007.

Crowell, Samuel. "The Gas Chamber of Sherlock Holmes: An Attempt at a Literary Analysis of the Holocaust Gassing Claim," 2000, www.codoh.com/incon/inconshr123.html.

DeLillo, Don. *Running Dog*. New York: Random House, 1978.

Dodd, Christopher J. *Letters from Nuremberg: My Father's Narrative of a Quest for Justice*. With Lary Bloom. New York: Crown, 2007.

Douglas, Lawrence. "The Shrunken Head of Buchenwald: Icons of Atrocity at Nuremberg." In *Visual Culture and the Holocaust,* edited by Barbie Zelizer, 275. New Brunswick, N.J.: Rutgers University Press, 2001.

Eckermann, Johann Peter. *Conversations of Goethe*. Cambridge, Mass.: Da Capo Press, 1998.

Foner, Eric. *Reconstruction: America's Unfinished Revolution, 1863–1877*. New York: Harper & Row, 1988.

Gedenkstätte Buchenwald, ed. *Buchenwald Concentration Camp 1937–1945: A Guide to the Permanent Historical Exhibition*. Compiled by Harry Stein. Frankfurt: Wallstein Verlag, 2004.

Gill, James. *Lords of Misrule: Mardi Gras and the Politics of Race in New Orleans*. Jackson: University Press of Mississippi, 1997.

Goethe, Johann Wolfgang von. *Faust*. Many translations.

Goldhagen, Daniel Jonah. *Hitler's Willing Executioners: Ordinary Germans and the Holocaust*. New York: Random House, 1997.

Gonen, Jay Y. *The Roots of Nazi Psychology: Hitler's Utopian Barbarism*. Lexington: The University Press of Kentucky, 2000.

Green, Lawrence, and Frederick Morton. *Lost Souls in the Cities of the Dead*. New Orleans: Divine Intervention Productions LLC, 2001.

Greene, Joshua M. *Justice at Dachau: The Trials of an American Prosecutor.* New York: Broadway Books, 2003.

Hackett, David A., ed. and trans. *The Buchenwald Report.* Boulder, Colo.: Westview Press, 1995.

Hair, William Ivy. *Carnival of Fury: Robert Charles and the New Orleans Race Riot of 1900.* Baton Rouge: Louisiana State University Press, 1976.

Halbwachs, Maurice. *On Collective Memory.* Translated by Lewis A. Coser. Chicago: University of Chicago Press, 1941.

Hale, Christopher. *Himmler's Crusade: The Nazi Expedition to Find the Origins of the Aryan Race.* Edison, N.J.: Castle Books, 2008.

Hall, Gwendolyn Midlo. *Africans in Colonial Louisiana: The Development of Afro-Creole Culture in the Eighteenth Century.* Baton Rouge: Louisiana State University Press, 1992.

Halow, Joseph. *Innocent at Dachau.* Newport Beach, Calif.: Institute for Historical Review, 1992.

Hamburg Institute for Social Research, ed. *The German Army and Genocide: Crimes Against War Prisoners, Jews, and Other Civilians, 1939–1944.* New York: The New Press, 1999.

Hammett, Dashiell. *The Maltese Falcon.* New York: Vintage, 1929.

Hartman, Chester, and Gregory D. Squires, eds. *There Is No Such Thing as a Natural Disaster: Race, Class, and Hurricane Katrina.* New York: Routledge, 2006.

Hauswald, Harald, and Lutz Rathenow. *Ost-Berlin: Life Before the Wall Fell.* Berlin: Jaron Verlag, 2005.

Hernon, Peter. *A Terrible Thunder: The Story of the New Orleans Sniper.* New Orleans: Garrett County Press, 2001.

Hoover, Herbert T. *The Chitimacha People.* Phoenix: Indian Tribal Series, 1975.

Hotard, Corey David. "Bombarding the City of the Dead: Who Has a Right to the Past?" Master's thesis, Department of Geography and Anthropology, Louisiana State University, 1999.

Institute of Women & Ethnic Studies. *Stories of Survival (and Beyond): Collective Healing after Hurricane Katrina.* New Orleans, 2007.

International Tracing Service, Annual Report 2007. Bad Arolsen, Germany.

Jablonski, Nina G. *Skin: A Natural History.* Berkeley: University of California Press, 2006.

Jung, C. G. *Jung on Evil*. Edited by Murray Stein. Princeton, N.J.: Princeton University Press, 1996.

Kahn, Catherine C., and Irwin Lachoff. *The Jewish Community of New Orleans*. Charleston, S.C.: Arcadia Publishing, 2005.

Kershaw, Ian. *The 'Hitler Myth': Image and Reality in the Third Reich*. Oxford: Oxford University Press, 1987.

Kertész, Imre. *Fatelessness: A Novel*. Translated by Tim Wilkinson. New York: Random House, 2004.

Kiernan, Ben. *Blood and Soil: A World History of Genocide and Extermination from Sparta to Darfur*. New Haven, Conn.: Yale University Press, 2007.

————. *The Pol Pot Regime: Race, Power, and Genocide in Cambodia under the Khmer Rouge, 1975–79*. New Haven, Conn.: Yale University Press, 2002.

Kleiman, Rabbi Yaakov. *DNA and Tradition: The Genetic Link to the Ancient Hebrews*. Jerusalem: Devora Publishing Company, 2004.

Kogon, Eugen. *The Theory and Practice of Hell*. New York: Farrar, Straus & Co., 1950.

Lerner, Daniel. *Psychological Warfare Against Nazi Germany: The Sykewar Campaign, D-Day to VE-Day*. Cambridge, Mass.: MIT Press, 1971.

Levenda, Peter. *Unholy Alliance: The History of Nazi Involvement with the Occult*. New York: Continuum, 1995.

Liebling, A. J. *The Earl of Louisiana*. Baton Rouge: Louisiana State University Press, 1961.

Linenthal, Edward T. *Preserving Memory: The Struggle to Create America's Holocaust Museum*. New York: Columbia University Press, 1995.

Lowenthal, David. "Authenticities Past and Present." *CRM: The Journal of Heritage Stewardship* 5, no. 1 (Winter 2008).

Lupton, Ellen. *Skin: Surface, Substance, and Design*. New York: Princeton Architectural Press, 2002.

Neumann, Klaus. *Shifting Memories: The Nazi Past in the New Germany*. Ann Arbor: The University of Michigan Press, 2000.

Niven, Bill. *The Buchenwald Child: Truth, Fiction, and Propaganda*. Rochester, N.Y.: Camden House, 2007.

Office of the Federal Register. 43 CFR 10 Subpart B: "Human Remains, Funerary Objects, Sacred Objects, or Objects of Cultural Patrimony from Federal or Tribal Lands."

Pringle, Heather. *The Master Plan: Himmler's Scholars and the Holocaust*. New York: Hyperion, 2006.

Przyrembel, Alexandra. "Transfixed by an Image: Ilse Koch, the 'Kommandeuse of Buchenwald.'" *German History* 19, no. 3 (2001): 369–99.

Ribowsky, Shiya. *Dead Center: Behind the Scenes at the World's Largest Medical Examiner's Office*. With Tom Shachtman. New York: Regan, 2006.

Ricoeur, Paul. *The Symbolism of Evil*. Boston: Beacon Press, 1967.

Robinson, Plater. *A House Divided: A Teaching Guide on the History of Civil Rights in Louisiana*. New Orleans: Southern Institute for Education and Research, 1995.

Rosenbaum, Ron. *Explaining Hitler: The Search for the Origins of His Evil*. New York: Random House, 1998.

———, ed. *Those Who Forget the Past: The Question of Anti-Semitism*. New York: Random House, 2004.

Saunders, Frances Stonor. *The Cultural Cold War: The CIA and the World of Arts and Letters*. New York: The New Press, 2000.

Schechter, Harold. *Deviant: The Shocking True Story of Ed Gein, the Original "Psycho."* New York: Pocket Books, 1989.

Semprún, Jorge. *Literature or Life*. London: Penguin Books, 1994.

———. *The Long Voyage: A Novel*. Woodstock, N.Y.: Overlook Press, 1963.

Shadows of Silence. Documentary film on Ken Kipperman. Written and directed by Martina Dase. Dokfilm, 2004.

Shalev-Gerz, Esther. *The Human Aspect of Objects*. Weimar: Stiftung Gedenkstätte Buchenwald und Mittelbau-Dora, 2004–6.

Shermer, Michael, and Alex Grobman. *Denying History: Who Says the Holocaust Never Happened and Why Do They Say It?*. Berkeley: University of California Press, 2002.

Simons, Andrew, and the Greater New Orleans Archivists. *The Jews of New Orleans: An Archival Guide*. New Orleans: The Greater New Orleans Archivists, 1998.

Smith, Alfred L. *Die Hexe of Buchenwald*. Böhlau, Köln, 1983.

Somers, Dale A. "Black and White in New Orleans: A Study in Urban Race Relations, 1865–1900." *Journal of Southern History* 40 (February 1974): 19–42.

South End Press Collective, ed. *What Lies Beneath: Katrina, Race, and the State of the Nation*. Cambridge, Mass.: South End Press, 2007.

Stein, Harry, and Sabine Stein. *Buchenwald: A Tour of the Memorial Site*. Buchenwald Memorial, 1993.

Sublette, Ned. *The World That Made New Orleans: From Spanish Silver to Congo Square*. Chicago: Lawrence Hill Books, 2008.

Tallant, Robert. *Voodoo in New Orleans*. Gretna, La.: Pelican Publishing Company, 2003.

Thompson, William Irwin. *Evil and the World Order*. New York: Harper and Row, 1976.

Tulkoff, Alec S. *Counterfeiting the Holocaust: A Historical and Archival Examination of Holocaust Artifacts*. Edited by Larry Urish. Atglen, Pa.: Schiffer Military History, 2000.

Vonnegut, Kurt. *Slaughterhouse-Five*. New York: Dell, 1969.

Watson, James D. *The Double Helix*. New York: Touchstone, 1968.

Weingartner, James J. "Law and Justice in the Nazi SS: The Case of Konrad Morgen." *Central European History* 16, no. 3 (September 1983): 276–94.

Williams, Tennessee. *A Streetcar Named Desire*. New York: Signet, 1951.

Zwerin, Mike. *La Tristesse de Saint Louis: Swing unter den Nazis*. Vienna: Hannibal, 1985.

Selected Web References

Germany, past and present

http://www.pitt.edu/~dash/faust.html Faust legends

http://www.pitt.edu/~dash/mythlinks.html Germanic myths and legends

http://www.scrapbookpages.com Remarkably complete, marginally scholarly account of concentration camps. Often updated. Recommended.

http://www.buchenwald.de/index_en.html Official website for Buchenwald Memorial.

http://www.amadeu-antonio-stiftung.de For information on neo-Nazi activity in the former GDR.

http://www.nsbm.org One of many National Socialist black metal music sites. For lyrics to Kommando Freisler's hideous "In Belsen," see **http://de.wiki pedia.org/wiki/Kommando_Freisler**.

Other Buchenwald information

http://www.nizkor.org/hweb/camps/buchenwald/diplomatic/georges
-vanier-042745.html

http://www.nizkor.org/features/techniques-of-denial/appendix-8-01
.html

http://www.jewishvirtuallibrary.org/jsource/Holocaust/buchtoc.html

http://www.youtube.com/watch?v=wYVn0hzcSs0 Murrow's speech

http://www.scrapbookpages.com/Buchenwald/Exhibits.html

http://www.axishistory.com/index.php?id=5198

http://www.ushmm.org/wlc/en/media_fi.php?MediaId=160 Color film
of the Weimar march and shots of the lampshade

Ilse Koch

http://www.inter-disciplinary.net/at-the-interface/evil/evil-women
-and-the-feminine

Holocaust museums and information

http://www.yadvashem.org

http://college.usc.edu/vhi USC Shoah Foundation Institute

http://www.ushmm.org United States Holocaust Memorial Museum

http://www.its-arolsen.org/en/homepage/index.html Recently opened
Red Cross Holocaust files

DNA and forensic examinations

http://www.bodetech.com

http://www.ornl.gov/sci/techresources/Human_Genome/elsi/
forensics.shtml

http://www.globaloptions.com

http://www.d.umn.edu/~jhamlin1/lombroso.html

Lampshade speculation, negative and positive

http://www.straightdope.com/columns/read/2511/did-the-nazis-make
-lampshades-out-of-human-skin

http://www.hlrecord.org/2.4462/books-bound-in-human-skin-lamp
shade-myth-1.579032

http://www.nizkor.org/features/techniques-of-denial/appendix-5-03
.html

Denier Bud's videos

http://www.holocaustdenialvideos.com

New Orleans hoodoo

http://www.luckymojo.com/lucky-mojo-inventory.html

http://www.spellmaker.com/witch.htm

http://www.sfgate.com/cgi-bin/article.cgi?f=/g/a/2006/07/10/find
relig.DTL

New Orleans Holocaust information

http://www.southerninstitute.info/holocaust_education/holocaust_
survivor_testimony.html

Race politics in New Orleans

http://www.withoutsanctuary.org/main.html

http://findarticles.com/p/articles/mi_m1295/is_n6_v57/ai_13773324

http://www.davidduke.com/general/my-awakening-chapter-15-the
-jewish-question-2_135.html

http://findarticles.com/p/articles/mi_hb6389/is_n4_v85/ai_n2869
7772/?tag=content;col1

http://www.gutenberg.org/files/14976/14976-h/14976-h.htm

http://www.wireheading.com/robert-heath.html

http://www.southerninstitute.info/index.jsp

http://www.ibiblio.org/laslave/index.html

http://www.eurekalert.org/pub_releases/2006-08/uog-stm081106
.php

New Orleans blogs

http://humidcity.com

http://neworleans.metblogs.com

http://www.yatpundit.com

http://neworleansmurderblog.blogspot.com

New Orleans cemetery theft

http://www.people.com/people/archive/article/0,,20128078,00.html

http://www.nytimes.com/1999/02/16/us/new-orleans-grave-theft
-nothing-s-sacred.html?sec=&spon=&pagewanted=all

Report on Jerusalem syndrome

http://bjp.rcpsych.org/cgi/content/full/176/1/86#BDY

APPENDIX

Bode Technology.

10430 Furnace Road, Suite 107
Lorton, VA 22079
Phone: 703-646-9740

Research Project Report
April 20, 2007

To:
Mark Jacobson
New York Magazine
444 Madison Avenue
New York, New York 10022

List of Evidence Received on February 21, 2007 for possible mitochondrial DNA analysis:

Bode Research Case #0702	Description
SYM0701-001	Small fragment cut from a Lampshade
SYM0701-002	Small fragment cut from a Lampshade
SYM0701-003	Small fragment cut from a Lampshade

BODE Sample #	Description
SYM0701-001-A1	Small Cutting of Lampshade SYM0701-001
SYM0701-001-A1-E1	DNA Extraction 1 from sample SYM0701-001-A1
SYM0701-001-A1-E2	DNA Extraction 2 from sample SYM0701-001-A1
SYM0701-001-A2	Small cutting from sample SYM0701-001
SYM0701-001-A2-E1	DNA Extraction 3 – re-extraction of undigested material from SYM0701-001-A1-E1

DNA was extracted twice independently from cuttings of SYM0701-001 using Qiagen DNA extraction techniques. Samples were tested with two sets of mitochondrial primers. Species testing was conducted through the amplification of a region of the Cytochrome b (Cyt b) gene using primers from Verma and Singh (2003) known to amplify across a wide range of vertebrate species including humans. Human specific testing was conducted through the amplification of a 214bp region of the Hyper Variable II (HVII) portion of the mitochondrial control region.

RESULTS:

1.) MtDNA profiles were obtained from extractions **SYM0701-001-A1-E2** and **SYM0701-001-A2-E1** for both Cyt b and HVII. These samples comprise two independent extractions from the SYM0701 source material carried out in parallel. **No profiles** were obtained from extraction **SYM0701-001-A1-E1**.

2.) The mtDNA Cyt b profile for extractions **SYM0701-001-A1-E2** and **SYM0701-001-A2-E1** were identical. No heteroplasmy (displays two nucleotides) was detected in the sequences.

3.) When the consensus sequence from extractions **SYM0701-001-A1-E2** and **SYM0701-001-A2-E1** were queried against the National Center for Biotechnology Information

NCBI database using the blastn searching tool, the results came back with a 0.0 E-value signifying a 100% probability that the cyt b sequence is human.

4.) Extractions **SYM0701-001-A1-E2** and **SYM0701-001-A2-E1** produced consistent profiles at the HVII loci. The evidence suggests two human contributors are present in sample **SYM0701-001**.

5.) In the HVII region, heteroplasmies were present at bp146 N(T/C), bp150 N(T/C), bp152 N(C/T), bp182 N(T/C), and bp194 N(T/C). The electropherogram levels were consistent with a mixture of two human samples: one major and one minor contributor.

6.) The HVII profiles from extractions **SYM0701-001-A1-E2** and **SYM0701-001-A2-E1** were checked against the laboratory database. Everyone who came into contact with the sample can be excluded as a possible contributor.

7.) The Cytb and HVII data for extractions **SYM0701-001-A1-E2** and **SYM0701-001-A2-E1** indicate that the sample is of human origin with a single minor contributor, also of human origin.

8.) Human mtDNA profiles were obtained from the lampshade material. The minor and major DNA sequences obtained from **SYM0701-001-A1-E2** and **SYM0701-001-A2-E1** were consistent with each other. The lampshade material **SYM0701-001-A1** was sanitized with 10% bleach prior to DNA extraction. Sample **SYM0701-001-A2** was not sanitized with bleach. The minor mtDNA HVII profile observed on sample **SYM0701-001-A1-E2** was less intense (weaker relative fluorescent units) than **SYM0701-001-A2-E1** mtDNA profile. The dominant profile of the two extractions was of the same intensity. This strongly suggests that the minor profile may be due to external handling of the lampshade, and the major profile is most likely from the lampshade material itself.

Recommendations for future work:

1. It is recommended that reference samples be obtained from any individuals that have handled the lampshade. These reference samples will be analyzed with the same mtDNA HVII primers to determine if they can or cannot be excluded as contributors to the DNA profile obtained from the lampshade.

2. DNA sequencing of the HV I region should be performed. DNA sequencing of the HVI and HVII regions will allow us infer the ethnicity of the donor.

3. To further confirm that the major DNA contributor is from the lampshade material, additional DNA testing could be performed from the cells internal to a histological cross section of the lampshade material. This additional analysis would permit us to state the DNA sequence is from lampshade material itself and conclusively rule out DNA from cells adhering to the external of the lampshade material.

See Table 1 for summary of mtDNA haplotypes reported for each sample.

Jared Latiolais MS, MFS   Robert Bever, Ph.D.

Research Scientist   Vice President of Research

Bode Technology   page 2 of 3   April 20, 2007

Table 1. mtDNA haplotypes for items SYM0701-001-A1-E2 and SYM0701-001-A2-E1 as compared to the standard Cambridge Reference Mitochondrial sequence.

Position	Cambridge Reference	SYM0701-001-A1-E2	SYM0701-001-A2-E1
73	A	G	G
146	T	N(C/T)	N(C/T)
150	C	N(T/C)	N(T/C)
152	T	N(C/T)	N(C/T)
182	C	N(T/C)	N(T/C)
194	C	N(T/C)	N(T/C)
263	A	G	G

The following notations apply:

a. Transition or transversion polymorphisms as compared to a standard sequence (Anderson, et al. 1981. *Nature* 290:457-465) are designated by the appropriate letter (base).

b. A deletion is designated by a "D."

c. An insertion is designated a ".1" for a one base insertion, and a ".2" for a two base insertion.

Note: Polycytosine stretches are often difficult to interpret. A possible cause may be the presence of a mixture of length variants in the mtDNA of an individual. A predominant length species is often apparent; however, the frequency of a particular length species cannot be determined accurately and may vary between maternal relatives. The sequence reported for Hypervariable Region 1 represents the first 10 cytosines observed, beginning at position 16184. The sequence reported for Hypervariable Region 2 represents the number of confirmed cytosines present in the predominant base sequence. When no predominant base sequence is observed, the insertions that could not be confirmed are designated by a "N."

d. A position that could not be confirmed is designated by a "N."

CHAIN OF CUSTODY
The Bode Technology Group, Inc.

Case Number:	SYM0701	Agency ID Number:	

Submitting Agency Information

Name		Victim	
Address		Suspect	

Contact/Attorney	Shiya Ribowsky, PA-C	Phone Number	
Additional Authorized Contacts		Phone Number	

Custody Record

Method of Delivery to Bode	FedEx	Condition	Good (Sealed)
Date Delivered	2/21/2007 Time: 9:40 AM		
Delivered By	FedEx	Signature TRK # 8567 7649 5536	
Delivered To	Shirley Salas	Signature	

Date/Time	Item No.	Released by (print)/(sign)	Received by (print)/(sign)	Purpose of change:
2/21/07 9:41 AM	001 to 003	Shirley Salas	Wendy Boone, for EMS	Accessioning/Storage
3/5/07 4:20 PM	001 to 003	Amber Bowman for EMS	Jon Davoren	Analysis
Date / Time	Item No.	Released by (print)/(sign)	Received by (print)/(sign)	Purpose of change:
Date / Time	Item No.	Released by (print)/(sign)	Received by (print)/(sign)	Purpose of change:
Date / Time	Item No.	Released by (print)/(sign)	Sent via: / Tracking No.	Purpose of change: FINAL DISPOSITION

Evidence Inventory

Bode Case #	Agency Item ID	Description
SYM0701-001		Labeled as "One white standard business envelope containing a small fragment cut from lampshade
SYM0701-002		Labeled as "One white standard business envelope containing a small fragment cut from lampshade
SYM0701-003		Labeled as "One white standard business envelope containing a small fragment cut from lampshade

Storage of Evidence: Secure Evidence Room

The Bode Technology Group, Inc.

Form COC1 Rev 5/31/05

INDEX

Page numbers in *italics* refer to illustrations.